Death Was Our
Bedmate

The stimulus for *Death Was Our Bedmate* was the book
Out of the Depths of Hell:
A Soldier's Story of Life & Death in Japanese Hands
by my late father, John McEwan.

Agnes McEwan

Death Was Our Bedmate

155th (Lanarkshire Yeomanry) Field Regiment
and the Japanese 1941–1945

by
Agnes McEwan
and
Campbell Thomson

Pen & Sword
MILITARY

First published in Great Britain in 2013 by
PEN & SWORD MILITARY
An imprint of
Pen & Sword Books Ltd
47 Church Street
Barnsley
South Yorkshire
S70 2AS

ISBN 978-1-78159-169-7

A CIP catalogue record for this book is
available from the British Library.

Typeset in 11/13pt Palatino by
Concept, Huddersfield, West Yorkshire

Printed and bound in Great Britain
by MPG Printgroup

Pen & Sword Books Ltd incorporates the imprints of Pen & Sword
Aviation, Pen & Sword Family History, Pen & Sword Maritime, Pen &
Sword Military, Pen & Sword Discovery, Wharncliffe Local History,
Wharncliffe True Crime, Wharncliffe Transport, Pen & Sword Select,
Pen & Sword Military Classics, Leo Cooper, The Praetorian Press,
Remember When, Seaforth Publishing and Frontline Publishing.

For a complete list of Pen & Sword titles please contact
PEN & SWORD BOOKS LIMITED
47 Church Street, Barnsley, South Yorkshire, S70 2AS England
E-mail: enquiries@pen-and-sword.co.uk
Website: www.pen-and-sword.co.uk

This book is dedicated to the Men of the 155th (Lanarkshire Yeomanry) Field Regiment, RA in acknowledgement of their courage and comradeship in the Far East throughout the Second World War.

Those of us who were privileged to observe both officers and men of the Lanarkshire Yeomanry during those years of captivity are able to testify to the value of a county association in that important relationship between officers and men. This yeomanry regiment set an example of behaviour as prisoners of war that simply could not be rivalled. Their outstanding part in the campaign, especially at Slim, is yet another story. They were like one great big family in which everyone took care of everyone. When small parties or even individual soldiers of the regiment were taken away by the Japs and transferred to remote camps, somehow or other an officer of the regiment would be sure to find his way. No single soldier of that regiment was ever allowed to feel forgotten. They seemed to possess a spirit that said 'we come through this as a regiment and not as individuals.' It was one of those things that sticks in the memory, which some of us talk about even today.

Lieutenant Colonel Denis Russell-Roberts
Spotlight on Singapore

Contents

Introduction viii

Acknowledgements ix

Glossary xi

Map of Malaya indicating battles involving the 155th xii

Map of Formosa with location of POW camps xii

Map of Thailand camps xiii

Chapter 1.   Off to War with the Fireside Soldiers   1

Chapter 2.   Japanese Blitzkrieg: The Battles for Jitra, Gurun and
              Kampar   18

Chapter 3.   'Hell was let loose in Malaya' – The Battles for Slim
              River and Johore   33

Chapter 4.   The Loss of the Impregnable Fortress   50

Chapter 5.   Singapore Interlude   61

Chapter 6.   The Drivers' Party Moves Out   72

Chapter 7.   The Track-Laying Gang   86

Chapter 8.   'D' for Damned – Hellfire Pass   100

Chapter 9.   F Force – Lies and Deceit   111

Chapter 10.   H Force – The Bridge at Hintock   128

Chapter 11.   'Dark and Gloomy Taiwan'   138

Chapter 12.   Spread Across the Far East   171

Epilogue   184

Nominal Roll of the 155th (Lanarkshire Yeomanry) Field
    Regiment, RA   191

Order of Battle on Japanese Invasion on 8 December 1941   212

Short Bibliography   214

Index   217

Introduction

I first learned of the 155th (Lanarkshire Yeomanry) Field Regiment, RA, from my late father, John McEwan, who had been a Gunner with the regiment and subsequently a prisoner of war in the Japanese hell camps at Kinkaseki and Kukutsu on Formosa, modern-day Taiwan.

Like all POWs who returned from the camps in the Far East, he believed himself betrayed by his own country. The men who had fought so bravely throughout the disastrous Malayan Campaign were made out to be cowards following the capitulation at Singapore.

To make matters even worse, he was saddened that his old regiment was little known, even in the county of its origin, and this book has been written to tell the story of those 'forgotten Gunners'.

Unlike most other military units that saw action during the Second World War, the Lanarkshire Yeomanry did not produce a regimental history or other official account of their wartime experiences in the Far East. Although not intended as a comprehensive history of the Malayan Campaign or the POW story, this book uses the stories of the men themselves to give a snapshot of their war and of their time as POWs.

It includes a full and detailed nominal roll of the regiment and by referring to it and the relevant chapters of the POW story, the reader can follow the individual footsteps of a loved one through the jungle, along the Death Railway or down into the depths of the copper and coal mines where they slaved and suffered.

They should not be forgotten.

Agnes McEwan
Newmains, Lanarkshire
2013

Acknowledgements

This account of the 155th (Lanarkshire Yeomanry) Field Regiment, RA, at war and as prisoners of the Japanese has been written in collaboration with Campbell Thomson, who became a close friend of my late father John McEwan after reading of his wartime experience in the book *Out of the Depths of Hell: A Soldier's Story of Life & Death in Japanese Hands*.

We are very grateful to the many families of former members of the regiment for their help, patience and understanding in our search for material about the involvement of the Lanarkshire Yeomanry in the ill-fated Malayan Campaign and their subsequent hell as POWs. There are too many to mention individually, but they know who they are.

This being our first foray into writing, we would like to acknowledge the critical help and advice given by friends Frank Morrison, Alan Coltart and Sally Dorrian. Their patience in reading and reviewing the manuscript was invaluable. The graphic art skills of my son, Patrick, were also put to good use in compiling the various maps and his *granda* would have been proud of his input into the story of the Men of the Regiment.

The work involved in researching a story such as that of the 155th was complex and we are grateful for the help and advice given by those experienced in the subject, including Terry Manttan of the Burma-Thai Railway Corp, Tony McQuade and Keith Andrews of the Children of the Far East POW Group, Ron Taylor of the Far East POW Community, Michael Hurst of the Taiwan POW Society, and Peter Gallagher, an independent researcher who generously did so much work for us at The National Archives at Kew.

We would also like to thank: Carol Cooper, founder of the Children of the Far East POW Group, for permission to quote from the diary of her father, Lance Corporal Bill Smith of the Norfolk Regiment, who died as a POW on the Death Railway; Tony Fasson, for the papers of his late father, Lieutenant Colonel James Fasson; Carrie Watson, for use of Jim's *Memoirs*; Betty Gwillim, for use of Dick's unpublished memoirs; Martin Moody, for excerpts from the diary of his father-in-law, John Mather, who served with the 155th in the Far East; the Changi Museum, for Peter Rhodes' *To Japan to Lay a Ghost*; Alan Ratnage, for research at The National Archives, Kew; Mike Heather, for material about the POW experience discovered while researching the story of his father-in-law, Ken Pett; and the indomitable Arthur Lane, who experienced the hell at first hand. We also acknowledge the use of quotes from the following books: *In the Shadow of Death*; *Railway of Hell*; *Out of the Depths of Hell*; *The Colonel of Tamarkan*; *One Fourteenth of an Elephant*; *The Rising Sun On My Back*; *The Inexcusable Betrayal*; *Bamboo Doctor*; *Sweet Kwai Run Softly*; *Yasume*; *War Diaries of Weary Dunlop*; *Bamboo and Barbed Wire*; *Branch Line to Burma*; *Spotlight on Singapore*; *Pristoner on the Kwai*; and *Banzai, You Bastards!*

We would also like to record our sincere thanks to the team at Pen and Sword for their help, guidance and encouragement; in particular, Henry Wilson, Linne Matthews, Matt Jones, Jonathan Wright and Pamela Covey.

However, without the kindness and understanding of some very special men – the remaining veterans of the regiment and their comrades in arms from other units who suffered alongside them – the compiling of this account would have been virtually impossible: Tom Hannah, Tom McKie, Pat Campbell, John Marshall, Andy Coogan, George Reynolds and Ken Pett. Sadly, since our work began, several others, including Jock Douglas, Benny Gough, Jim Watson, Bobby Findlater, David Paton, Les Puckering and Willie Clark have passed on.

Gentlemen, we salute you all!

Glossary

Attap	rough palm-like leaves used for roofing and hut construction throughout the Far East
Bango	number off (Japanese)
BSM	Battery Sergeant Major (British)
Bukit	mountain or high point (Malay)
Bully beef	tinned corned beef
Chunkel	hoe-like tool widely used throughout the Far East
CiC	Commander-in-Chief (British)
CO	Commanding Officer (British)
GOC	General Officer Commanding (British)
Godown	warehouse, or sheds, particularly on the dockside
Gunso	Sergeant (Japanese)
Hancho	name given to the overseers in the Kinkaseki Copper Mine, usually a local Taiwanese
Havildar	a non-commissioned officer in the Indian Army corresponding to a sergeant
Kampong	village (Malay)
Kioski!	attention!, a command given by a Japanese guard
Kwai Noi	Little River (Thai)
Kwai Yai	Big River (Thai)
Kwali	large, shallow metal cooking pot
Leggi	leftover food, extras
RAF	Royal Air Force
RSM	Regimental Sergeant Major (British)
Sampan	shallow draft native boat common throughout the Far East
Sungei	river (Malay)
Tenko	roll call (Japanese)
Yasume	rest (Japanese)

Note: Up until June 1939 modern-day Thailand was known as Siam. From 1939 until Sept 1945 it became Thailand before once again reverting to Siam. Since 1949, it has been Thailand and this is how it is referred to throughout this story.

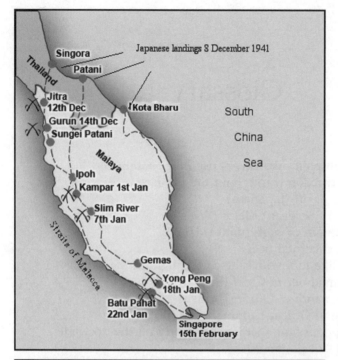

Map of Malaya
indicating battles
involving the 155th

Map of Formosa with
location of POW
camps

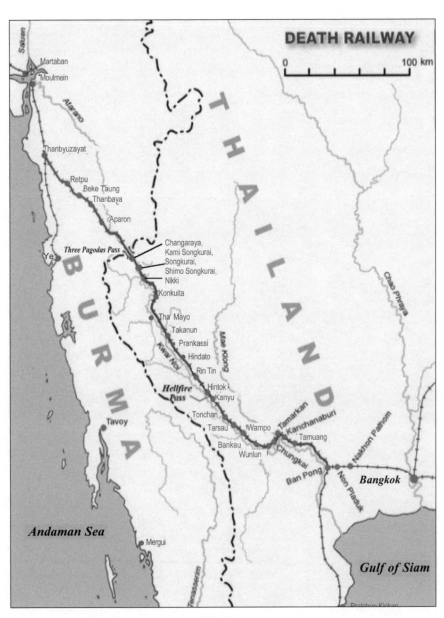

Map of Thailand camps

Chapter 1

Off to War with the Fireside Soldiers

'Away an' fight the bloody Jerries, ye' useless fireside sojers!' were the cries ringing in the ears of the young Gunners of the 155th (Lanarkshire Yeomanry) Field Regiment, RA, as they marched through the streets of Lanark on their way to the railway station. Defiantly singing back the words of their regimental marching song, 'We're no awa ta bide awa, we'll aye come back and see ye!', the Gunners happily responded to the taunts coming from the young men of the town who, for the last two years, had played second fiddle to them in the affections of the Lanark lassies.

Climbing aboard the carriages of the train that was to take them off to war, their bravado quickly wore off as they wondered where they were going. The consensus was North Africa. For months they had been preparing to go into action and the former Territorial cavalry regiment, with the induction of professional Royal Artillery Gunners into their ranks, had been moulded into an efficient – but as yet unblooded – field artillery unit.

Pushing and squeezing their haversacks into the overhead luggage racks of the carriages, they continued to belt out their regimental song, *Carnwath Mill*, which ends with the promise, 'We'll aye come back and see ye'. Little did the eager young Gunners know that for many, there would be no return. In the years to follow, scores of them would die fighting in the hot and humid jungles of Malaya or as POWs in Japanese hell camps spread across the Far East.

Much had happened since that fateful day in September 1939 when they had been mobilized.

As serving Territorials in the Lanarkshire Yeomanry, some, like teenager John McEwan, an apprentice butcher from Motherwell in Lanarkshire, had been anticipating their call-up. The previous May,

1

18-year-old John and his 20-year-old brother Richard had walked the mile distance from their home to the Marshall Street Drill Hall in the nearby town of Wishaw. There they signed on as Territorials with the local cavalry regiment in the hope that, if war did come, they would serve together.

The Lanarkshire Yeomanry was an old county regiment with its origins in the rural heartland of central Scotland. Raised in 1819 as a volunteer cavalry regiment, its officers were from old Lanarkshire families – the landed gentry – with its troopers drawn from tenant farmers or estate workers. That had all changed after the First World War: now the troopers were from all parts of the community, although the officers were still drawn from the same land-owning families with a tradition of 'handing down the sword' from father to son. The Territorial Lanarkshire Yeomanry, with its headquarters in Lanark, was made up of squadrons that met at various drill halls throughout Lanarkshire and Dumfriesshire and, for most, war had been the last thing on their minds when they initially signed on. Now it was fast becoming a reality.

Following the end of the Great War, where the regiment had served with distinction as 'dismounted cavalry' at Gallipoli, Palestine and on the Western Front, the Lanarkshire Yeomanry had reformed as a cavalry regiment of the Territorial Army. The troopers were from all backgrounds and included Tom Moore, from Glassford, a plasterer; Tom Gordon, from Auchenheath, a farm worker; and Carluke man George Brown. These young, and in some cases not so young, men had joined as Territorials for the small bounty paid. Some, like Bill Anderson, from Kirkfieldbank, near Lanark, a Territorial with nine years' service but a barman by trade, were married men with families to keep and, in the straitened years of the 1930s, the few extra pounds made a difference to household budgets. However, for the Anderson family, and the families of Tom Moore, Tom Gordon and George Brown, the cost would be heavy.

On 1 September 1939, the call-up papers for the troopers were prepared at the Regimental Offices in Lanark and handed in at the local Post Office later that night. It is to the credit of the postal system at a time when it was under immense pressure that the letters were successfully delivered to homes throughout Lanarkshire and Dumfriesshire the following day.

A good number of the men of the Lanarkshire Yeomanry were from Dumfriesshire, where D Squadron of the Territorial Regiment was based. Mobilized the day before war broke out, members of the squadron mustered at Annan in Dumfriesshire. No billets had been organized for them and they slept in a barn on bales of straw. The following day,

3 September 1939, while on the train north to Lanark, they learned that war had broken out and that they were now full-time soldiers.

On arrival at Lanark they found themselves among a large batch of men from all over Dumfriesshire and Lanarkshire who had been hurriedly called up and were now being billeted in halls and disused factories throughout the town.

But, for a good number of them, their stay at Lanark was brief. A few days after call-up, Tom McKie and Dick Gwillim, along with other Territorials from Dumfriesshire and Lanarkshire who had only just arrived at Lanark, were told that they were on their way south. No explanation was given and for them this was the start of a strange spell of duty in France during what came to be known as the Phoney War. Then, in November 1939, the regiment's commanding officer, Lieutenant Colonel Alan Murdoch, was advised by the Army Council that the Yeomanry were to be absorbed into the Royal Artillery, converted to mechanized units, and given the choice of becoming field regiments, medium regiments or anti-tank regiments. Following consultation with officers, warrant officers and NCOs of the regiment, agreement was reached that the Field Branch of the Royal Artillery was the closest to their former role as mounted cavalry and, in communicating the reply to the Army Council, the colonel stressed that the regiment wished to retain its identity as the Lanarkshire Yeomanry and keep its cap badge, a double-headed eagle. On 10 January 1940, it was confirmed that their former role as a cavalry unit had been superseded and that from 15 February 1940, a day and month to be etched into the psyche of the regiment just two years later, it would become the 155th (Lanarkshire Yeomanry) Field Regiment, RA.

The regiment lost the first of its number about this time.

Gunner John Scott died in Roadmeetings Hospital, Carluke, on 10 March 1940, of pneumonia.
John, from Wishaw, Lanarkshire, was twenty years of age.
The cold and drafty billets of Lanark had taken their toll.

The following month, the first of the field guns arrived at Lanark. On 8 April 1940, two 4.5-inch howitzers arrived complete with sights but the next batch of four, delivered six days later, were old, unserviceable and without sights. But at least the newly-fledged field regiment now knew what their new charges looked like and, while still prone to kick out at unwary Gunners, they at least didn't need to be mucked out!

Up until then the regiment had been made up of former Territorials and others who, on the outbreak of war, had hurriedly joined up with their local regiment. But, with conscription being introduced that month, new recruits began appearing from all over the country.

Included among them were many Glaswegians. As hundreds of fresh recruits milled around the platforms of Glasgow Central Railway Station in April 1940, their anxious families fretted and worried about when they would next see them – none more so than the family of Frankie Divers, a married man in his mid-thirties who was a less than enthusiastic conscript. As Frankie boarded the crammed train he pushed his way to an open corridor window and stuck his head out. Over the hubbub of noisy conversations taking place all around the busy station came the loud and emotional exchange between Frankie and his wife, who was standing on the platform. 'Ah luv ye, Frankie' wailed the distraught wife. 'Ah luv ye tae, Bella' shouted back Frankie, only to follow the endearment with other fond remarks: 'Awe Bella, gonnae no forget me!' and 'Ah luv ye, Bella, ah really luv ye!' For ever after, Gunner Francis Divers was known to his hard-headed and unromantic comrades as 'Bella' Divers. Later, when in action in Malaya, where Gunner Divers assisted with the supply of munitions to the gun positions, the incongruous cry 'Haw, Bella, we need mair ammo' would ring throughout the jungle.

Bella and the others were soon to be Gunners with the 155th (Lanark-shire Yeomanry) Field Regiment, RA, and at Lanark were put through their paces by the drill instructor, Sergeant 'Mick' Flaherty, a professional soldier from the Irish Guards. Under his relentless and sarcastic tongue they either learned to march or suffered the consequences – and woe betide those, like John McEwan, the young butcher from Motherwell, who had a penchant for wearing their forage caps at a jaunty but precarious angle. The drill periods were carried out on the playground of St Mary's Primary School in Lanark, and could go on for hours until Big Mick was either satisfied or gave up in complete frustration. And the latter seldom happened as the drill sergeant was a true Guardsman. As the young soldiers began to wilt under the constant haranguing, their heads could drop momentarily, and this was fatal for those whose caps were not stuck firmly and squarely on their heads.

Said John McEwan: 'I could feel my cap beginning to slip and as I put my hand up to stop it, Big Mick roared at me and I had to let it fall off. I received another roar from him as I tried to bend down and catch it before it landed on the ground. And that was that. Big Mick had us drilling up and down until the drill squad had virtually pressed my cap into the ground. It didn't happen again!'

The horses were now all gone, much to the disappointment of the many country lads in the regiment, including Tom Hannah from

Kirkfieldbank, whose father had served with the Lanarkshire Yeomanry in the Great War. Tom had been brought up to hard work and after elementary schooling – where he had to walk 3 miles across rough moorland to and from school – he began work as a farm labourer. Accordingly, for Tom, this new army life was really not too bad; the only thing he hated was the constant square-bashing (military drill) under the lashing tongue of the tyrannical Sergeant Flaherty. So when the opportunity arose to become batman to Major Jock Wilson, he grabbed it with both hands.

Major Wilson, from a wealthy Lanarkshire mine-owning family, lived with his young wife and baby daughter in a house provided at Mousebank Road in Lanark, where a nanny for the infant was employed. Tom, as batman to the major, maintained the officer's uniform and equipment and generally acted as his valet. Another of the duties of batman – which initially came as a surprise to Tom – was that of acting as the officer's bodyguard during combat. This was first drawn to his attention when he accompanied Major Wilson through to the family seat at Dunning, in Perth, where he was introduced to Sir James Wilson, the major's father. To his bemusement, Tom was handed a Colt automatic pistol by Sir James, with the instruction to look after his son's safety.

While the young former farm labourer had no objection to becoming a bodyguard, he was less than happy with other aspects of his duties. The nanny, who was initially expected to include basic housekeeping in her role, soon objected and, to his disgust, the disgruntled Tom became the family housemaid. That was until one day, while cleaning in the master bedroom, he happily vacuumed up the delicate, and hard to replace, underwear that the lady of the house had discarded on the floor while she had her bath. Not surprisingly, Tom's spell as batman came to an abrupt end and the next day he was back square-bashing.

Meanwhile, in France, other members of the regiment were in trouble of a more serious kind.

Since October 1939, Dick Gwillim and the others of the Yeomanry who had left for France had been attached to the British Expeditionary Force on a variety of duties. Some, like Dick, had been escorting German POWs, while others, including Tom McKie, had been working alongside French gunners.

For Dick and the others on escort duties, life was not unpleasant. However, conditions dramatically changed when the Germans invaded France and cut off the British Expeditionary Force at Dunkirk, and Dick's safe haven at Dieppe soon became a target for German dive-bombers. Another of the 155th in a similar position was Tom McKie. He

5

had been with a group helping out the French on the famous – but ill-fated – Maginot Line, the series of defensive fortifications established along the French-German border. By 5 June 1940, the heavy Panzer tanks of the German Wehrmacht had outflanked the Maginot Line and pushed deep into France and, said Tom, 'Once the Germans had broken through in the north, there was nothing we could do but get out. It was utter confusion and the British units there got all mixed up. I ended up in a truck with men I had never met before. No one really knew what they were doing and we just set off across France.'

Meanwhile, with Dunkirk cut off, Dick made his way to St Nazaire in the hope of finding passage to England. Lying off the Loire River estuary was the former British Cunard liner, RMS *Lancastria*, requisitioned as a troopship and now waiting to embark the thousands of British troops and civilians who had been stranded after the fall of Dunkirk.

It was now 17 June 1940, and Dick and thousands of others were ferried out to the ship by a fleet of smaller vessels. The *Lancastria* had capacity for about 2,200, including crew, but the captain, 54-year-old Rudolph Sharp, had been ordered to take on board as many as possible. By the time that Dick was on board there were at least 5,000 others and, tragically, just before 1600 hours, they were attacked by German Ju 88 bombers. The ship received three direct hits and sank within twenty minutes, with the loss of more than 4,000 lives. Luckily, Dick was not among them. This was to be the first of his many amazing escapes during his time with the 155th.

Meanwhile, Tom McKie and his newfound comrades had driven west with the intention of joining up with a British unit, but none of those they did meet up with appeared to know what they were doing. Eventually, Tom's group reached the west coast of France, where, in a tiny fishing village on the Bay of Biscay north of St Nazaire, they found a young French fisherman who was willing to sail them across the Channel in his small fishing boat as he was intent on joining the Free French Forces. Once back in England, Tom was given a rail pass and, on his return to Lanark, found himself a stranger in the newly-formed 155th Field Regiment.

On arrival in Plymouth, those like Dick Gwillim rescued from the *Lancastria* received a warm welcome from the townspeople, who lined the roadway in their hundreds to cheer the survivors from the ill-fated ship. Following a short train journey to Southampton, a medical examination and a brief spell of recuperation, Dick and the others were sent north to Liverpool for what was considered a lighter spell of duty escorting German POWs and Italian civilian internees to Canada.

At Lanark, the regiment was required to provide additional personnel for the same duty, and Tom McKie, being 'spare', once again found himself among those selected. Arriving at Liverpool, he met up with others from the Lanarkshire Yeomanry who had been in France, including Gunners Sammy Frew, Tom Moore and Jim McKenna, and they boarded their new ship, the SS *Arandora Star*. They were impressed. Said Dick Gwillim: 'Our first meal on board the *Arandora Star* was a pleasant surprise. The thick-carpeted dining room and excellent food were an unexpected treat.'

On 1 July 1940, the fully-laden ship sailed from Liverpool, and the following day was making good headway into the Atlantic when it was spotted by *U-47*, a German hunter submarine commanded by Gunther Prien, the celebrated U-boat ace. The previous October, *U-47* had crept through the defences at Scapa Flow and triumphantly sunk the battleship HMS *Royal Oak*. Now making its way back to its base on the west coast of France after another successful spell of hunting down merchant ships in the Atlantic, *U-47* had only one torpedo left – enough for an attacking run on the unescorted *Arandora Star*.

The ship, a former cruise liner with the Cunard Line, was carrying more than 1,200 Germans and Italians, plus a full crew and escort. At 0658 hours that morning, about 75 miles off the west coast of Ireland, the single torpedo struck home and the *Arandora Star* began to sink. Attempts were made to launch the thirteen lifeboats – one had been destroyed in the attack – but with limited success, and many men ended up in the water. Once again, luck was with non-swimmer Dick Gwillim. He managed to clamber aboard one of the lifeboats as it was being lowered into the sea, as did most of the others of the 155th, including Sammy Frew and Tom McKie, but Tom Moore and Jim McKenna were both lost.

Gunner Thomas Dunn Moore was from Glassford, Lanarkshire.
Thomas was twenty-three years of age.

Gunner James McKenna was married and from Penicuik,
Midlothian.
James was thirty years of age.

But at Lanark life went on. Colonel C.A. Russell, an experienced Royal Artilleryman, had earlier arrived as instructor and the new Gunners were taught how to handle the field guns and to give and implement fire orders. Much of the instruction was of a technical nature and during one of the geometry lessons a veteran sergeant of the Lanarkshire

Yeomanry, more used to looking after horses, was overheard to say, 'It's awe right for youse educated yins,' before stalking off!

In September 1940, training on the guns was intensified, with a trip being made to the barren moorland at Beattock, some 30 miles south of Lanark. Peter Rhodes, a Gunner surveyor, recalled, 'It was announced that the guns were to be calibrated and all the measuring and checking done by the Regimental Survey Section. Six of the surveyors went onto the target area, a bleak stretch of moorland, to observe and measure the fall of shot. This was the first time that any of us had been near a gun when it fired and several among the gun crew, ourselves included, were scared at first.'

But not as scared as Gunner Tom McKie, the *Arandora Star* survivor now back with the regiment. Having no permanent role owing to his frequent spells of duty elsewhere, Tom was supernumerary and, in his words, had become the 'odd job man'. And there was no odder job than the one he was now undertaking. Huddled down in the cold and wet moorland with a thin covering of a single sheet of corrugated iron and clods of turf as shelter, it was now his job to spot those shells that failed to explode on landing so that they could later be located and destroyed. Shivering from an unpleasant mixture of fear and cold, he often wondered what it would be like if a shell – live or otherwise – landed on his 'shelter'.

In October 1940, the regiment moved to Haddington, on the east coast of Scotland, to man the 6-inch guns of the Coastal Defences and to relieve the 70th Field Regiment, RA, who had been on protective duties at the RAF aerodromes at Drem and Macmerry. RAF Drem was the base for 602 City of Glasgow Squadron, an air defence unit whose function was the protection of Edinburgh and the shipping channels of the Firth of Forth. The previous October, during what was the first Luftwaffe attack on Britain, Flight Lieutenant George Pinkerton, flying a Spitfire of 602 Squadron, gained the second 'kill' of the war when he shot down a Junkers Ju 88 bomber. Only minutes earlier, Spitfires from 603 City of Edinburgh Squadron, flying from RAF Turnhouse, near Edinburgh, had achieved the first.

The Gunners were billeted and spread out over the Haddington area, with A Battery based at Gosford House, near the town – the troops in various huts about the grounds and the officers in the basement of the large country house. The men of B Battery had the unusual experience of being billeted in brand-new council houses in the village of Gifford, which had been requisitioned by the Army on the outbreak of war. As a result, the Army was not particularly popular in the area.

Back at Lanark, one member of the rear guard preparing to join the regiment at Haddington was equally unpopular with a member of the local community. Sergeant Charles 'Chuk' Lowther, in charge of the remaining group, was fast asleep in the regimental billet located in St Mary's RC Church Hall in St Leonard Street when he was awakened by a local special constable with a ticklish problem. It appeared that an item of clothing had been stolen from a local lady. Having got dressed, Sergeant Lowther wakened the sleeping billet with the straightforward question, 'Which wan o you has a girl's knickers?'

Receiving no reply from the bleary-eyed and bemused Gunners, he had the 'girl' brought into the billet while ordering the men to 'sit to attention'.

The female in question, now recognized by the Gunners as 'Carnwath Kate', a local lady of easy virtue, then walked down the row of beds accompanied by the constable and Sergeant Lowther. Reaching the bed of a still sleeping figure, Sergeant Lowther pulled off the bed covers to reveal a fully-clothed Gunner, complete with boots. As the man sat up and sleepily rubbed his eyes, the gleeful Kate squealed, 'That's him, and there's ma knickers!' pointing to the irrefutable evidence lying under the bed. Grabbing the offending item off the floor, she strode triumphantly out of the room to the cheers of the delighted and by now fully awake Gunners!

Later that month, the regiment had its first taste of war when the B Battery motor transport park at Gifford was machine-gunned by a German fighter bomber. However, their spell of duty at Haddington was coming to an end and on 23 December, the regiment received word that they were to be relieved and should be ready to move to 'a tropical climate' by the middle of January. It appeared that their time as 'fireside soldiers' was coming to an end.

The first of several cancellations came on Wednesday, 8 January 1941, when the departure date was rescinded. Instead, the regiment returned to Lanark, where they were once again dispersed throughout the town. During February, rumours grew but it was only when they were finally issued with lightweight khaki uniforms and ordered to attend for their tetanus and typhoid 'jags' that they knew they were definitely on the move. Their new uniforms were khaki drill shirts and strange-looking baggy shorts, which, although knee-length, could be folded down, supposedly for protection against mosquitoes. From the nature of the equipment issued to them, the Gunners concluded that they were destined for the Western Desert. They should have paid more attention to the film then being shown in the local cinema – Bing Crosby, Bob Hope and Dorothy Lamour in *The Road to Singapore*.

The morning of 21 March 1941 was a typically dreich and cold early spring day and following their short parade through the town, the Gunners assembled in the car park adjoining the railway station ready to board the troop train. Among those waiting was Tom Hannah, the young Gunner from Kirkfieldbank, who was once again in trouble. The previous evening, being aware that the regiment was on the move the next day, he had taken the opportunity to make a hurried visit to his home a few miles away. Unfortunately for Tom, on making his way back to Lanark he had been stopped by the local police, who insisted on giving him a lift back to the billet and straight into the custody of Regimental Police Sergeant Roy Russell. Tom now awaited his fate.

The journey from Lanark to the Firth of Clyde was relatively short and after alighting from the train at Gourock Railway Station, the still whistling and jaunty Gunners marched cheerfully to the nearby docks. And instead of the jeers and insults they had experienced at Lanark, the shouts from the watching crowd of factory girls out on their lunch break were both cheering and enthusiastic.

'Where are you off to?' shouted one of the girls, only to receive the chirpy reply, 'We're off to see the Wizard', and at that, the marching column of Gunners picked up the exchange with a rousing chorus from the current hit film *The Wizard of Oz*! But it was not the Wizard, or even the Wicked Witch of the North whom they were about to meet. Instead, they were destined for a nightmare date with the evil 'Devils of the East'!

Ferried out to the waiting troopship, the SS *Strathmore*, the Gunners were distributed throughout the ship, with officers quartered in cabins on C and D Decks, warrant officers and sergeants in cabins on D Deck, and other ranks on Mess Deck G, where their quarters doubled as both sleeping and messing areas. On Deck G there were long linoleum-covered mess tables to seat fourteen men, and at night, hammocks were slung from the deck beams for the Gunners to sleep in. All except for Tom Hannah! Sentenced to be confined to ship for the duration of the voyage, Tom found himself in the 'brig', which had previously served as the nursery in civilian times. So while his mates sweated in the cramped conditions below, Tom travelled first class on the upper deck and when the ship's captain decreed that there could be no locked cabins owing to the ever-present U-boat threat, the young Gunner, when not actually scrubbing the decks, had the virtual run of the ship, much to the exasperation of Sergeant Russell.

Following a six-week-long voyage via Cape Town, South Africa, the SS *Strathmore* arrived safely in India on 5 May. Said Gunner Peter Rhodes: 'I didn't believe it when a few old hands assured us that we should be able to smell Bombay from 200 miles out at sea. But it was true. We could!'

After docking in the busy Bombay Harbour, the Gunners disembarked and, with haversacks slung over their shoulders, marched through the bustling docks to the railway station, astonished at the strange and unfamiliar sights all around them.

Sitting on hard wooden seats in stifling, dirty carriages, the hours passed uncomfortably as the train slowly wound its way higher and higher until it reached the elevated dusty plains of the Deccan Plateau. Early the following morning, after what had been a hot and sticky journey, they reached their destination – Ahmednagar. They were now part of the 9th Indian Division.

Located on a hot, dry and dusty plain, their new quarters were the large black basalt stone barracks from a bygone Victorian era. Previously the home of the British Indian Army, the inappropriately-named Sandhurst Barracks were far from clean and sleeping facilities were fibre-latticed beds with compressed straw mattresses.

However, the tired and hungry Gunners had more pressing matters on their minds. Where was their grub? On learning that the kitchen would not be in place until later in the day, they dejectedly lined up alongside a mess truck, where they were each handed a tin plate containing two slices of bread and butter and two boiled eggs. And as they made their way back across the dusty parade ground towards their new barracks, they had their first experience of dive-bombers. From high out of the blue sky, fast-moving kites – a type of small hawk – swooped on the Gunners' exposed plates.

'The man in front of me swore loudly at the birds and held his left hand spread to protect the bread and eggs. A second later and he had lost the tip of a finger! From that day on we all regarded these predators, soon to be known by all of us as shite hawks, with the greatest respect,' said Gunner Peter Rhodes.

Ahmednagar was to be the Gunners' new home for the next four weeks and their introduction to colonial life. Gunner Jim Johnston, in a letter back home to his mother, wrote: 'You might not believe what I'm going to tell you now, Mother, but it's perfectly true. Before you are awake in the morning you are shaved by the shaving wallah. The first morning I nearly died with fright. The wallah came in and lashed the soap on my face before I was awake. Of course, I woke up and saw a black man bending over me with an open razor. I thought he was going to cut my throat but he just said, "Shave, Sahib." I just managed to gasp out, "tec aie" [Hindi: phonetic for "OK"] and he shaved me.'

11

On 14 June, the regiment packed all their gear into the hotchpotch of vehicles assigned to them and drove the hundred or so miles from Ahmednagar to the arsenal town of Kirkee, a few miles north of Poona. Life was pleasant for the Gunners. After reveille and breakfast, there was foot drill, PT and training of all kinds until tiffin, or lunch, which was followed by a compulsory siesta in the afternoon. Despite the words of the popular song by Noel Coward that only mad dogs and Englishmen go out in the midday sun, Gunners of all nationalities were more than happy to comply with this not unpleasant order. The searing heat of the early afternoon sun was not to be trifled with and going down with sunstroke, or even sunburn, as a result of not wearing the obligatory pith helmet, or topee, was sufficient for a disciplinary charge.

But it was not all fun and games. On the firing ranges around the Kirkee area, the Gunners familiarized themselves with their 4.5-inch howitzers while some locals found dubious and dangerous employment.

Said Gunner Tom Hannah: 'During my time at Kirkee I was never away from the range as once again I found myself an "RSM volunteer". Whenever there was an unpleasant job, the regimental sergeant major would parade the troop and ask for volunteers only to follow up with the order "Gunner Hannah, two paces forward, march!" And there I was on the firing range, where it was my job to look after the ammunition and make sure that everything was safe. After a practice shoot, local natives were allowed onto the range to look for misfires. It was my job to detonate them after they were piled in a heap!'

A common sight on the congested roads around Kirkee were carts drawn by a pair of bullocks with the male head of the family sitting in the cart while the women, bundles on their heads, walked silently alongside or behind. Those strange social customs were once again to bring the unfortunate Gunner Tom Hannah to attention.

On one particular occasion, while making his way along one of the roads around Kirkee, the gallant but misguided Tom decided to intervene: 'I was driving along the road about the middle of the day when I saw a bunch of locals up ahead. When I got up to them I saw that it was an Indian man sitting astride a donkey, which was so small that the man's feet almost touched the ground. Behind the man and the donkey walked a line of women, the oldest at the front. They were all carrying packs on their head and the youngest one at the back was heavily pregnant and seemed to me to be struggling in the intense heat.

'I stopped the truck, got out and yanked the man off the donkey. He just stood and stared at me as I got the pregnant woman – presumably one of his wives – and sat her on the donkey. As I was getting back into the truck, the man was ranting and raving at me but I just ignored him and drove away.

'Later that day when I got back to the barracks, I was pulled up by one of the sergeants who said that I had set the cat amongst the pigeons and that I would have to pay the man compensation for his injured feelings. I remember thinking "What a bloody country!" but I didn't get involved again!'

Elsewhere in the world, events were beginning to impinge on the regiment's idyllic spell in India. In early June, with the Dutch East Indies having failed to meet her demands for oil, the situation for Japan was compounded when the United States, owing to a shortage in home production, placed an embargo on oil exports to countries other than Britain and her other immediate allies. Although she had amassed considerable stocks of oil, the position was still problematic for Japan. Then, on 22 June 1941, without warning, Germany invaded Russia, Japan's traditional enemy.

Once over their initial surprise, the 'hawks' in the Japanese establishment were quick to appreciate the opportunity. The first target was French Indochina. In July, despite pleas from the US that French Indochina should be considered a neutral country irrespective of the situation in Europe, Japan sent troops into the former French colony. In retaliation for this flagrantly hostile act, the US and Britain froze all Japanese assets in their respective countries and imposed a total trade embargo and, crucially, this action extended to the Dutch East Indies – an essential source of Japanese oil.

Oil was the lifeblood of Japan. And, with no natural resources, it was also dependent upon imports of rubber, tin and iron ore. Despite efforts by more conciliatory elements in Japan to mediate and compromise, the belligerent and militarily-influenced government greedily looked towards the natural assets of Malaya and the Dutch East Indies.

Back in India, the Gunners of the 155th remained oblivious to the implications of all this political activity in the Far East for they were busy preparing for action against Rommel and his Afrika Korps in the Western Desert. Then, in August, a shocked regiment learned that they were being restructured and would lose one of their three batteries. A Battery was being sent north to Quetta to make up the nucleus of the 160th Field Regiment, while B and C Batteries were to remain the 155th Field Regiment but now destined for Malaya to bolster defences in light of the increasingly hostile tone of Japan.

On 23 August, B and C Batteries, with all their guns, vehicles and equipment, embarked at Bombay on the SS *Ekma*, part of a convoy bound for Port Swettenham on the west coast of Malaya. Left behind was Jim Johnston, the young Gunner from Wishaw. Sadly, since arriving in India, he had been bedevilled with ill health, which was subsequently diagnosed as tuberculosis, almost certainly caught on board the *Strathmore* on its outward journey. He did not recover.

Gunner William James Johnston died at the Military Hospital, Poona, on 19 October 1941.
William was nineteen years of age.

The Gunners' journey to Malaya was so unlike their previous experience on board the SS *Strathmore* as the *Ekma* was a stinking tramp ship of the worst kind. The smell aboard was appalling and the Gunners gagged at the stench from the galleys. The ship was alive with cockroaches and instead of the deck games and housey-housey previously enjoyed on board the *Strathmore*, the men passed the time holding cockroach races on the long mess tables. At night this same area was used as sleeping quarters, with hammocks slung above the tables, although many of the men preferred to sleep on the open deck despite having to be awake before the native crew sluiced down the surface with sea water.

Arrival in Malaya on 3 September was a complete contrast with India. The searing dry heat of the Indian plains was replaced with a humidity that immediately sapped the Gunners' energy. As the guns and transport were being unloaded and hitched up, the sweat-soaked men entrained for Ipoh. The metre-gauge railroad looked strange and out of place to the Gunners and they wondered how the wide coaches could balance on such a narrow track. In the coming years, hundreds of the men would become very familiar with this type of railroad when they slaved and, in many cases, died on the infamous 'Death Railway' driven at enormous cost in human life through the jungles of Thailand and Burma.

It was already dark when they arrived at Ipoh and they were met at the railway station by dozens of 3-ton trucks driven by a crowd of cheerful and mocking Australians. Once aboard, the Gunners were driven at a crazy speed along the narrow roads until they reached Canning Camp, about 2 miles outside the town, where their accommodation consisted of 100-foot-long *attap*-roofed huts raised about 4 feet off the ground on concrete posts to allow air to circulate. Ipoh was initially out of bounds to the Gunners but they were made welcome at the nearby Australian camp, where they quickly became accustomed to being assailed with the greeting 'G'day, ya Pommie bastards'. They soon found that this was the normal friendly form of address from their

Aussie comrades, with no insult or offence intended. From Ipoh the regiment moved to Sungei Patani, where they were housed in similar-style *attap*-roofed huts but this time under the dense canopy of a rubber plantation. It was impressed upon the Gunners that rubber was the lifeblood of the country and crucial to the war effort and that under no circumstances were trees to be damaged, never mind removed.

Despite the limitations inflicted by the conditions and demands of the rubber plantations, training continued and each day units went north to Jitra to locate and prepare gun positions. Since 1 October, the regiment had been attached to the 11th Indian Division with a remit to provide artillery support to the infantrymen of 6th and 15th Indian brigades. Those two brigades were a mixture of Indian regiments, which included the Jats and Punjabis, and two British battalions, the 2nd East Surrey Regiment and the 1st Leicestershire Regiment.

At Jitra, the infantrymen were preparing for Operation *Matador*.

In August, following the increasingly icy relations with Japan, the Commander-in-Chief, British Far East Command, Air Chief Marshal Robert Brooke-Popham had prepared a plan of action – Operation *Matador* – for implementation in the event of a likely invasion of Malaya by the Japanese. In 1937, Major General William Dobbie, then Officer Commanding Malaya, had indicated that Malaya would be vulnerable if the Japanese gained access to the Kra Isthmus by making landings at Singora and Patani in Thailand, but his findings were ignored. Now his recommendations were hurriedly being reviewed and the nub of the plan was for a pre-emptive strike into Thailand by units of the 11th Indian Division to prevent any seaborne landings by Japanese forces. While militarily straightforward in concept, the plan was bedevilled by political reservations.

That same month, the newly-appointed General Officer Command-ing, Malaya Command, Lieutenant General Arthur Percival, who had previously served in the area, told the War Office in London that his estimate of the troops required for an effective defence of Malaya was six divisions, including, most importantly, two tank regiments.

The shortage of experienced infantrymen and the absence of those two tank regiments was to be pivotal to the subsequent, and disastrous, Malayan Campaign.

On 16 October 1941, the more conciliatory Japanese Prime Minister, Prince Konoye, was replaced by General Hidaki Tojo, and, as the military historian S. Woodburn Kirby has noted, 'The military had now taken control in Japan and war was inevitable.' Back in Britain, the prevailing view remained that Japan could be held in check and that an attack on Malaya was unlikely. However, as a safeguard, it was decided to send

HMS *Prince of Wales* to the Far East as it was believed that the presence of a capital ship would act as a significant deterrent to those elements in the Japanese government who were pressing for military action as a means of territorial expansion.

On 21 October, HMS *Repulse* was ordered to accompany the *Prince of Wales* but the Admiralty insisted that this small fleet be augmented by the aircraft carrier HMS *Indomitable* to provide air cover as it was recognized that the RAF in Malaya was well below the recommended minimum strength. Unfortunately for those concerned about the lack of air protection for the two capital ships, now considered essential for the defence of the Far East, HMS *Indomitable* ran aground in Kingston Harbour in Jamaica on 3 November.

Throughout November, the Gunners of the 155th continued their almost daily trips to Jitra, where the Survey Section made the necessary calculations, the Signallers laid field telegraph wire and the gun crews prepared sites for their precious 4.5-inch howitzers. At that time, the defensive preparations being made at Jitra were undoubtedly over-shadowed by the possibility of Operation *Matador*. Unfortunately for all those involved, *Matador* was dogged by indecision – as was all political activity in the area.

Political manoeuvring finally became irrelevant when, on 4 December 1941, a Japanese invasion force comprising the 25th Army set sail from Hainan Island in the South China Sea under the command of Lieutenant General Yamashita. Although its presence in the area was known, its final destination was not. Nevertheless, it was still sufficient for alarm bells to be set ringing and, on 5 December, Brooke-Popham sought guidance from London about the possible implementation of Operation *Matador*. Once again, political wavering was evident and the decision was left with him, if and when he considered it appropriate.

During a meeting on 6 December with Brooke-Popham and Sir Shenton Thomas, the Governor of Singapore, and with the situation continuing to deteriorate, Lieutenant General Percival recommended that Operation *Matador* be immediately put into action. But the hapless Brooke-Popham remained unconvinced. The following day, a Catalina flying boat of 205 Squadron operating from Singapore spotted the Japanese assault force in the South China Sea heading in the direction of the Kra Isthmus – gateway to Thailand and north-east Malaya. Before it could send off full details of the invasion fleet, the RAF plane was attacked and shot down. But sufficient alarm had been given and once again the authorities on Singapore were left with a decision. And, once again, Brooke-Popham vacillated. He feared that it was a Japanese ruse to force the British into making a pre-emptive strike on neutral Thailand, so allowing the

Japanese an excuse for an all-out war. Whether such indecision was justified from a purely political standpoint was one thing; for the military, it was simply disastrous.

For weeks they had been on standby for just such an eventuality. The ongoing indecision and uncertainty was having a toxic effect on morale and the overall effectiveness of the units involved was being seriously undermined.

Shortly after midnight on 7/8 December, elements of the Japanese fleet were seen off the Malayan coast at Kota Bharu and by dawn a task force from the Japanese 18th Division was landing on the beaches, despite fierce resistance by the 3/17th Battalion of the Dogra Regiment supported by the guns of the 5th Field Regiment. The fighting was bloody and hand-to-hand, but having achieved a beachhead, the tenacious and determined Japanese were not for losing it. Meanwhile, other units of the 25th Japanese Army were landing at Singora and Patani, in Thailand.

An all-out assault on northern Malaya by the powerful Japanese 25th Army was now imminent.

Chapter 2

Japanese Blitzkrieg: The Battles for Jitra, Gurun and Kampar

The uncertainty and waiting were now over, for the inevitable had happened. It was now too late for *Matador* as the opportunity had been lost through dithering and incompetence and others were about to pay the price. The men of the 11th Indian Division, who had been keyed up to make the dash into Thailand to prevent a Japanese landing, were instead ordered to the prepared positions at Jitra.

As dusk fell, the Gunners left Sungei Patani armed with sixteen 4.5-inch howitzers, the heavy field guns that were to play such a vital role in the days ahead. The journey, hazardous enough under normal circumstances, was made even more treacherous as it was undertaken during the monsoon season and constant torrential rain filled the monsoon ditches on either side of the narrow roads.

The main body of the regiment, held up by rain and crumbling estate roads, reached Jitra in the early hours of the morning and in the downpour and darkness sought out their so-called 'prepared positions'. The men were in for a shock for the positions were now flooded and little more than quagmires. Cursing and swearing, the tired and stressed-out Gunners struggled and squelched their way through the morass, eventually manhandling the heavy howitzers and fully-loaded ammunition limbers into some sort of order. They had been told that the guns were to be ready to fire by 0700 hours that morning – 9 December 1941.

Sergeant Jim Watson of D Troop vividly remembers that first hectic night: 'After a lot of hard work and sweat we finally got our guns established and ready to fire. We were just inside a clump of rubber trees and had about 100 yards of clearing ahead of us. In this area

18

monkeys were swinging around the treetops and we killed several snakes.'

It was a long, hard night, with no sleep for anyone. When dawn broke, the bleary-eyed Gunners took in the scene before them. All around was mud and desolation. However, despite having had to work in the dark, plagued by myriad buzzing mosquitoes that swarmed around their sweating bodies, they had successfully concealed and camouflaged the guns under the cover of rubber trees. A store of sixty artillery shells was dumped at each gun position, with a further reserve in boxes a few hundred yards away. Quads and limbers were kept fully loaded and, once action began, this was to prove crucial.

As the day progressed, the artillery troop commanders checked out their observation posts (OPs), usually sited far out in the front line amongst the infantry positions and manned by an officer, a bombardier as his OPA (assistant) and a Gunner as signaller. On this occasion, all the OPs were north of Jitra, just in front of a hurriedly-commenced – but still incomplete – anti-tank ditch, where a solitary mechanical digger lay forlorn and abandoned not far in front of the Leicesters' lines. The OP for D Troop of the 155th was located in a pillbox to the right of the road in a small wooded area where a company of the 2/9th Jats were dug in. To their left were C Company of the 1st Leicesters, who had the difficult role of covering both sides of the trunk road, and the OP for C Troop of the 155th was embedded in their lines.

Said Bombardier Pat Campbell, the C Troop OPA: 'When we got up to the prepared OP we found it flooded. There was enough water in it for us to drown so Captain Mackenzie arranged a trench in the forward position of the Leicesters, where "Dally" Duncan, "Titch" Walker and I spent some uncomfortable moments.'

Similarly, the OP for E and F Troops was located on the west flank of the Leicesters' position where it met with lines of the 2nd East Surreys, close to the *kampong* at Manggoi. In the oppressive and humid conditions around the positions, the gun crews relaxed as best they could. Night fell abruptly and the presence of creepy-crawlies – the ever-present snakes, centipedes, biting red ants and leeches – made things unpleasant.

Perhaps not surprisingly, the Gunners' nerves were becoming frayed.

That day witnessed the beginning of saturation bombing of British airfields in northern Malaya. The airfields at Alor Star, Sungei Patani, Butterworth, Ipoh and Kuantan were soon all but out of action and already steps were being taken to abandon what was left.

Events of 10 December came as a shock to the Gunners. Without any warning being given to the men of the 11th Indian Division who were preparing to meet the Japanese at Jitra, the hurried evacuation of the Alor Star airfield began in earnest and fuel and buildings were blown up. The resulting pall of smoke could be seen by the anxious troops waiting at Jitra and did nothing for their confidence or morale, particularly as the presence of the airfields was largely the reason for them being there!

And things got even worse when, later in the day, news percolated through to the shocked and disbelieving troops of the loss of the two capital ships, HMS *Prince of Wales* and HMS *Repulse*.

On the evening of 8 December, on news having been received of a possible Japanese invasion force heading for the north-west coast of Malaya, the *Prince of Wales* and *Repulse* had set sail from the naval base at Singapore. At 1140 hours on 10 December, the British fleet came under sustained attack from waves of Japanese aircraft and by 1318 hours, the two capital ships were at the bottom of the South China Sea.

Now the men of the 11th Indian Division were to face the might of the Japanese Army with no navy and no air force!

In the early hours of the following morning, 11 December, heavily-camouflaged warriors from the Japanese 5th Division, including a tank company of 15-ton Model 97 medium tanks and the ever-present engineering unit, crossed the border from Thailand. The invasion of Malaya was now under way.

Aware that the defences at Jitra were still far from complete, Major General Murray-Lyon, the 11th Indian Division Commander, ordered the Japanese halted north of Jitra.

This nigh impossible task fell to the inexperienced infantrymen of the 1/14th Punjab and 2/1st Gurkha battalions, who had been intended as divisional reserve. Their remit was to hold the Japanese advance long enough for the Jitra position to be strengthened and then disengage and withdraw.

The Punjabis dug in at Changlun about 10 miles north of Jitra on the trunk road into Thailand. Their sole anti-tank weapons for use against the expected Japanese armour consisted of the two Breda anti-tank guns of the 4th Mountain Battery. About 1130 hours that morning, following a heavy mortar attack on the Indian positions, Japanese tanks crossed the Changlun Bridge and appeared in front of the Punjabi lines. For several hours, the beleaguered Indian troops withstood the attack but by early afternoon, they were ordered to fall back and regroup some miles further south of Asun.

In appalling weather, they were making their way south when, without warning, the first of the tanks caught up with them. Trudging their way down the road, they were totally unaware of the enemy closing on them as the monotonous sound of the torrential rain bouncing off the rubber trees masked the rumble of the oncoming tanks. The tanks simply mowed their way through the hapless and horrified young soldiers who, taken completely by surprise, had little chance of fighting back. Many were little more than teenagers from the back streets of the Indian sub-continent and had never seen a tank before. It was a complete and total rout.

The Japanese assault force rapidly advanced on the Asun Bridge just 2 miles further south, which was being held by the 2/1st Gurkhas. Although they had no Breda guns, the Gurkhas responded desperately with two Boys .55 anti-tank rifles and successfully brought two of the tanks to a halt, effectively blocking the road. The Japanese infantry reacted immediately and, wading swiftly across the Sungei Asun, attacked the Gurkha positions from all sides. Forty-five minutes later, the fight was over.

At Jitra, the 6th Brigade was located on the left of the trunk road. Covering a front of 18,000 yards of marshy country west to the coast were the 2/16th Punjab, with the 2nd East Surrey Regiment on their right. In front of the East Surrey lines were rice paddy fields spreading east into 15th Brigade's area, where the 1st Leicester Regiment held a crucial position astride the trunk road. On their right were the 2/9th Jats, with jungle and rubber plantations spreading further east to the heights of Bukit Penia.

Morale among the infantrymen was poor. With *Matador* cancelled they had despondently returned to their positions at Jitra to find, like the Gunners of the 155th, that they were sodden and waterlogged. Having to repair and rebuild defences, the weary and dispirited infantrymen were still laying out barbed wire as the Japanese swept through Asun.

Behind the infantry were the four troops of the 155th (Lanarkshire Yeomanry) Field Regiment.

The four howitzers of E Troop were located just south of Jitra village, with the four guns of F Troop half a mile further back – all covering the front of the East Surrey and Leicester positions. The eight guns of C and D Troops were sited on the east side of the main road, south of the Sungei Bata, and provided fire for both the Leicester and Jat positions – considered to be the most likely target of a Jap assault.

The defensive line held by D Company of the 2/9th Jats was vital. It was situated just a short distance east of the main road, with only limited protection from the partly-completed anti-tank ditch. Both this part of the defensive line and that covered by the adjoining C Company of the Leicesters, which sat astride the main road, were an obvious point

21

for a Japanese thrust and located in this area were the two OPs of C and D Troops of the artillery of the 155th.

As darkness fell, a Jap tank, moving slowly southwards along the road, reached a culvert almost in front of Lieutenant Brian France in the D Troop OP, where demolitions had been laid. As the gunners in the OP frantically signalled back to Regimental Headquarters, a Japanese soldier leapt from the tank and cut the demolition leads with a sword. As quickly as it had appeared, the tank reversed and disappeared into the darkness.

The demolition charges that had been laid on the culvert and a bridge over the anti-tank ditch then disastrously failed to detonate. Tanks then began rapidly moving down the road but were initially halted by a makeshift roadblock hastily put up by the Leicesters. Fire from the guns of the 215th Anti-Tank Battery, concealed in a copse of trees near the Leicesters' C Company position, knocked out two tanks, creating an effective block on the narrow embankment. The Gunners from the 155th now fired their opening salvo on the Japanese tanks, forcing them to hurriedly withdraw. This was the first time that the Japs had experienced artillery and the lesson was salutary.

In the early hours of 12 December, the enemy were once again on the move and under cover of darkness, Japanese infantry stealthily crept forward towards the Leicesters' C Company positions alongside the trunk road. However, keen eyes in the artillery OPs paid off and the Japanese were spotted, with the inevitable artillery barrage being immediately brought down on them.

The air around the guns was thick with acrid smoke and, eyes stinging from the cordite that pouring sweat brought into their eyes, the Gunners kept up the barrage. Continually in action, there was no break for them during that night. Said Sergeant Jim Watson, the No. 1 on a D Troop gun: 'When we got our orders we started to shell the enemy, continuing through the night until we were absolutely exhausted. My gun by this time had embedded itself into the soft ground up to the breech block and was out of action until we managed to pull it clear onto a fresh slot.'

So much ammunition was being expended that Gunner Tom Hannah and his escort, Gunner 'Bella' Divers, were incessantly on the move, drawing full limbers of ammunition from the wagon lines and returning with empties.

Tom said, 'It was bloody awful. We never stopped all night and at one time I was driving a Quad with six limbers hooked together like a train as we tore up and down the road.'

The ubiquitous Quad was the workhorse of the artillery and was used to tow the field artillery pieces used by the 155th; the 4.5-inch howitzer and 25-pounder, along with their ammunition trailer, or limber. Manufactured in Britain as the Morris Commercial field artillery tractor, it was better known in the British Army as a Quad from its four-wheeled-drive capability. Weighing just over 3 tonnes, its 3.5-litre petrol engine had a top speed of 50mph. More than enough for the muddy jungle tracks around Jitra!

Tragically, the regiment's first casualty of the campaign came early that day when the guns of E and F Troops were brought into action on the left. During the firing of E Troop's first task, a shell from one of its 4.5-inch howitzers hit a tree and prematurely exploded, killing Bombardier Hall and wounding Lance Bombardier Ben Carson and Gunner Reg Spooner.

Bombardier Maurice 'Nobby' Hall was from Acton, Middlesex.
Maurice was twenty-three years of age.

As dawn broke, the next two fatalities were even more shocking. About 0600 hours that morning, just as Captain Forster and his OPA, Bombardier Bennett, were taking over the D Troop OP situated between the Leicesters' and Jats' positions, they were rushed by a force of Japanese infantry who suddenly arose from out of the undergrowth. The young Indian troops from the Jats who were providing the escort for the vital OP were quickly overwhelmed by the ruthless and determined killers, who were masked in a very effective camouflage of twigs and leaves. The shocked OP signaller, who was nearby removing equipment from a truck, was able to jump into the vehicle and make a rapid escape through a hail of bullets.

Captain Alfred Ronald Forster, a married man, was killed
during the encounter.

Bombardier George J.E. Bennett was killed alongside
Captain Forster.
George, a married man from Harrow Weald, Middlesex, was
twenty-five years of age.

They were later buried in a joint grave.

About the same time as this attack was being sprung on the Jats' position on the right-hand side of the road, the Leicesters on the left became aware of movement in the paddy fields in front of them. Said

23

Lieutenant George Chippington: 'I noticed tiny figures begin to flit across the open spaces between the trees beyond the paddy, moving in from the direction of the main road. Some carried loads, which, without field glasses, I could only guess were machine guns and probably mortars, no doubt with the intention of providing covering fire for others crawling in the paddy.'

His guess was right. Within minutes, the Leicesters' lines were under intense fire – first from machine guns and then from mortars falling amongst them. From the figures rapidly wriggling through the paddy towards their lines, Chippington realized that his platoon was heavily outnumbered. On a scrap of paper, he hastily drew a rough diagram of his position and sent it off by runner to Company Headquarters with a request for artillery support.

After what seemed to him like an eternity, the first salvo arrived but fell short between his position and the crawling Japanese in the paddy. The next salvo, and those following, were dead on target.

Said Lieutenant Chippington: 'Scores of tiny figures scuttled away at high speed, dodging and weaving through the rubber trees while we fired, more in hope than anticipation. After a few more rounds for luck, the artillery must have considered my request for assistance dealt with and all went quiet.'

Unknown to Chippington, at the same time as he had witnessed the Jap advance on his front, his platoon had also been the target of Japanese troops creeping in from his right. He was later told that when the shells started falling, the enemy had 'melted away as quickly and as quietly as they had arrived.'

By mid-morning that same day, Captain James Mackenzie of B Battery had established an OP on the slopes of Bukit Penia, a high point to the right of the village. From there he could clearly see further attempts by the Japanese to use the cover of the paddy to encircle the outer flanks of the Jats and just after midday, a battalion-strength attack by the Japanese was made on the Jats' D Company position, and the guns of B Battery were once again brought into action.

The ammunition around the field guns was rapidly being depleted owing to the amount of firing and whenever there was a lull in the artillery fire, the Japanese used it to advantage and crept closer to the Jats' position. The Indian troops were coming under increasing pressure.

Japanese troops had gathered in large numbers in the anti-tank ditch in front of the Jats' D Company position and 21-year-old Captain Cyril Holden requested permission from his CO, Lieutenant Colonel Tester, to withdraw as their weapons had become unserviceable owing to the clinging mud and the extreme heat of continual use.

'The men cannot fire, Sir,' he reported.

'I cannot give you permission to withdraw,' was the reply.

'Ok, Sir, we will fight it out with grenades and bayonets. The men are splendid. I reckon we have about five minutes left.'

'Good luck to you,' was the final reply.

The young captain was last seen throwing grenades at the oncoming hordes of screaming Japanese infantry.

The situation for the troops of the 11th Indian Division was deteriorating rapidly and the advancing Japanese infantry, aided by their highly effective and deadly use of mortars, were rapidly moving in on the gun positions of C and D Troops of the 155th's B Battery. The Gunners were themselves alarmed by the panic on the faces of young Indian soldiers who were running through the gun positions discarding their rifles. Before long, the encroaching Japanese advance made the gun positions untenable and C Troop – in the forefront – and then D Troop, hurriedly began to fall back. Extricating the guns from the boggy ground was sheer hell and, despite their best efforts, D Troop was forced to abandon an ammunition limber that was stuck firmly in the mud. The confused and exhausted Gunners tried their best but the rapid, and seemingly unstoppable, Japanese advance had unnerved them.

On the other side of the trunk road, E and F Troops of C Battery were also now coming under pressure. Their OPs in front of the East Surrey and Leicester lines had become vulnerable to Japanese infiltration through the paddy fields.

The E Troop OP in the Leicesters' lines was first to go as their gun positions, some distance further back, came under sustained mortar attack. There was little that the infantry could do as they were experiencing difficulties themselves.

With little other option, the F Troop OP was then abandoned and the OP officer, Second Lieutenant, The Hon Edward Douglas-Home, his assistant, Bombardier Sidney Stone, and signaller, Gunner William Barnes, struggled to make their way back through the paddy fields. Then, to add insult to injury, they were fired on from both sides.

A furious Douglas-Home, in an attempt to stop the 'friendly' fire from the lines of the East Surrey Regiment, was shot in the chest for his efforts.

Gunner Barnes recalls: 'We helped the lieutenant back as best we could but during one of the spates of firing, I flung myself down and broke the bottle of Teacher's whisky that I was carrying. When I told the lieutenant, the air was blue as he had been taking sips to ease the pain from his wound. When we finally reached the East Surrey positions, he was not in a good mood. And I don't blame him.'

Meanwhile, the 155th were running short of ammunition and about 1400 hours, Lieutenant Colonel Murdoch reported to Brigadier Carpendale of 15th Brigade that he would have to reduce the rate of artillery fire. A decision was made to try to recoup some of the abandoned ammunition left by D Troop at the previous gun position and this unenviable task fell to Battery Sergeant Major Robert Bennett, who, along with half a dozen Gunners, was sent back to the gun position with a Quad and a 3-ton truck to retrieve the ammunition and extricate the limber from the mud. Arriving on the position, they found Gurkhas from the 2/2nd Battalion engaged in a bitter shoot-out and under fire from Japanese concealed in the undergrowth and rubber trees. Bennett and his gunners desperately loaded the dumped shells into the back of the 3-ton lorry but, despite their best efforts amid much cursing and swearing, they could not pull the limber from the mire. Mortar shells began falling all around them and with the constant whine of machine-gun bullets in their ears, they had little option but to make an undignified and rapid exit under the protective fire of the brave little mountain fighters from Nepal.

The situation along the whole Jitra line had become totally confused. Following the disintegration of the Jat position, the Leicesters' right flank was dangerously exposed and a decision was hurriedly made to deploy what was left of the two brigades into a supposedly better disposition. To the consternation of the Leicesters, who felt that they were holding their own against the Japanese, they were ordered from a relatively strong location to one running north-west from the iron bridge at Tanjong Pau over the Sungei Batu. This area had not been reconnoitred and, despite protests, they were ordered to occupy this new and more exposed position, which, to their great credit, they did early that evening. Unfortunately, the move led to misleading reports that they were withdrawing in the face of the enemy and matters just went from bad to worse as panic-stricken troops fired on non-existent targets. And worse, they often opened fire on their own side.

In the afternoon, Captain Fraser Stewart of B Battery, while trying to set up an OP on the bridge at Tanjong Pau in an attempt to give some artillery support to the besieged Leicesters, had to take cover when a 25-pounder of 350th Battery, 137th Field Regiment – then under the command of the 155th – shelled the bridge while he was still there!

The situation was now impossible. The C Battery command post was under constant gunfire – from whose side will never be known – and the guns were in danger of being overrun and lost. The battery commander, Major Philip Gold, reluctantly passed on the order to pull back.

Left behind at Jitra was Lance Bombardier Winslow of the 155th. It was only when the regiment reassembled at the abandoned airfield at Alor Star that it was realized he was missing. The last sighting of him had been at Jitra, when he was seen along with some Bengali sappers, but nothing was ever heard of him again.

Lance Bombardier Walter Winslow was reported missing, believed killed at Jitra.
Walter was single and had lived with his parents in Leicester.

Late on the evening of 12 December 1941, the situation on the main road south was chaotic. It was pitch dark and men and units – as in the case of the unfortunate Lance Bombardier Winslow – were inextricably mixed up. And in these hectic and confused conditions, the 155th lost yet another member when Lieutenant Wynne was knocked off his motorcycle by a speeding Bren carrier.

Lieutenant Jack Wynne died from his injuries in hospital on 20 January 1942.
Jack was single and had lived with his parents in Winchmore Hill, Middlesex. He was twenty-one years of age.

And during it all the monsoon rain continued to pour down.

For the tired and dispirited men of the 11th Indian Division, the withdrawal from Jitra late on the evening of 12 December 1941 came just in the nick of time. Hard on their heels was the Japanese 9th Infantry Brigade.

Driving throughout the night, the Quads and guns of the 155th were caught up in the mass exodus. Now the plan of action for the 11th Indian Division – or at least what was left of it – was to fight a delaying action at Gurun. But, as at Jitra, no attempt had been made to construct meaningful physical defences and although hasty efforts were considered following the disastrous failings at Jitra, it was now too late. Once again the dejected and physically exhausted British and Indian troops were left to complete the 'digging in'.

Unlike the 'poor bloody infantry', feverishly digging in up ahead of them, the dishevelled Gunners of the 155th had the unexpected luxury of fresh clothing, which had just arrived from their former base at Sungei Patani. In the afternoon, B Battery was recalled to Bedong, some distance south of Gurun, ostensibly to prepare for re-equipping with the more manoeuvrable 25-pounder field guns and, for those of C Battery left at Gurun, the afternoon brought the inevitable monsoon downpour.

Some miles further north, the battle raged on. Despite determined and brave resistance, the infantrymen of the 6th Brigade were taking heavy losses from repeated Japanese attacks and in the early hours of the morning of 15 December 1942, following a heavy mortar bombardment on the British and Indian positions, Japanese tanks and troops came rushing straight down the road. A mistaken belief that Japanese troops had infiltrated behind the position had led to an early and, at that stage, unnecessary withdrawal, leaving the sector totally undefended. The result was mayhem. Rapidly infiltrating through the jungle, Japanese troops fell on the headquarters of the 2nd East Surreys, killing the commanding officer and six other officers, including the medical officer and padre, who had been tending the wounded in the ambulance post attached to battalion HQ. Shortly afterwards, 6th Brigade Headquarters was similarly overwhelmed and once again all the staff were killed, with the exception of Brigadier Lay, who had fortunately left the hut just before the attack

And, as at Jitra, panic-stricken Indian troops were seen retreating through the artillery gun positions. A group of Punjabi infantrymen, accompanied by a *havildar*, appeared in the area and only two still had rifles.

Said Lieutenant Andrew Sewell: 'They appeared to have lost heart and disappeared into the rubber when no one was looking.'

Although aware from the sounds coming from the front that a fierce fight was ongoing, the Gunners, as a result of the loss of both the brigade and battalion HQs, had no real idea as to what was actually happening. On the west sector, the East Surreys and the Punjabis had taken the brunt of the attack but the 1st Leicesters, on being sent forward in support, had also come under sustained attack from tanks, mortars and small arms.

About 0930 hours, a warning was received by the gun crews of a possible Japanese infantry attack on their positions and small arms were hastily issued to the Gunners. The two field guns of the section commanded by Lieutenant Sewell had already been pulled back to the battery wagon lines and were hurriedly being brought ready for action when they were attacked by Japanese dive-bombers. Most of the men scrambled for cover and safety, but one, Gunner Edgar of F Troop, was killed outright during the attack.

Gunner Tom Edgar had lived with his sister in Wallasey, Cheshire.
Tom was twenty-nine years of age.

28

As the situation just ahead of them quickly deteriorated, the order was received for C Battery units to withdraw and rendezvous further south, at Bukit Mertajam.

The following day they continued on to Ipoh, where they reformed with B Battery. The regiment was in desperate need of re-equipping and with artillery cover now available from the 137th and 88th Field regiments, they were able to catch up with a few days' much needed rest.

With the loss of the northern states of Malaya and the apparently unstoppable Japanese advance, Lieutenant General Percival was under pressure to hold central Malaya in order to slow the enemy progress for as long as possible to enable the withdrawal of the 9th Indian Division from the east coast before it was cut off.

The 12th Indian Infantry Brigade from the Malaya Command Reserve was brought up to the front to allow the 11th Indian Division to withdraw through them and prepare for the proposed prolonged stand at Kampar.

On the morning and afternoon of 21 December 1941, reconnaissance parties from the 155th Field Regiment's Survey Section travelled south from Ipoh to the mountainous outcrop of Gunong Bujang Melaka, near Kampar. There they surveyed the area to the east – the defensive position allocated to them and the Gurkhas of 48th Brigade – soon to be euphemistically known to the Gunners as 'Happy Valley'.

The following day – 22 December – advance parties from the 155th moved down to Happy Valley, where they began preparing the gun locations for the regiment's 4.5-inch howitzers and newly-acquired 25-pounders. And, for the first time since the campaign began, they were in a good defensive position as the valley was bounded on either side by steep cliffs – some 2,000 feet high in places.

The slopes leading up from the valley floor were covered by rubber and banana trees and long grass known as lalang, which provided excellent camouflage and concealment for the guns. The Gunners themselves were well catered for as the locals had left behind most of their livestock. As a result, eggs, poultry and fresh meat were in plentiful supply.

The Gunners were in a buoyant mood and cheerfully set about working on the gun positions and the slit trenches surrounding them. Such was their confidence and morale that the commanding officer, Lieutenant Colonel Murdoch, remarked that the men had better not eat up all the chickens as some were required to lay eggs as their stay would be for some time!

During the night of 28/29 December, the guns of B Battery were brought into action on predicted targets in the Dipang area, as Japanese troops could be seen gathering en masse just north of the *kampong*. Fire directions from Captain Mackenzie in the C Troop OP proved particularly effective and achieved success on a number of targets, most notably the bridge at Dipang. Earlier attempts by Indian sappers to completely blow up the bridge had been unsuccessful and as Japanese engineers began to repair the damage, the artillery finished the job – and the engineers!

The OPs provided good observation of the valley floor and repeated attempts during the day by Japanese infantry to infiltrate forward were quickly spotted and resulted in devastating barrages being brought down on them. The accuracy of the artillery spotters was again demonstrated when Captain Mackenzie, scrutinizing the area through his field glasses, saw enemy soldiers carrying boxes of ammunition into a distant tin-mining building and was able to accurately pinpoint fire directly onto the structure, with the inevitable result.

While the location of the OPs and the skill of the Gunners operating there was of crucial significance, earlier work carried out in the area by the Survey Section the previous week, where they identified and predicted probable targets, was key to much of the success and one of the regiment's officers remarked, 'In spite of the good observation much of the shooting was off the map or on previously surveyed points. The success of these shoots again showed the accuracy of the work of the Survey Section.'

On their arrival in the valley, the Survey Section had only standard 1-inch Ordnance Survey-style maps on which to make their calculations. It is an indication of their skill and ability that they were able to carry out such accurate surveying in the time available. However, during one surveying expedition not long after arriving in the valley, they caused consternation when they attempted to drive through the Gurkha front line.

Said Gunner Peter Rhodes: 'No infantryman likes to have people walking out through his lines and so we were challenged by our friends, with the familiar grin but great firmness. As our ability to communicate was limited to a grin and "Hello, Johnnie", we explained our presence to their officer. He knew what we had to do and waved us on our way with his best wishes, but even so, his Nepalese friends still looked apprehensive as we drove off in the general direction of the enemy.'

Rhodes' next encounter with the young Gurkhas a day or so later was more gruesome. He and several other surveyors had again gone forward to fix positions, which involved yet another walk through the Gurkha positions. However, on this occasion they were greeted enthusiastically by the young Nepalese, who were clearly delighted to see them. Calling them across to their trenches, the grinning Gurkhas produced cotton bags secured with drawstrings, from which they proudly produced dozens of human ears, the produce of their nightly 'murder patrols' into enemy lines!

His subsequent meeting was even more macabre. Later that day, while acting as a temporary despatch rider, he was riding his motor-cycle along a track when he was waved down by another group of cheerful Gurkhas who were sitting eating by the trackside. Walking across to where they were sitting in a circle, he was astonished to see on the ground in the middle of the group an enamel plate with the severed head of a Japanese soldier still wearing his cap! Never had Rhodes been so glad that the Gurkhas were on his side!

It was now the evening of 31 December 1941. For the many Scots in the regiment, this was Hogmanay and a New Year was rapidly approaching, and back home a toast to welcome the new arrival would have been customary. But these were not normal circumstances and the Gunners, bunkered down in a foreign land, were instead getting ready to engage with a brutal and fearsome enemy. So how were they to suitably celebrate the event? The answer soon came when the Scots CO of the 155th decided on an appropriate way to mark the occasion. Between five minutes to midnight and five minutes past, every gun would fire continuously into the Japanese positions. The subsequent effect on the enemy remains unknown but it certainly cheered up the Gunners.

Following the midnight artillery barrage, the early hours of the first day of the New Year were marked by a huge, glorious yellow moon, which shone over Happy Valley. Sitting concealed in the B Battery OP on the hillside, Bombardier Pat Campbell and his signaller, Gunner 'Titch' Walker, silently stared out onto a night now only disturbed by the regular and constant chirping of millions of insects and let their thoughts wander off to their homes in Dumfries and Coventry. The OP officer, Captain Mackenzie, as was his norm, had gone off to confer with the Gurkhas, leaving Pat and Titch to their quiet contemplation and dreams.

Suddenly, the peace and serenity were shattered. The terrifying sound of loud and unrelenting gunfire behind them instantly brought the shocked Gunners out of their reverie. It quickly became obvious that the Gurkhas were battling it out with the enemy but the two hapless Gunners had no idea how it had come about! Unbeknown to them, during the night, and by the light of the very moon that they had been

31

so taken with, the enemy had skilfully and silently infiltrated through the position and had unknowingly crept past the well-concealed OP. It was only when the Japanese met the ever-alert Gurkhas and their waiting kukri knives that all hell broke loose.

Just as dawn was breaking, the fierce and seemingly endless firing petered out and, to their profound shock, Pat and Titch became aware of Japanese soldiers creeping back to their own lines as silently as they had come. They were only a short distance from the OP and still oblivious to its existence. Fully aware of this, Pat had his hands full in preventing the determined Titch from having a pot shot at them with their solitary rifle. To have done so would have been suicidal.

The dawn brought unexpected news. Gurkha patrols returning from their sorties into no-man's-land in pursuit of the retreating Japanese reported that the enemy had disappeared and looked to have pulled back from their positions in the valley. The puzzled Gunners wondered what the 'cunning buggers' were up to now but in no time received their answer. From the other side of the mountain came the sound of a massive artillery barrage. The Japanese were now advancing on the British Battalion and the Battle of Kampar was moving into a new and devastating phase. Over the next twenty-four hours, the former infantrymen of the decimated 1st Leicesters and 2nd East Surrey regiments, now joined as the British Battalion, wrote themselves into the pages of history with their magnificent and heroic stand at Kampar. Sadly, it was to little avail.

Having successfully held the position in Kampar valley for four days against a determined force, the Gunners, to their profound shock and disbelief, were told to prepare for yet another withdrawal. Despite their tenacity in halting the Japanese over the preceding days, they learned that the enemy had once again bypassed their position and were threatening from the rear.

Accordingly, the Gurkhas of 48th Brigade and the guns of the 155th were withdrawn from the positions in Happy Valley, which they had held so successfully. The Gunners were gutted, for they believed that, at long last, they had shown the Japanese just what they could do. Earlier thoughts, on the dawning of the New Year, of a fresh impetus to push back the Japs had evaporated. Now, at the end of the first day of January 1941, they were facing retreat once again. It was as if nothing had changed.

Chapter 3

'Hell was let loose in Malaya' – The Battles for Slim River and Johore

Following the disheartening yet inevitable withdrawal from Kampar, Lieutenant General Percival had decided on a further tactical delaying action north of Kuala Lumpur to prevent the advancing Japanese from capturing the airfields at Kuala Lumpur and Port Swettenham. The overall strategic aim was to stall any Japanese advance south of the state of Selangor, at least until sufficient reinforcements for the defence of Singapore were available, and the next defensive position identified was at Trolak, north of Slim River. The original intention was to hold the position for several days to allow time for final work at Tah Jong Malim, where a strong divisional defence line was being prepared. Holding the front line at Trolak were the 12th Indian Brigade, made up of the 4/19th Hyderabad Regiment, the 5/2 Punjab Regiment and the 2nd Argyll and Sutherland Highlanders, with the 5/14 Punjab Regiment in reserve. The three Gurkha battalions of 28th Brigade were holding the area around Kampong Slim.

The anti-tank defences prepared along the length of the road were pathetically insufficient and although over 1,400 mines should have been made available for use, only twenty-four had been issued. The 5/2 Punjab formed the main defensive line between Milestones 61 and 62, with support from the 2-pounder guns of a single anti-tank troop. About 8 miles further south, two artillery batteries of the 137th Field Regiment were harboured in the Cluny Estate. Some 6 miles south of Slim River, 11th Indian Division's other Field Regiment, the 155th (Lanarkshire Yeomanry) were held in reserve in a rubber estate at Behrang.

Meanwhile, the bridges north of Trolak, which had earlier been blown by sappers of the retreating 11th Indian Division, were swiftly repaired and brought back into use by the skilful Japanese engineers.

In clear moonlight, at 0330 hours on the morning of 7 January, an armoured unit of twenty medium and light tanks, followed by truck-loads of motorized infantry, attacked the Hyderabads' position. Within minutes, the Indians' solitary anti-tank gun was destroyed and the tanks rolled on past, spraying machine-gun bullets into the jungle after the fleeing Indian troops. The convoy did not even bother to stop. In the following hours, the Japanese would destroy most of the 12th Indian Brigade and the 28th Gurkhas. During the action, communications between the various battalions of the 12th Brigade were severed and by 0600 hours, the fast-moving Japanese tank column had surprised the Argylls, who were holding a position at Trolak. Next was the reserve battalion of the 5/14th Punjab moving up the trunk road to hold a check position. The leading Punjab company scattered but those coming behind were mowed down by the machine guns of the looming tanks, the survivors fleeing into the jungle on either side of the road.

Further south, the Gurkhas of 2/9th Battalion were also caught unawares, only to be followed by their comrades of the 2/1st approaching from the rear. With nothing to take on the oncoming tanks, there was little they could do but dive for cover into the jungle to avoid the scything destruction of the tanks' machine guns.

Rolling past the jungle clearing at the Cluny Estate, where the vehicles and 25-pounders of the 137th Field Regiment were parked up, the clanking Jap tanks simply stopped and for five minutes turned their fire on the unprotected field guns and crews before moving on.

It was a complete disaster.

Just before 0800 hours, the 155th Field Regiment, held in reserve some miles south of Slim River Bridge, was ordered into action and hurriedly began the move north towards Slim River.

With little information as to what was happening up ahead, the Regimental Headquarters staff and commanding officer set off to find suitable positions and to open an advanced headquarters. Leading at the front in a 15cwt truck was Lieutenant Eustace, his assistant Lance Bombardier Levitt and Gunners Limb and Holton. They had only gone a short distance, eyes searching for the inevitable Jap planes, when they were brought to a halt by a bomb crater in the road. This probably saved their lives, for as Lieutenant Eustace was arranging to have the crater filled to allow passage for the field guns following up behind, they were passed by others.

On a motorcycle were Lieutenant Wilmer and Bombardier Edel of the Survey Section, followed by the orderly officer, Lieutenant Brocklehurst, also riding a motorcycle. Behind them at a short distance were the CO, Lieutenant Colonel Murdoch, as pillion passenger on a motorcycle ridden by Gunner Bobby Warwick and then Lieutenant Kepple, the Signal officer, and eleven Signallers, with four of the Signals' trucks.

Next in the spread-out convoy came Captain Mackenzie and Lieutenant Hinton, the troop commander and gun position officer of C Troop, followed by Battery Sergeant Major Billings with the first of the C Troop 25-pounders. Next were Second Lieutenant Ronaldson and Sergeant Keen, and one of the gun crews of E Troop drawing one of the old 4.5-inch howitzers. All were stretched out at a distance of 400 yards as a precaution against the ever-present Japanese planes, which flew up and down the road, bombing and machine-gunning anything that moved.

Unknown to them, the first column of Japanese armour, made up of six medium and five light tanks, had broken through the forward and other defences around Slim and were heading in their direction. Lieutenant Wilmer and Bombardier Edel were first to meet them south of Kampong Slim and during the encounter, Bombardier Edel was killed and Lieutenant Wilmer taken prisoner.

Bombardier Bernard Edel was from Stoke Newington, London.
Bernard was twenty-three years of age.

Shortly thereafter it was Lieutenant Brocklehurst's turn to meet the oncoming enemy and although he managed to escape into the jungle, he was subsequently captured before he could make his way back to his unit.

Tragically, the regiment's popular commanding officer was next to be killed, when he and Gunner Warwick came face to face with the advancing tanks. While engaged in a frantic attempt to turn the motorcycle around, they were fired on by the leading tank's machine gun. Colonel Murdoch was killed outright and Bobby Warwick seriously wounded and later taken prisoner.

Lieutenant Colonel Alan Murdoch was married with a young
daughter and lived in New Abbey, Dumfries.

Following behind the CO, Lieutenant Kepple and the Signallers spotted the tanks just in time. They stopped their trucks and quickly scrambled into the undergrowth. Unfortunately, only Lieutenant Kepple managed to get back to his lines at that time, while over the next few days the other eleven Signallers were either killed or taken prisoner. In any event, it made little difference as Lieutenant Kepple was to become a POW a few weeks later after the fall of Singapore.

Some distance behind the Signallers in a 15cwt truck, Captain Mackenzie, Bombardier Pat Campbell, Gunner 'Titch' Walker and Gunner Hector McKay had a lucky escape. They had just crossed over the Slim River Bridge, when a British officer rushed out into the road in front of them waving his arms, shouting, 'Tanks, tanks!'

'We stopped immediately and abandoned the truck,' said Pat. 'Everybody ran into the rubber and watched the tanks come along and just push the 15cwt aside.'

The tanks rolled on and over the Slim River Bridge and it wasn't long before the crew of the leading gun of C Troop became the next victims. Sergeant Major Billings was killed in the brief encounter.

Sergeant Major Francis John Billings was married and
from Sutton, Surrey.
Francis was forty years of age.

The gun crew were luckier and managed to escape into the jungle.

Next to meet the tanks were Second Lieutenant Ronaldson with the leading 4.5-inch howitzer of E Troop. He was surprised to have caught up with Lieutenant Eustace, the gun position officer, who he had thought was further ahead on the road. By this time Lieutenant Eustace had been alerted of the situation ahead and, after warning him of the tanks advancing towards them, went back to alert the rest of the battery while Ronaldson brought the howitzer into action in an anti-tank role. He positioned the gun in a steep-sided cutting to the right of the road, about 40 yards south of a sharp left-hand bend. Tanks approaching from the north would have no prior warning of the gun's presence until they turned into the straight.

As the gun was being manoeuvred into place, the regiment's adjutant, Captain Gordon Brown, arrived on a motorcycle and took command of the gun crew. Lieutenant Ronaldson then went forward to the bend, taking up a position on some high ground from where he could see to the next corner.

The gun crew under Sergeant Oliver Keen hurriedly prepared six rounds of armour-piercing shells and waited by the howitzer for the tanks to appear. Captain Brown and the Quad driver, Lance Bombardier George Mair, armed with rifles, were ready behind some concrete-filled barrels.

Suddenly, a truck loaded with Indian sappers came racing round the bend from the direction of Slim River and screeched to a halt right in front of the Morris Quad, which by this time had been turned around ready for a quick getaway. Before anything could be done about moving the truck, the sappers jumped from the vehicle and scattered into the rubber trees at the side of the road.

Within minutes the clanking rumble of approaching tanks could be clearly heard and up ahead on the banking, Lieutenant Ronaldson blew his whistle as prearranged.

Said Gunner John Ogden, the gunlayer on the howitzer: 'The first tank came round the corner and I waited until it was in my open sights and then fired: the shell struck the tank dead centre and seemed to shake it, but did not stop it. It came on slowly and we put another round into it; it stopped and burst into flames.'

Immediately after the first strike on the tank, two Japanese soldiers jumped from the turret and were brought down by fire from the rifles of Captain Brown and Lance Bombardier Mair. The cannon on the tank had been bent upwards by the first artillery shot and rendered useless. The second tank was unable to pass its disabled neighbour and stopped alongside, just an arm's length from Lieutenant Ronaldson, who was clearly visible from the left-hand side of the tank. Fortunately for him, the two Japs who emerged from the turret of the tank carrying automatic weapons climbed down the other side.

Said Gunner Ogden: 'Between the firing of the first two rounds, the second tank had come round the corner and was hidden by the first. Sergeant Keen ordered me to try and penetrate the first one and so reach the second; we fired the remaining four rounds, with what effect I could not see. We were told to limber up and mount and as we started up we heard machine-gun fire from the cutting and two awful bangs. I turned and saw Captain Brown lying wounded.'

With all the ammunition expended, Lance Bombardier Mair had started up the Quad and was beginning to pull out from behind the sappers' abandoned truck. It was immediately seen by the second tank, which fired on it. Amazingly, the tank shell entered through the Quad's rear offside shot locker and then exited through the nearside door, miraculously with no injury to those in the vehicle.

Sadly, Sergeant Keen and Captain Brown were not so fortunate.

Sergeant Keen had delayed mounting the vehicle until he was sure that the gun was properly hooked in and was running after the Quad, which was already on the move, when he was killed by a burst of automatic weapon fire from one of the tank crew who had climbed onto the embankment.

Sergeant Oliver James Keen was married and from Barnsley.
Oliver was thirty years of age.
For his conduct during the incident he was later posthumously
Mentioned in Despatches.

Captain Brown was similarly shot and although he survived his injuries, he lost his right arm and several fingers from his left hand. Prior to the war, he had been a gifted pianist. For his leadership and bravery during the incident, he was later awarded the Military Cross.

Word of what was happening around Slim River had got back to the main body of the regiment and guns were hastily brought up nearer the bridge and put into anti-tank positions, with efforts being made to strengthen the defences with improvised anti-tank blocks. Manning one of the 4.5-inch howitzers, Gunner John McEwan from Motherwell celebrated his twenty-first birthday. The Japanese tanks had had enough for the time being and pulled back to the bridge and the respite was enough to allow hundreds of Allied troops the opportunity to make their escape.

Owing to the general confusion, there was no infantry available and B Battery sent up a Bren carrier and a 15cwt truck with a party of twenty men under Battery Sergeant Major Charles Road-night [*sic*] to patrol forward of the destroyed enemy tank. Once past the stricken tank, the Gunners had only travelled about 400 yards when they came under machine-gun fire from the right-hand side of the road. Hurriedly taking to the jungle, they engaged the enemy, who had come from the two tanks on the box girder bridge at Slim River. During the encounter they killed several Japanese and beat off the rest, while suffering only one casualty – Gunner Jimmy Graham – who was slightly wounded by a rifle bullet. During the fight, Thompson light machine guns – the famed 'Tommy gun' – and hand grenades were used for the first time by the Gunners, although, in their ignorance and inexperience in the use of the latter, they ended up throwing the grenades before the fuses had been inserted! But thereafter, Sergeant Major Road-night was known to the Gunners as 'Machine Gun Charlie'!

All around the Slim River area, shocked British and Indian troops were making their way south – either through the thick jungle or down the railway. Their stories were all the same – a sudden and unexpected meeting with the tanks – taking cover in the rubber as the tanks rumbled by – a moment to collect themselves and then a march south through rubber and jungle to their own lines. Even the famed Gurkhas of 28th Brigade had received a mauling and many were drowned when, in a futile attempt to escape, they tried to swim the swollen Sungei Slim and were swept to their deaths by the fast current.

The previous day, the 155th's much-liked and respected CO, Lieutenant Colonel Murdoch, had sent a long and surprisingly uncensored letter to his brother where he began:

> I hardly know where to start in the telling of this little war and its position and effect on us and Malaya but I am quite determined to let you have the full story censor or no, so that you may pass it round to influential people as all should know what a disgraceful show it has been from the very beginning.

He continued thereafter with a detailed criticism of the campaign and the lack of preparation to meet the Japanese invasion.

The letter ends:

> Postal services having more or less broken down I have not been able to send this till today [6 Jan] no doubt when air force and reinforcements appear this show will stabilize. Am really OK.

The following day, 7 January 1942, he was killed in action following yet another debacle in what was fast becoming an ill-fated campaign.

In a letter sent home to his wife at Lanark only days later, Bombardier James Fergusson of C Troop, B Battery, had written:

> Since I wrote my last letter, Hell was let loose in Malaya. Many and varied have been my experiences since we set forth to meet the might of the Japanese Empire with forces which we were led to believe were adequate not only to hold the Japs but to take the offensive and hurl her back through Thailand. But alas we found ourselves hopelessly outnumbered and with absolutely no air support, and with a fifth column against us probably larger than any army has had to deal with. So far it has been a tale of withdrawal after withdrawal but at each stage we have been able to inflict heavy loss on the enemy before we withdraw to await them again.

On the morning of 8 January, following the tragic losses of the previous day, the regiment was reorganized and Major Philip Gold, C Battery Commander, assumed command of the regiment. The defence of Central Malaya had become extremely precarious and the remnants of the 11th Indian Division and 12th and 28th Indian brigades were basically all that was left to stem any further Japanese advance down the Malay Peninsula. They were all in a poor state; the men were both physically and mentally drained and, on the chance of a brief respite, they were withdrawn some distance south to Serendah, where hopefully, after some rest, they could help prevent the enemy access to Kuala Lumpur – at least for a couple of days.

The 155th had likewise begun the familiar withdrawal – retreat was not a word recognized – and although coming under repeated air attacks on the busy road, they reached their destination at Serendah without further mishap. As was normal in the monsoon season, heavy rain poured down during the afternoon, but the Gunners were now used to this and pulled and pushed the 25-pounders and 4.5-inch howitzers into their inevitably muddy emplacements ready for action.

The Serendah position could easily be turned by the now familiar Japanese tactic of outflanking through the rubber plantations on either side, and during the wet night of 9/10 January, the two weak battalions were feverishly trying to dig themselves in, the Gurkhas having nothing but some hoes found in the village and their own bayonets as entrenching tools.

Just after dawn on 10 January, fierce fighting broke out on the forward positions when large numbers of Japanese infantry, adopting their usual enveloping tactics, met with the Gurkhas. The resulting hand-to-hand fighting was savage and, under force of numbers, the Gurkhas were driven back until the guns of the 155th were themselves in danger of being overrun. The Japanese were everywhere and, by 1100 hours, the leading 4.5-inch howitzers of F Troop, set up near the main road at Sungei Choh, just south of Serendah, were hurriedly pulled out in the face of the encircling Japanese.

The main road through Serendah was to all intents now in the hands of the enemy and Captain Mackenzie, in the D Troop OP alongside the Gurkhas, lost his transport when his vehicle was destroyed by a Jap dive-bomber. Another to come face to face with the enemy was 21-year-old Gunner Tom McKie, from Thornhill, near Dumfries. The regiment was running low on ammunition and Tom and his mate, Gunner Harry Stokes from London, were sent south with a 15cwt truck to collect fresh supplies and on their way back were fired on from the dense jungle at the side of the road, forcing the truck into a ditch. In their haste to get away from the deadly machine-gun fire, Tom and Harry were separated and, with his instincts telling him to make as much distance from the hidden Japanese as quickly as possible, the unarmed Tom set off in the opposite direction, into the jungle. He had only gone a short distance when, to his relief, he encountered a Gurkha patrol led by a young English officer. But his relief was short-lived when they heard the sound of Japanese infantry moving noisily through the jungle towards them and Tom was handed a rifle with a bayonet already fixed and told to get ready. Panic-stricken, he tried to explain that he had never used a rifle and bayonet before, but merely received the calm direction from the young officer: 'Don't worry, my men will look after you. Just you stand behind that tree and as they come forward, stick it in them and give it bully!' Terrified out of his wits, Tom did as he was told and, in his words, 'Of course, it happened. All of a sudden I couldn't get the bloody thing out and I panicked and someone shouted, "Pull the trigger," and I did. If you pull the trigger on someone that close to you there is nothing but bits flying all around. I was alright that day but the day after, boy was I sick. I couldn't move for being sick but surprisingly, after that nothing ever bothered me again about being in action.'

During his brief but torrid experience of hand-to-hand combat, Tom had received a bayonet wound to his own leg but only become aware of it afterwards when the adrenalin stopped flowing. His respect for the Gurkhas was boundless!

Irrespective of the risk of being overrun, the regiment's guns continued firing throughout and scored a number of successful hits on predicted targets previously identified by a survey team of the Federated Malay States Volunteer Force. But their effectiveness was undoubtedly hindered by the frequent and accurate attacks by enemy dive-bombers who pounded the area, forcing the guns to be continually moved from position to position. During one of the raids on the C Troop position, the B Battery commander, Major Jock Wilson, was wounded in the head and his driver, Gunner Graham, killed.

Gunner George Graham, a married man, came from Glasgow.
George was twenty-six years of age.

On 13 January, the survivors of the 15th Indian Brigade, who had taken such a pounding at Jitra, Gurun and Kampar, arrived from reserve and took up their positions. Once again they were covered by the guns of the 155th but before any contact was made with the enemy, orders were received from 11th Indian Division HQ for the regiment to take up a mobile reserve role at Kluang and to remain there in reserve for a month to rest and retrain reinforcements.

General Wavell, on speaking with some of the survivors of the 11th Indian Division, had realized that they were at the end of their endurance and immediately ordered the division out of the front line to rest, and the responsibility for holding the Japanese advance was given over to the Australian 8th Division, who had not yet been in action and were ready, spoiling for a fight.

On their way south, the Gunners of the 155th met with a great deal of traffic congestion as the fresh Australian units moved up to relieve the exhausted British and Indian troops. The battle-weary Gunners were furious and enraged at the insults and taunts thrown at them by the Australians who, to be fair, had no idea what they had been up against since the Japanese invasion in December.

As Lieutenant Andrew Sewell of the 155th more delicately put it, 'Some of the Australians, who were doubtless unaware of the situation, were misled by the withdrawal of the regiment into casting aspersions on the morale of the 11th Indian Division.'

The Australian troops were about to experience the reality of the situation for themselves.

With Central Malaya now in his hands, Lieutenant General Yamashita, the Japanese commander, considered that Muar was the last real obstacle facing him and his plan was to send the Imperial Guards down the west coast to outflank the Allied defences while the Japanese 5th Division kept them busy on the front. On 16 January 1942, the Guards landed at Telaga Jetty, on the west coast near Batu Pahat, and began moving inland. The Japanese forces were also on the move some 30 miles further north near Muar and, once again, as at Kampar, there was a danger that the Allied forces would be outflanked by landings from the sea.

Soon, in the area around Muar and Bakri, the Australian 27th Brigade and the 45th Indian Brigade were engaged in fierce fighting with various units of the Japanese 5th Division, while at Batu Pahat the 15th Indian Brigade were up against the Japanese 1/4th Battalion.

At Gemas, Australian troops scored an initial success when they staged a very effective ambush on the advancing enemy but, unhappily, they were destined to suffer the same fate as all other Allied units when the Japanese quickly reinforced with fresh troops. As a result, 53rd Brigade were sent to Ayer Hitum as back-up, with artillery support provided by B and C Batteries of the 155th Field Regiment, who had hurriedly been brought back out of reserve.

The 53rd Brigade was a Territorial infantry unit made up of the 2nd Battalion of the Cambridgeshire Regiment and the 5th and 6th Battalions of the Norfolk Regiment. Part of the 18th Division, they were ill-prepared for combat, having arrived in Singapore only three days previous, after eleven weeks at sea.

From the headquarters of the 11th Indian Division at Ayer Hitum, the 2nd Cambridgeshires were directed to the Batu Pahat area with artillery assistance from eight 25-pounder field guns of B Battery of the 155th, while the 6th Norfolk Regiment was fated to hold the Bukit Pelandok Defile at Milestone 78 on the Muar–Yong Peng Road, backed by C Battery's 4.5-inch howitzers. The next few days were a literal baptism of fire for both the Norfolk and Cambridgeshire Regiments.

The infantrymen of C and D Companies of the Norfolks were deployed at the strategically important steep-sided defile backed by the four 4.5-inch howitzers of F Troop of the 155th with the artillery OP positioned high on the side of Bukit Belah, which made up one side of the steep-sided gap.

The four field guns were set up on the right of the road near a small *kampong* and as they were in open ground, they had to be concealed with shrub and bushes, which quickly turned brown in the heat. Every night the camouflage had to be replaced under cover of darkness.

And action for the nervous and untested Norfolks was not long in coming. On the morning of 18 January, Japanese infantry infiltrating through the jungle on the lower slopes of Bukit Pelandok surprised the Norfolks' C Company, which had been positioned there to guard the Yong Peng Road. This was the inexperienced Norfolks' first taste of close combat and they were caught completely unawares by the speed and ferocity of the attack and quickly dislodged from the hill. By 1430 hours, the Japanese 5th Battalion had taken control of Bukit Pelandok but the Norfolks, now over their initial shock, were fighting back. Two platoons of D Company, dug in on the opposite slopes of Bukit Belah just below the F Troop Artillery OP, and opposite the enemy now in control on the slopes of Bukit Pelandok, were holding their own despite taking casualties from persistent and accurate sniping from the Japanese. Firing for the Gunners of F Troop was fast becoming problematic – and dangerous – as one gun section had to fire over the position of the other in engaging the unseen enemy now entrenched on Bukit Pelandok. As a result, a section was withdrawn to the wagon lines, leaving the remaining two guns firing on the area where the Japanese were known to be concealed. Under the weight of the attack, the Norfolks were forced to pull back, and with no forward protection, BSM Charles Road-night, now better known to the Gunners as Machine Gun Charlie following his exploits at Slim River, once again lived up to his nickname. Taking six Gunners with him, he went out in front to defend the two guns. Coming across some Japanese troops moving forward in a small *kampong*, he and his men brought their favoured Tommy guns into use and when the enemy dived into some huts for cover, dealt with them by lobbing in hand grenades. But this time, unlike at Slim River, the fuses were inserted!

Above them in the artillery OP on Bukit Belah, the newly-promoted Captain Andrew Sewell and his OP assistant, Bombardier Joe Shone, were fighting their own personal war against a large group of Japanese troops who had managed to get across the road and were now scaling the heights towards them. The action is best described from the citations submitted for their award of the Military Cross and Military Medal, respectively:

Sewell:

For conspicuous gallantry and devotion to duty on 17 [sic] January 42 during the action of the Yong Peng-Muar Road. When his OP party was cut off from the troop which he was firing, Capt. Sewell and his men brought into action two mortars which they had found in the vicinity and, though never having fired a mortar before, inflicted such casualties on the enemy that they were able to rejoin their battery. Later during the night he went out in front of the forward troops and assisted in salving an anti-tank gun.

Shone:

Gunner Shone has throughout the whole campaign shown great courage and resourcefulness. He was O.P/A [Observation Post Assistant] to Capt. E.R.A. Sewell at the defile on the Yong Peng-Perit Sulon road and while Capt. Sewell was otherwise engaged shot the Troop himself with success. He assisted Capt Sewell in rigging up the sites for two Mortars and later, firing them, inflicting heavy casualties on the enemy. On one occasion the Mortar misfired and after waiting a minute, Gnr Shone emptied the bomb from the Mortar and threw it at the enemy, the bomb exploding some thirty feet in front of the OP.

Throughout the incident, the Gunners in the artillery OP continued to direct the fire of the guns, but at 1730 hours, a withdrawal was finally ordered and the OP evacuated while the guns of F Troop disengaged just in time. As the last gun was pulling out, Japanese troops appeared and opened up on them with machine guns – fortunately without success.

F Troop's involvement in the defile had come to an end and by 22 January, they and E Troop were withdrawn from action and safely harboured at Johore Bahru.

Meanwhile over on the west coast, near Batu Pahat, their mates in B Battery were taking a pounding.

On the same day that C Battery had moved with the 6th Norfolks to the defile, the Gunners of B Battery were despatched to Batu Pahat in support of the 2nd Cambridgeshire Regiment, who had been given the job of holding the town and surrounding area.

On 20 January, the Gunners were spread thinly. D Troop of B Battery was located on Hill 127 to the east of Batu Pahat and the four 25-pounders of C Troop were hidden in the rubber of the Bukit Banang Estate to the south of the town. The Japanese plan of attack was for the Guards Reconnaissance Battalion to attack Batu Pahat from the north-east and pin down the defenders, while the 4th Guards Regiment made a landing on the coast to the west of the town and then moved south towards Senggarang. The 5th Guards would then make a pincer move on Rengit and in so doing, effectively cut the escape route for those in Batu Pahat while at the same time preventing any attempt at reinforcing from the south.

Throughout Southern Johore, the British, Indian and Australian forces were in trouble and it was clearly evident that a withdrawal to Singapore was inevitable.

About 0900 hours on 22 January, on the east side of the town, D Troop and their escort from the British Battalion were attacked by a group of about 100 Japanese troops who unexpectedly appeared in front of their position. Aware of the sudden danger, the Gunners rapidly lowered the barrels of the 25-pounders and prepared to fire over open sights at the fast-approaching enemy.

Said Sergeant Jim Watson: 'Suddenly ahead of us silhouetted against the skyline was a large contingent of Jap infantry covered in camouflage. We engaged them, firing with open sights, whereupon they split up to our right and left, blending into the undergrowth.'

Within minutes, the relentless Japanese infantrymen returned to the attack, and, along with their British Battalion escort, the Gunners moved out in front of the gun position and fought them off with their other favourite weapon – the Tommy gun. There was now a real danger of the 25-pounders being overrun if the Japanese repeated their sudden, fanatical tactics and help was called for from the guns of C Troop and it is recorded that their troop commander, Captain Michael Anderson, very effectively brought down a heavy salvo of fire 'onto several patches of dead ground' where the Japanese infantry were known to be con-cealed. To the relief of the beleaguered Gunners, this brought about a brief but welcome respite in the attack. However, it did not last long and to the consternation of the Gunners and the men of the British Battalion, mortar shells soon began falling on the gun position and in amongst the shallow trenches of the infantry escort.

Even when there was a let-up from the damnable mortars, persistent sniping from the jungle caused mayhem around the gun positions and about 1600 hours that afternoon, it resulted in yet another severe blow to the regiment. The B Battery commander, Major Jock Wilson, who was still recovering from injuries sustained in the bombing attack at Serendah on 10 January, arrived in a carrier to check out the situation and was inadvertently driven just beyond the gun position and, before anyone had a chance to warn him of the presence of snipers, he stood up in the carrier and was immediately shot in the head and killed.

Major John 'Jock' Wilson was married with a young child.
He was the son of Sir James Wilson and Lady Wilson, from Dunning, Perthshire.
John was buried in a nearby rubber plantation following a brief funeral service by Padre Noel Duckworth.

The decision was then taken to pull out the guns while there was still a relative lull in the fighting. Over the next thirty minutes, taking advantage of the slow-down in enemy fire – it was thought that they were replenishing their ammunition as firing up until then had been extremely heavy – the guns were frantically, but successfully, removed from the position. That is, all except the 25-pounder of Sergeant Jim Watson.

The Quad tractor units used to haul the limbers and field guns were parked at the wagon lines about a mile back from the gun position and Jim had been kept busy helping bring up the vehicles to the front as there was a shortage of drivers owing to the day's confusion. As a result, his gun was the last on the position and when he arrived from the wagon lines in the final Quad, his crew feverishly began hitching up the gun. Said Jim: 'All hell then broke loose as the Japs in the trees opened up with all their weapons.'

As the gun crew scattered for cover, Jim leaped from the Quad but with bullets shrieking all around him, he had little option but to crouch down and take shelter behind the front offside wheel of the vehicle. Bullets peppered the Quad and punctured the tyres, including the one on the wheel behind which Jim was sheltering but fortunately for him, the large steel wheel rim continued to provide him with protection and the wheel's manufacturer – Sankey – whose name his face was firmly pressed against, remained forever in his memory.

From his hiding place behind the wheel, Jim frantically wriggled over the path and into the ditch beside the others where, without a weapon among them, they crouched down and wondered what to do next. Their minds were soon made up when a large group of yelling Japanese infantry, with fixed bayonets, suddenly came rushing out of the jungle towards them.

Said Jim: 'The six of us took to our heels and ran down the same gulley I had used to get to the wagon lines. I think that was one of the most humiliating experiences for me in the entire campaign and, of course, we left behind a Quad and gun, which we had tried so hard to salvage.'

Others from the gun position, attempting to escape from the encircling Japanese, also ran into trouble and Gunners Dick Gwillim and John McGuinness were both seriously wounded during the hurried evacuation. Dick was shot through the right elbow, with the bullet exiting at his hand, while John was hit in the chest. Luckily for them, as they staggered down the road bleeding heavily, Jim Watson and others from the 155th came along in a truck and picked them up. Jim and his crew, after their escape from the gun position, had retrieved an abandoned truck and were moving south to make contact with the rest of the battery when they came across Dick and his mate. War for the two wounded Gunners was over for the time being.

The situation at Batu Pahat was now critical and, with a real risk of the British troops being cut off, preparations were made for a complete withdrawal from the area.

The dilemma was what to do with the many seriously wounded. Just days before at Parit Sulong, near Muar, the Japanese had murdered 150 Australian wounded who had fallen into their hands. There was a real fear that the same would happen at Batu Pahat. The courageous Padre Noel Duckworth and Captains Walsh and Marks, and twenty-six others from the 198th Field Ambulance Company, volunteered to stay behind with those considered too ill or injured to attempt the tortuous trek through the jungle. Little hope was given for their survival but, thankfully, on this occasion the Japanese who accepted their surrender were more merciful and they were spared.

During the morning of 26 January, the others all assembled on the Senggarang Road – trucks and Quads nose to tail – and moved southwards until brought to a halt by heavy machine-gun fire from a crossfire roadblock half a mile north of Kampong Senggarang.

With their escape route blocked, the order was finally given for the trapped British troops to destroy their transport and equipment and make for the coast through the jungle. With the wounded having to be left behind, it was considered foolhardy to enrage the Japanese by 'spiking' the guns and instead essential parts were removed and retained by the Gunners.

The Gunners making their escape through the jungle at Batu Pahat were split into small groups and some joined with other units and were led into the jungle. The narrow jungle trails, initially firm underfoot, were soon churned up by hundreds of trudging boots. Forging their way through thick jungle undergrowth and swamps, the dispirited soldiers quickly became exhausted and as Japanese patrols were known to be in the area, talking and unnecessary noise was banned. The closer they got to the coast the worse the going became as tired men got caught up in underground roots and then mangrove swamps. This led to much stumbling and pushing, leaving men muttering and swearing under their breath in sheer frustration. In the early hours of the following morning, a brief halt was called and exhausted men fell where they had stopped. Most of them had not eaten all day and the only food and water available was what individual men had brought for themselves. The initial intention had been to reach the coast and then follow it south before heading back inland once the Japanese roadblocks were bypassed.

Said Gunner Tom McKie: 'I was with quite a few of the 155th to begin with and then we got split up. You would maybe stop for a minute to catch your breath and then tag onto whoever was coming along behind you. It was dark and some men stopped where they were when it got too dark. Others kept going, sometimes with a hand on the shoulder of the man in front. I was with a group of about six lads at that time but I couldn't tell you who they were. You just joined up with anyone.'

As dawn broke on 27 January, the weary soldiers had to be careful not to be seen from the air as Japanese aircraft were constantly flying overhead and at times the sound of Japanese trucks travelling south down the coast road could be clearly heard. There was now little point in heading back inland as the enemy had obviously taken control of the whole road and the only hope left was for the men to be somehow taken off by boat. But with little navy to call upon, it appeared a forlorn hope.

Plodding their way slowly down the coast, the Gunners' group caught up with the others later in the day when they learned that some officers had left in a small boat to try to make contact with the Navy at the southern end of the west coast of Johore.

Later that day the group was back on the march towards the fishing village at Kampong Ponggor, 5 miles further south, as the sea there was less affected by tidal mud flats and it was a better prospect for a rescue attempt. It was a long and arduous trek through the night, with countless tidal streams having to be forded or crossed by narrow wooden bridges, and when they eventually reached the coast near Kampong Ponggor on the morning of 28 January, the mud-plastered and mosquito-bitten men were dead on their feet. Unbeknown to them, successful contact had been made with the Navy and arrangements were in place to have the stranded men rescued by two naval gunboats, HMS *Dragonfly* and HMS *Scorpion*.

Later that night, the two gunboats made the hazardous trip up the coast but had to lie some distance out at sea owing to the tidal mudflats at the mouth of the Sungei Ponggor. Strong swimmers among the men made it out to the boats by their own steam, despite fears of sharks, sea snakes and seagoing crocodiles, while the non-swimmers, and the more faint-hearted, were taken off in a flotilla of small rowing boats. On the first night, the bulk of the men were evacuated on the two gunboats and taken back to Singapore.

Said Gunner Tom McKie: 'I was one of the last to be taken off – there was no reason for that – you just had to wait your turn. I waited a good day and a half. There was nothing you could do but sit around and wait – even during the night. We had no food – we had nothing with us.'

The last of the men – including a few of the 155th – were taken off on 30 January. It was a remarkable feat, with a total of 1,500 men rescued without a single loss. Not surprisingly, it became known as the 'Malayan Dunkirk'.

Chapter 4

The Loss of the Impregnable Fortress

The Battle for Malaya was now coming to its inevitable and tragic end. On the evening of 27 January, C Battery and Regimental Headquarters, still unaware of the fate of their mates in B Battery, left Johore Baru in Malaya and crossed the causeway onto Singapore Island, where they took up a position about a mile south of the Singapore Naval Base on the Nee Soon Road.

The Island of Singapore is approximately the same shape and size as the Isle of Wight and linked to the State of Johore and the Malay Peninsula by a mile-long causeway, although parts of the Straits of Johore, separating Singapore and the mainland, are barely 700 yards wide. Prior to the Japanese invasion of Malaya, Singapore had been considered a strong defensive position, a virtual fortress, with its large guns pointing out to sea. This was where any invasion would come from and the thick, impenetrable jungles of Malaya to its rear posed no threat. The rapid Japanese advance down the peninsula had shown this belief to be little more than wishful thinking.

Singapore of that time was largely a series of extended rubber plantations and small *kampongs*, with Singapore City on the south coast being the main centre of population. Following the massive influx of refugees from the mainland, the numbers in the city, principally Chinese, had swollen to such a degree that there were now close to 1 million. The streets of the city, particularly the Chinese districts, were full of refugees living in tents, in doorways – anywhere – while on the fringes of the city were the spacious residential suburbs of wealthy and professional Europeans who continued to delude themselves that it was only a matter of time before the Japanese were taught the error of their ways. However, the daily and constant pattern bombing of the city by the inevitable formation of twenty-seven Japanese planes was bringing public services and the basic infrastructure of the city to near breaking-point and those on the receiving end had no illusions as to the true state of affairs.

With the mainland about to fall into Japanese hands, the disposition of the troops available on Singapore was of vital importance and the island was divided into three defensive sectors – the Western, Northern and Southern Areas. In the west were the Australian 8th Division, in the north the 11th Indian Division and 18th Division, with various other units, including the 1st and 2nd Malay Infantry brigades, making up the Fortress Troops to the south.

In the Northern Area the 155th Field Regiment settled their field guns in and around the district of Nee Soon and a lot of hard work was done digging gun pits and laying and burying cable as it was anticipated that the Gunners would have to provide their own close protection in the event of an enemy landing. The OPs were established in the Naval Base overlooking the Straits of Johore and on their first visit to recce the area, the Gunners were shocked at the sight. The large base, with its extensive docking and repair facilities, had been hastily evacuated on 28 December 1941, and all naval personnel previously stationed there had sailed from Singapore three days later. In the wardrooms and mess area, half-eaten, and by now putrid, meals lay evidence to the hurried departure. Like the men of the British Battalion now guarding the deserted base, the Gunners were disgusted at having been abandoned by the Navy but were still more than happy to help themselves from the well-stocked stores.

Meanwhile, fresh from the Serangoon Road evacuation centre in Singapore after their escape from Batu Pahat, the newly-kitted-out Gunners of B Battery had returned to the regiment along with their replacement 25-pounders. The battle for Malaya was now over and the evacuation of all troops from the mainland to Singapore Island was planned for the morning of 31 January. As lorryloads of troops crossed from Johore throughout the night, Indian sappers were setting their charges on the concrete causeway that spanned the Straits. At 0730 hours, the last troops to cross over to Singapore – the Argyll and Sutherland Highlanders – left the mainland to the strains of their regimental marching song, *Hielan' Laddie*, and they had no sooner reached the island when the charges were blown.

The event was witnessed from a distance by Sergeant Jack Edwards of the 155th's Signals Section who, along with his team, were laying cable to an OP overlooking the Straits.

Said Sergeant Edwards: 'With a tremendous explosion and clouds of debris, the demolitions were fired. We were shattered – dumbfounded – by what we saw. There was a pitifully small gap. We had hoped for a complete demolition or at least a wide breach. My cheerful, hard-working driver from South Wales, Eddie Morris, summed up the feelings of thousands of the soldiers who had watched. "Sarge," he said, "the fucking Japs will spit across that. It won't stop them an hour."'

He wasn't far wrong. The gap of about 60 feet would be bridged in a matter of days by the skilful and experienced Japanese engineer troops.

The Gunners had by now become used to living and surviving in the stifling heat of the jungle. No longer did the cacophony of strange sounds and screeches coming from the varied creatures that inhabited the deep recesses hold any fear for them, although they still despised the ever-present leeches. However, their overfamiliarity sometimes had uncomfortable repercussions.

On a trip into the jungle to verify bearings from one of the gun positions, two of the regimental surveyors, Peter Rhodes and 'Tiger' Robinson, were hailed by one of their friends, Sergeant 'Ginger' Brown from Glasgow, who called them over to admire the gun position that he had set up. Finding good positions was always a trial for the Gunners as a good arc of fire was essential both for the effectiveness of their shooting and to guard against premature detonations if a shell struck a nearby tree. However, on this occasion, the two Gunners from the Survey Section had to admit that the site was well chosen. The camouflage was very effective and the gun was skilfully positioned under the over-hanging branch of a large Flame of the Forest tree, which was itself covered with camouflage netting.

Having duly expressed their admiration, Rhodes and Robinson were turning to leave when a fire order was received and the proud Ginger impressed upon them to stay and watch 'real' Gunners in action. Both Rhodes and Robinson were more amused than offended for they were well aware of the possessiveness, even fondness, that the men developed for 'their' guns. Calling on the gun crew to do everything by 'drill order', Sergeant Brown smartly stood at attention and shouted out to the gun position officer, 'Number One gun ready, Sarr!' On receiving the command to fire, he sharply rapped out the order, 'Number One gun, fire!'

Said Peter Rhodes: 'There was the expected bang and suddenly the strictly disciplined crew began to dance around like madmen as they tossed away their steel helmets and tore off their shirts. Tiger and I, standing a few yards away, were both amazed and amused, but it took only a moment to understand such strange behaviour. It was indeed an excellent gun position but what Ginger and his crew hadn't noticed was the long line of red ants, notorious for their vicious biting, that had climbed up the tree trunk and out over the big branch and the net above the gun. When it was fired, all the ants fell off onto the heads and shoulders of the crew below. Being Ginger's friends, Tiger and I departed immediately.'

Over the next few days, food and ammunition were collected in large quantities and at the gun placements everything was dug in and sandbagged. Incessant shelling by the Japanese artillery – who appeared to have guns of all calibres from 6-inch howitzers to 105mm field guns – made conditions uncomfortable for the crews on the gun positions and the regiment had to employ a system of roving sections to prevent their permanent positions from becoming too obvious. It was a nuisance for the Gunners having to haul the guns in and out but at least for those in B Battery, the 25-pounders were a lot more manoeuvrable and easier to handle. However, it was not all one-sided and the OPs sent back flash and sound bearings of enemy guns on the Johore coastline. As a result, both batteries were kept fully engaged, although the need to conserve ammunition was an ever-present consideration notwithstanding earlier calculations that there should be sufficient artillery ammunition available to withstand a three-month siege.

In the early hours of 4 February, all twelve of the large oil fuel tanks at the Naval Base went up in flames. The whole area was soon enveloped in a huge pall of black oily smoke, which could be seen from all over the island. During daylight hours, the accumulation of smoke had the effect of permanent twilight and at night the burning tanks lit up the jungle for miles.

Later that day, in anticipation of a possible Japanese assault on the north-east coast, all civilians living in the Northern Area were evacuated to Singapore City, which was already bursting at the seams. It had long been the opinion of the General Officer Commanding, Lieutenant General Percival, although not shared by others, that the most likely point for an attack would be the north coast of the island to the east of the causeway and this was the area where the majority of the garrison was now disposed.

The following day the whole island was in for a shock. On the night of 6/7 February, when the expected assault did come, it was in the Western Area, held by the Australian 8th Division. Following a horrendous bombardment of artillery fire, which effectively destroyed what little defences existed on the north-west coastline of Singapore, the Japanese 5th and 18th Divisions made their move. It was those two experienced, and recently rested, divisions, which just weeks before had wreaked so much havoc at Khota Bahru and Jitra, that now began the assault on Singapore Island from a flotilla of small barges and boats. Within hours, over 13,000 Japanese assault troops had landed on Singapore Island and were progressing speedily inland despite pockets of fierce resistance by infantry battalions of the Australian 8th Division.

For those manning the 155th's gun positions in the Northern Area, the ferocity of the attack in the west could be clearly heard. The noise was like continual rolling thunder but the experienced Gunners knew exactly what it was – a massive artillery barrage.

In the days to follow, the fighting in the Western Area was savage and ongoing and despite a brave and stubborn fightback by Australian and Indian troops, the Japanese were soon advancing and taking ground throughout the west and north of the island.

'Another day of artillery duels', was how the 155th's CO, Lieutenant Colonel Gold, described the action of 8 February, and the battle of the guns raged for hours, with the 155th getting more than its share with shells falling all around their own gun positions and Gunners having to jump in and out of the prepared trenches between firing. The Regimental Sergeant Major, Peter Scullion, a veteran of the Great War, described it as 'just like the bombardment on the Somme'.

By this time the restriction on the use of artillery ammunition had been lifted – there was now little point in attempting to conserve ammunition in the face of the enemy and Lieutenant Colonel Gold records: 'It was calculated that the enemy had six regiments of artillery opposing us consisting of 105mm and 75mm and some 4.5-inch howitzers and a 25cm howitzer gun of very long range. During the course of the day, we definitely destroyed one troop, which came into action on the water's edge [off the coast of Johore] and left its guns wrecked on the shore. Two other guns were also destroyed, an ammunition dump blown up and another battery silenced.'

And in a directive sent to Percival, General Wavell emphasized the point that:

There must be no thought of sparing the troops or civil population and no mercy must be shown to weakness in any shape or form. Commanders must lead their troops and, if necessary, die with them. There must be no question or thought of surrender. Every unit must fight it out to the end and in close contact with the enemy.

That same day, the 155th were still busily in action. From the OPs overlooking the Straits of Johore, barges and *sampans* loaded with enemy troops were seen crossing from the mainland, and the regimental record describes how F Troop, 'After engaging an enemy battery and destroying its ammunition in the morning, sank five barges loaded with troops and later in the afternoon, a motor boat towing another five.' As the enemy moved ever closer south towards Singapore City, firing from the 155th's guns increased to such an extent that each was firing in excess of 300 rounds a night.

An instruction from the GOC was received 'to withdraw all troops from the northern and north-eastern shores of the island because the time had come to establish a perimeter defence round the city.' As this order was being received, the Japanese Imperial Guards were already engaged in heavy fighting around Nee Soon. On 13 February, the 155th were withdrawn to the Farrer Park district on the northern outskirts of the city and Regimental Headquarters set up in a square of bungalows in a nearby residential area just off Lavender Street, the notorious red light district of the town.

Japanese air attacks continued relentlessly and a large bomb fell on another of the B Battery gun positions set up near Government House. Although narrowly missing one of the 25-pounders, it threw Sergeant Sam Lockhead from Dumfries, and Glasgow man Gunner Dick Docherty a distance of nearly 50 feet. Unbelievably, neither man was seriously injured. Sergeant Jimmy Bingham from Lanark was another to cheat death during that same bombing raid. He was standing in the middle of the road when he was caught between two bombs, which miraculously landed in the deep monsoon drains on either side of the road.

Later that morning, with artillery stocks running short on the positions owing to the constant firing, 20-year-old Lieutenant Maurice Graham was given the hazardous and unenviable task of returning to the former wagon lines at Nee Soon in an attempt to retrieve ammunition concealed there. The rapid Japanese advance meant that their current position was uncertain and there was a strong possibility that they had already reached the Nee Soon area. Leading a convoy of a dozen 3-ton lorries, Lieutenant Graham and his unhappy band of reluctant Gunners set off, and at Yio Chu Kang, a few miles north of Nee Soon, the inevitable happened. They were ambushed by Japanese Imperial Guards who had set up heavy machine guns in trenches, which, ironically, had been dug by the Gunners during their earlier spell in the area.

In the leading truck, Bombardier Bob Pennington from Thurnscoe in Yorkshire was first to be killed. A popular member of D Troop, he had faithfully and cheerfully kept Nos. 3 and 4 guns supplied with ammunition throughout the fighting on the mainland.

Bombardier Robert Pennington was a married man from
Thurnscoe, Yorks.
Robert was thirty years of age.

Bombardier Bill Glencross, from Sanquhar in Dumfries, riding in the front of the following truck, amazingly avoided a similar fate when his vehicle was likewise riddled with machine-gun bullets. However, Jim McDonald, the Gunner sitting beside him, was not so lucky and was killed outright by a bullet between his eyes.

Gunner James McDonald was from Port Glasgow.
James was twenty-four years of age.

Another victim was 20-year-old John Kelly, a former joiner who had joined the Lanarkshire Yeomanry as a territorial in April 1939 along with a close friend, Ian Scott, another young Biggar man.

Lance Bombardier John McKay Kelly was from Biggar,
Lanarkshire.
John was twenty years of age.

One of the lorries in the middle of the column, hastily attempting to turn on the narrow road, unfortunately got stuck and effectively blocked the escape for those in front. With little option but to abandon their vehicles, the Gunners dived into the deep monsoon drains that ran along both sides of the road in order to avoid the machine-gun bullets whining all around them. One of the men, big Jim Armstrong from Ferniegair in Lanarkshire, came to grief when, in his haste to get under cover, he struck himself under the chin with his own knee and knocked himself out! A large, solidly-built man who had played rugby for the regiment, he was cursed roundly by his mates as they dragged his heavy unconscious body along the drain to safety.

As the fighting continued on the outskirts of the city, every conceivable open space suitable for a gun position was utilized and guns from different field regiments were mixed in together. There was no real order or pattern to their use as gun crews responded to individual calls for fire and there were even occasions when guns were firing over each other in opposite directions. The command post of B Battery had a fortunate stroke of luck when a 25-pounder of 135th Field Regiment, firing on a target over open sights, narrowly missed the building where they were situated. And, to add to the mayhem and misery, the Gunners remained under constant attack from enemy shelling and bombing, with the ever-present large mortars being particularly deadly.

Said Sergeant Jim Watson: 'We were still defiantly shelling the enemy whenever targets presented themselves. My gun was located between two private houses where we had sandbagged an area round the gun and underneath one house to form a shelter. We crawled under the house when there was a lull in our firing but one crew member was required to stay on the gun as a guard. We were coming under enemy fire when Gunner Joe Wileman, the guard, popped his head into the shelter and said, "It's getting hot out here, Sergeant," so I said, "Just come in for a wee while till it quietens down." He was no sooner under cover when our gun position received a direct hit. I went outside and there were ammunition boxes ripped up with live ammunition scattered all over the gun position but only minor damage to the gun. I picked up a large piece of shrapnel and dropped it smartly – it was red hot. I think that we had been hit by a 3-inch mortar shell as the crater behind the gun was quite shallow, but nevertheless it was a lucky escape for the gun crew.'

Ferocious fighting continued throughout the day and at one point a group of about fifty Japanese soldiers appeared on cycles just in front of the D Troop OP and, as a result, were 'blown off the road'. The regiment was in action fighting hard all day and a Bofors AA gun manned by Gunners of F Troop successfully brought down three Jap planes. The shelling of the 155th Regiment's positions continued unabated: first, the command post of C Battery was hit and set on fire and then an ammunition truck suffered a similar fate. As it burst into flames, 23-year-old Bombardier Alex Downie from Lanark, at considerable risk to himself, bravely jumped into the vehicle and drove it some distance away from the position, where the fire was tackled and safely extinguished. Sadly, during this same attack, the regiment sustained further fatalities. Twenty-year-old Captain Eustace, who had featured in so many of the regiment's exploits, was mortally wounded when a large mortar shell landed between his legs. He died on the way to hospital.

Captain Maurice J.R. Eustace was from Newstown, Co Carlow.
Maurice was twenty years of age.

Bombardier Bob Gaillard was also wounded by an incoming shell and died shortly afterwards in hospital. Another casualty of the same attack, 23-year-old Bombardier Fred Anniss, would later die of his injuries on 11 April 1942, while a POW in Roberts Hospital at Changi.

57

Bombardier Robert Philip Gaillard was from Aylesbury, Bucks.
Robert was twenty-one years of age.

A further attack on the E Troop gun position near the polo ground brought fresh casualties. John Carroll, a 22-year-old Gunner from Annan in Dumfriesshire, was killed and his body later buried in the garden of a nearby house, while at Regimental Headquarters, Gunner Bert Quertier of the 155th and a Gunner McDonald, who had been attached from the 137th Field Regiment, were both killed during a bombing raid. There was little time for mourning or ceremony.

Gunner John Joseph Carroll was from Annan, Dumfriesshire.
John was twenty-two years of age.

Gunner Albert George Quertier was married and from Wakefield, Yorkshire.
Albert was thirty-two years of age.

As darkness descended, Japanese troops were up as far as the OPs and about a mile from the gun positions, and hasty arrangements were made for a 'defensive ring of bayonets' around the guns to prevent them being rushed in the night.

One man who did have a truly miraculous escape that day was Dick Gwillim, the Gunner who had been shot and seriously wounded during the fighting at Batu Pahat. After he and Gunner John McGuiness had been rescued and picked up by others from the 155th, they were moved on through the system until, eventually, Dick ended up in the Alexandra Hospital on the outskirts of Singapore City.

Between 12 and 14 February, during the battle for Singapore, the advancing Japanese Army was held at Pasir Panjang to the west of the hospital by the 1st Malaya Infantry Brigade. In the vicious and bitter hand-to-hand fighting that ensued, the tenacious Malays stood their ground and inflicted heavy losses on the Japanese 114th Regiment until finally, the maddened Japanese, supported by tanks, successfully forced a way through the Malay lines. In the afternoon of 14 February, heavily-camouflaged Japanese infantry were spotted approaching the hospital, which still held more than 200 patients and staff. A British officer, holding a white flag, went out to meet them and was immediately bayoneted to death. The Japanese troops then rushed the hospital and systematically set about murdering patients and staff, many of whom were lying helpless in bed. A patient undergoing surgery was bayoneted while under anaesthetic on the operating table.

Said Dick: 'At this point we were not sure what was happening as we heard shouts of "No, no", followed by silence and then more cries. A patient appeared on our veranda saying he had been bayoneted. He collapsed and one of the doctors and an orderly took charge of him. A bullet ricocheted off the floor and we took cover.'

What happened thereafter was the stuff of nightmares. In an attempt to shield him from the shooting, two Royal Army Medical Corps orderlies helped Dick into a small kitchen adjoining the ward. One of the orderlies then left while the other, 23-year-old Private Arthur Bruce, stayed to tend Dick, who was now lying on the floor. The orderly was in the process of re-dressing Dick's wound, which had started to bleed, when two Japanese soldiers, in a mad killing frenzy, burst into the kitchen. As Private Bruce stood up and turned towards them, he was deliberately shot three times in the stomach although unarmed and clearly wearing a Red Cross armband. His blood splattered everywhere – much of it over Dick, who was still lying on the kitchen floor. Rigid with fear, Dick watched through half-closed eyes as one of the Jap soldiers stood over him with a rifle and bayonet pointed at his chest. After what seemed like an eternity, he heard one soldier grunt something to the other and then they both left the kitchen, obviously believing that the blood-soaked and ashen-faced Dick was also dead.

Within thirty minutes of the murderous attack, at least fifty patients and staff had been killed and during that afternoon a further 200 were removed and later murdered. Dick Gwillim was one of the very few to survive this act of outrageous barbarism.

The last of the regiment to die in action was Gunner George Taylor, who was killed by a shell in the early hours of 15 February.

Gunner George Taylor was from Winton, Manchester.
George was twenty-three years of age.

As the afternoon wore on, the shocked and disbelieving Gunners heard rumours of a possible surrender. Said Sergeant Jack Edwards: 'Lieutenant Kepple called me and said, "We are packing in at four o'clock." Just those few words. We were dumbfounded and couldn't grasp what he meant. For a mad second I thought that the Japs must have had enough and were evacuating the Island.'

Unknown to Jack Edwards, some of their own number had already evacuated the stricken island. The 155th's CO, Lieutenant Colonel Gold, and six others – BSM Road-night, who was later to be awarded the Distinquished Conduct Medal for his bravery throughout the campaign, Sergeant D. Lindup, Lance Sergeant R.A. Brown, Bombardier

W. Smith and Gunners J. Hamilton and T. Johnstone – had been ordered to attempt an escape from Singapore and had left in a small boat the previous evening. Similar orders had been given to key personnel in other units as it was considered essential that a nucleus of knowledge as to what had befallen the disastrous campaign should be available for future planning. Few of those escape parties were successful in breaking through the Japanese naval and air blockade although the 155th were one of those that did. After many adventures and mishaps they eventually reached Ceylon.

However, at 1600 hours, after an uncanny and eerie period of silence with no incoming artillery or mortar fire, those still on Singapore received confirmation of the capitulation and, contrary to the surrender agreement, began destroying guns and equipment. Said Peter Rhodes: 'The silence was shattered by a series of very loud noises, best described as a mixture of a loud bang, a do-ingg and a mournful whine. Some of us had heard that sound before and we felt very sad, knowing that it was the death cry of a gun destroying itself.'

After the guns had been destroyed, the strange silence returned and, in the residential area where Regimental Headquarters was located, the Regimental Sergeant Major, Peter Scullion, instructed the Gunners to set up a defensive ring using the remaining small arms that had not yet been destroyed. As he began to direct the men to their positions, the RSM saw that they were instinctively gathering into small groups of friends and decided that, as they had fought together as friends, they might as well enter into captivity in the same way. These friendships would serve them well in the dreadful years of suffering and privation that were to follow.

Chapter 5

Singapore Interlude

Their disbelief was palpable. Shocked Gunners gathered around the tennis courts, polo fields or wherever they had made their last stand, wondering what was going to happen next. The last do-ingg of a 25-pounder as it was destroyed with a shell up the spout was now a memory. In compliance with the capitulation terms, all small arms had been gathered into piles, although most would never fire again as barrels had been deliberately bent and firing mechanisms irretrievably damaged.

The Regimental Sergeant Major had begun marshalling the Gunners and jobs were found to keep them occupied. Some were not pleasant. Burial parties were urgently required to deal with the many dead – both soldiers and civilians – lying all over the ruined city and here the Gunners had their initial taste of life as prisoners of the Japanese.

Sergeant Jack Edwards and others were busily engaged in this grisly duty when the first Japanese soldiers arrived. Said Edwards: 'They pointed their rifles at us, motioning at our wristwatches. We looked over at RSM Scullion nearby. He shouted, "You'd better hand them over, boys, or take the consequences."' As they handed them over, Sergeant Edwards saw that one of the Japs had six already on his arm.

Their next encounter was worse. A Japanese soldier, carrying a Bren gun over his shoulder, appeared casually leading a group of about forty Chinese civilians, all with their hands tied. Other soldiers walked alongside the straggling column, clubbing at the stumbling Chinese. The group moved off in the direction of a nearby creek and the Gunners had no illusion regarding what was about to happen. All morning the sound of machine-gun fire had been heard coming from that area. All over Singapore, the Japanese were carrying out similar atrocities on the Chinese community. Retribution was in the air.

61

The following day, 17 February, the regiment learned that all British and Australian troops had been ordered to assemble at Changi on the east of the island. At Changi there were several military barracks and installations and, with no idea what to do with the tens of thousands of prisoners who had fallen captive, the Japanese simply wanted them out of their hands, at least for the time being.

So, carrying whatever they could gather together, the vanquished troops began the long march to Changi. Some vehicles were allowed by the Japanese, but not many, and each individual soldier was responsible for carrying on his back what he considered essential.

Soon a long snaking column of trudging men – it could hardly be called marching – was making its way out of the devastated city. All around was the detritus of war – bombed-out buildings, burnt-out trucks and the all-pervading smell of putrefying bodies.

It was a long hard march in the heat of the sun and the exhausted men were relieved to arrive at Changi later that day, where they sought out shelter in the various buildings making up the former Roberts Barracks. The first couple of days were confused and a bit of a free-for-all but when the Gunners were moved into Changi Jail on 21 February, they were far from amused. The fact that the men selected for incarceration were from the 9th and 11th Indian divisions, who had fought the Japanese all the way down the peninsula, led to the belief that they had been especially singled out.

The jail had accommodation for up to 650 civilian prisoners but thousands of British troops were somehow packed in. Small individual cells for one civilian prisoner, with a concrete sleeping platform in the middle of the floor, now housed four POWs and their belongings. It was a tight squeeze.

Food, such as it was, was provided by the Gunners' own cooks and consisted largely of bully beef and biscuits brought with them from Singapore. No rations were provided by the Japanese at this time and they did not become involved in the day-to-day running of the POW administration for some time.

They were too busy elsewhere and the men of the regiment were not long in finding out where.

On 24 February, dozens of men from the 155th were sent out on working parties. The thought of getting away from the claustrophobic atmosphere of Changi Jail was not unwelcome and the Gunners enjoyed their walk out in the sun to the nearby beach. Their pleasure soon turned to horror when they viewed the nightmare scene in front of them. The beach and shoreline were littered with the bodies of Chinese civilians – men, women and children. From the impassive faces of the heavily-armed Japanese soldiers who were on the beach, the stunned Gunners thought that their time had come and that they were next to be dealt with.

Said Gunner Tom McKie: 'We instinctively sidled up to mates and began to shake hands. I remember saying things like, "It's been good to know you," and "All the best, see you up there." We were sure our time had come.' But to their relief, the POWs gathered from the gestures of the guards that they were there for another purpose – they were there to dig burial pits and retrieve the bodies from the edges of the sea, where they bobbed about in a sickening and disgusting fashion.

Said Sergeant Jack Edwards: 'Lying grotesquely entangled in rolls of barbed wire, were hundreds of Chinese men, women and youngsters of all ages. Their hands were still bound together on long ropes. They had been herded together into the water and then either shot or bayoneted.'

Equally horrified was Gunner Peter Rhodes: 'Looking back on my time as a prisoner of war, this was not the most arduous or the most dangerous job I had to do, but it was certainly the most revolting.' He continued, 'There seemed to be corpses everywhere, some washed up on the sand, others bobbing about in the shallows. There was a line of Chinese women and children, all roped together and all shot in the back of the head.'

The experience of Gunner John McEwan was, if anything, even worse. As he retrieved bodies from the shallows, he became aware that one of them, a young teenage girl, was still alive although bleeding heavily. He picked up the frail body in his arms and stood in the warm sea, wondering what to do next. He soon found out when he received a blow to the side of the head from an enraged Japanese soldier who pointed in the direction of a pit where the bodies were being buried. In a daze and with the girl still in his arms, John staggered over to the pit, where he stood teetering on the edge, uncertain what to do next. His mind was made up for him when a savage blow to his back propelled both he and the girl into the gory pit, which was already half full of blood-stained corpses. As he struggled out, panic-stricken, he was conscious of her pain-filled eyes. For the rest of his life, those eyes would haunt him.

All over the island similar atrocities were being committed by the Japanese. Old scores were being settled and it has been estimated that up to 50,000 Chinese civilians of all ages were murdered. It became known as Sook Ching – a 'purge through cleansing'.

The Gunners' spell in Changi Jail came to an end during March and they were moved out to allow the incarceration of civilian internees – men, women and children who had either decided to stay and tough it out or who had failed to get a place on the many ships attempting to escape the island. In many ways they were the more fortunate for although their time under the Nipponese would be harsh, they were still alive, unlike many who had made the escape attempt only to be lost when their ships were sunk by the ever-present Japanese war planes.

Birdwood Camp was the next home for the men of the 155th. The *attap*-roofed huts were very similar to those they had occupied at Ipoh and were a luxury after the crowding at Changi Jail. Although the buildings had been damaged during the fighting on the island, the POWs, as they had now come to regard themselves, quickly had them habitable. In the same area, the Australian and other British troops were being similarly detained. In effect, the whole Changi area had become a series of POW camps where tens of thousands of prisoners were held. Each individual camp was encircled with barbed wire put up by the men themselves and they joked that it was there not to keep them in, but to keep the Japs out. However, the immediate problem was not the Japs but the POWs former allies, Indian troops of their own 9th and 11th Indian divisions.

Following the fall of Singapore, freedom had been offered to those Indian troops who were prepared to join the Indian National Army, set up by Captain Mohan Singh, a former officer in the British Indian Army, and work alongside the Japanese. Pre-war conditions in the Indian Army had never been good and, with their negative experience of British Command during the disastrous Malayan Campaign, there was no shortage of volunteers and almost 12,000 changed sides.

With so many prisoners to watch, the task of supervising the POW camps at Changi was given over to the renegade Indian National Army and if the former Gunners thought that they would garner sympathy from those for whom they had provided artillery support all the way down the Malay Peninsula, they were in for a rude awakening. The Indians, mainly Sikhs, were brutal and took great delight in humiliating their former allies. The POWs, officers included, were required to salute the Indian guards and failure to do so immediately resulted in a slap, punch or worse.

Returning from an outside work party to collect wood, Jack Edwards had his first experience of the new regime. When the young officer in charge of the work party did not salute and call the others to attention quickly enough, he was punched and kicked. The others were all lined up and repeatedly slapped on the face. Missing from the Indian National Army were the Gurkhas – to a man they had refused to be involved in any form of collaboration and paid the penalty when later sent up onto the Death Railway.

Food brought with them from Singapore had all but run out and the Japanese were issuing rice – an inferior, poor quality rice that was contaminated with lime. It was thought that it was probably the sweepings from rice held in the *godowns*, or warehouses, at Singapore Harbour and intended for planting. The cooks' first attempts at producing meals from this poor mixture were barely edible. They had no previous experience of mass-cooking rice and they ended up serving up soggy dollops of rice to hungry men. In time the cooks came to grips with their new basic ingredient and rice in all shapes and forms – boiled, rissoled, fried and even ground into a type of flour – became commonplace but ultimately monotonous. Bombardier Benny Gough, a former baker from Hamilton and now one of the 155th's cooks, learned to make yeast by fermenting the rice flour using liquid from green coconuts. He had Sergeant Sam Lockhead, the lucky survivor of the bombing at Singapore, and Lance Bombardier Irving 'Kitty' Carlyle from Annan, source steel doors from a nearby deserted gun position and the ingenious trio manufactured a rough but effective oven from which Benny conjured up rice flour goodies. He famously became known as the 'Pie Man of Changi'.

Inevitably with such a limited diet, the POWs began to suffer the effects of vitamin deficiency and related illnesses became prevalent. The embarrassing 'Changi balls', a painful skin rash on the scrotum and upper thighs, competed with 'Changi belly', a distended stomach from wet and soggy rice. Unlike Changi belly, which disappeared in time once the cooks had mastered how to cook the rice, Changi balls resulted in serious discomfort, which made walking extremely difficult or even impossible. The best treatment available to the doctors treating the afflicted POWs was Marmite, the well-known yeast extract spread, rich in vitamin B. On one occasion when dispensing some of the precious paste, the medical orderly assumed that the sufferer was familiar with its use and was startled when the patient shortly returned, dancing in agony. Instead of consuming the spread orally, he had spread the Marmite on the raw and sensitive afflicted area, with the inevitable painful result.

But the lack of vitamin B1 brought on the more serious condition of beriberi. Found in two forms, dry and wet beriberi, the condition was endemic in poorer regions of the Far East, where polished rice – rice with the husk, bran and heart removed, a natural source of B1 – was the staple diet. Dry beriberi resulted in lethargy, tiredness and a painful tingling in the feet, which the POWs came to know as 'happy feet'! The searing stabs of pain were like fire but if the agonized victim dared put his feet into cold water, the converse happened and the sufferer would feel as if they were immersed in ice. There was no happy medium. The wet form was, if anything, even more dangerous, as it could lead to heart failure. Beriberi became one of the main killers of POWs throughout the Far East and could have been simply dealt with by the provision of B1.

Accommodation in the camps in the Changi area was reasonable, with little of the overcrowding experienced in Changi Jail, although in the hospital established in Roberts Barracks, this soon changed. The sick and wounded who had been transferred from hospitals in Singapore, including the survivors of the Alexandra Hospital Massacre, were soon joined by the increasing number of sick from the local POW camps. Beriberi was soon followed by that even greater killer – dysentery.

Bombardier Thomas Sinclair died in Roberts Hospital, Changi, on 1 June 1942, from dysentery.
Thomas, from Glasgow, was twenty-three years of age.

Dysentery is a serious condition caused by bacterial or parasitic infestation. A disorder of the intestines, it leads to violent diarrhoea and, if untreated, can be fatal. Effective hygiene is essential in the control of the disease and in the basic and relatively primitive conditions of the POW camps, this was not often possible. As a result the doctors in the hospital were overworked and not always sympathetic, as Bombardier Pat Campbell found out.

On an outside working party, he was wading in the sea when he was stung or bitten by something – he never did discover what – and had to be half-carried back to the camp and then to the hospital. On examining the hole that had developed in the foot, the puzzled doctor asked Pat where the exit wound was. Equally puzzled, Pat had explained that he was not suffering from a bullet wound but had been stung or bitten by a sea creature. The impatient and harassed doctor gave Pat a long stare, and without another word, turned and strode out of the examination room, leaving Pat to hobble back to the camp, once again assisted by his mates. Bites and stings, no matter how painful, were not high on the priorities of the pressured medical staff.

Bombardier Fred Anniss died in Roberts Hospital, Changi, on 11 April 1942, as a result of wounds received during the battle for Singapore.
Fred was twenty-three years of age.

During April and May, groups of POWs were sent from Changi on work parties throughout the island. Two of the largest demands for labour were in the building of a shrine to the Japanese war dead on the top of Bukit Timah in the centre of the island and in the many *godowns* spread along the 6-mile length of Singapore Harbour.

For those who laboured at Bukit Timah, the work was varied and many were involved in the building of a road to the shrine high on the hillside. This was heavy work and the POWs were organized into work parties under very junior Japanese NCOs, who were not particularly bright or intelligent, and the wily POWs soon found ways of making the work less onerous with opportunities to sabotage or slow down progress whenever the guards were not watching. Lookouts were kept and men only worked when watched, but the more astute Japanese engineers soon got wise and set each group a specific piece of work with the promise of rest when it was finished. As the POWs would find out later when on the railway or in the mines on Taiwan or in Japan, these were idle promises and the engineers just kept increasing the workload.

Gunner Tom Hannah, the former ammunition Quad driver with the 155th, found himself hauling loads of a different kind. He was now part of a small group of former drivers of the regiment, including Pat McCready and Geordie Shannon, who were employed in hauling stones from quarries for road ballast or timber for the shrine. On one occasion he was loading up with timber at a nearby mill and protested that the lorry was being overloaded, but from the attitude of the over-seers, quickly concluded that the best plan was to keep his mouth shut. Joining the convoy of overloaded vehicles, the inevitable happened. The lorry in front suddenly stopped without warning and Tom ran heavily into the back of it. Through stunned eyes, he was amazed to see the figure of a Jap soldier who had been sitting on the pile of timber on the vehicle in front rising high into the air and flopping over a telephone wire to land with a thump at the side of the road. Before he had a chance to draw himself together, the cabin door was violently pulled open and Tom was physically yanked from the vehicle, despite the fact that his feet had been trapped under the brake and clutch pedals.

Said Tom: 'This Jap officer appeared from nowhere. He was about 6 feet 6 inches tall and pulled me effortlessly from the cabin and began to give me a good hiding. I thought to myself, "Don't fall or he'll kick you to death – stay on your feet!" However, he stopped as suddenly as he had begun and walked away, leaving me stunned.'

Later that evening, back at his billet in the former private houses in the Adam Park district, and still sore from the earlier beating, Tom received a visit from a different Jap officer who was accompanied by some junior ranks and an interpreter. Through the interpreter, the officer began to question Tom about the incident. The interpreter had the usual habit of adding an 'O' at the end of certain words, such as 'You understand-o?' and Tom could not contain himself when the interpreter, to emphasize the seriousness of his position, said to him, 'You will die-o.' He rashly let an amused grin momentarily flit across his face. But it was enough of an excuse for yet another, even more serious, beating.

The following morning, the bruised and battered Tom was unexpectedly detailed as driver to the same Japanese officer who had questioned him the previous evening. He apprehensively drove the officer throughout the day and other than commands such as, 'Stop soldier' and other incomprehensible grunts, barely a word was spoken by the Jap. At the end of the day, when Tom had dropped the officer off, he noticed two packets of cigarettes lying on the passenger seat. Thinking that it was some kind of trick, Tom had spoken to the British officer in charge of his group who reassured him that it was almost certainly a 'present-o'. The Japanese had come to the conclusion that Tom wasn't to blame for the previous day's accident, but would not admit it without losing face. This was their way of acknowledging it. This was yet another of the difficulties that the POWs had in their dealings with their new masters – they were so contrary and inexplicable.

In the house in Adam Park where Tom and his mates Geordie Shannon and Paddy McCready were billeted, things had become unpleasant. They had been there only a matter of days when they became aware of the presence of a large number of rats. On exploring the garden area at the back of the house they discovered why. The rats had disturbed the beheaded bodies of the former Chinese occupants of the house. Things now began to fall into place for Tom and the others and they were able to relate to their grisly find of the severed heads of Chinese civilians displayed on benches further along the road.

Down at the docks, others of the 155th were being put to work.

It had been a bad start. Dozens of men of the regiment were transported from Changi standing up in the back of uncovered 15cwt trucks. The Japanese drivers were neither competent nor careful and they hurtled along the rutted roads heedless of the men clinging desperately to each other in the rear of the vehicles. The hair-raising journey had its inevitable conclusion and on a bend taken recklessly at speed, Gunner Alfred Street was thrown from a truck onto the road.

Gunner Alfred Charles Street died at Roberts Hospital, Changi,
on 9 May 1942, from a fractured skull.
Alfred, a married man from Fleetwood, Lancashire, was
twenty-five years of age.

The POWs were accommodated in the former Great World Amusement Park in the middle of Singapore. Initially there was no proper shelter other than the few small administration buildings and the men sought bed space in amongst the now-redundant amusement stalls or even on the roundabouts themselves. Divided into groups of roughly a dozen, the following day they were marched about 3 miles through the city down to the waiting *godowns*.

These warehouses were crammed to capacity with goods and materials of all kinds. For days prior to the capitulation, the holds of the many ships tied up along the harbour had been hurriedly and haphazardly emptied of their cargoes to allow the evacuation of civilians. The POWs were now set to work putting the material into order and loading it onto ships bound for Japan. The loads were made up of materials of all kinds. Some days the men would spend uncomfortable and unpleasant hours hauling bags of cement, which would burn the skin off their bare, sweating backs and form solid lumps in their hair. On other occasions, they would fall lucky. Bombardier Pat Campbell recalls one incident; when working in a *godown* his party came across crates filled with bottles of Guinness stout. This was manna from heaven for the sweating stevedores and throughout the day they would surreptitiously remove full bottles from the crates and then replace the empties. Things seemed to be going well until a sharp-eyed guard noticed that a group of Australian troops at the other end of the large *godown* were doing likewise. All hell broke loose and the half-cut workers were lined up to be berated by the furious guards. Unfortunately, one of the 155th, Gunner Sammy Frew, the survivor of the SS *Arandora Star*, had possibly consumed more than his fair share and, with his hungry stomach empty of food, the drink had gone straight to his head. Standing swaying from side to side under the maniacal rantings of the guards, the grinning Sammy was not the least bit concerned. Not even when a furious guard, who had to stand on a wooden crate to do so, brought the flat of his sword repeatedly down on the head of the unfortunate Sammy, did he flinch or stop his swaying. Only the fact that he was wearing one of the ubiquitous pith helmets saved him from serious injury and the next day it was a toss-up as to whether it had been the beating with the sword or the amount of Guinness consumed that was the cause of Sammy's splitting headache!

69

The POWs became expert at stealing from the *godowns*. Almost everything had a value and on making their way back up to the Great World, the groups of prisoners would be met by dozens of young Chinese urchins who ran in and out of the marching ranks gathering the various items that had been liberated from the *godowns*. It was a never-ending mystery to the POWs how, the next day when returning to work, they would be met by the same boys who would instinctively identify the man who was to be paid for the previous day's trade. The POWs still speak of the incredible honesty and bravery of those young boys and their elderly Chinese Fagins who ran enormous risks when carrying out the forbidden trade.

In the months between May and going up onto the Death Railway or being transported to the copper mine on Taiwan in October, the prisoners stole and traded anything that could be moved – thread, hacksaw blades, bicycle chains, small machine parts, anything that was sufficiently small enough to be concealed and pass the search of the careful guards. All the POWs were at it – some more skilled at thieving than others – but the Australian troops were the masters. Gunner Tom McKie joked: 'We stole sewing machine needles but the Aussies stole the sewing machines.' And he wasn't kidding! Realizing that they had to have transport to get the sewing machines out of the *godowns*, some enterprising diggers succeeded in plying a Jap driver with so much drink that one of them took his place and, wearing the Jap's hat pulled low over his face, drove the piled-up lorry out of the docks.

And the Ten Commandments didn't come into it. Said Bombardier Pat Campbell: 'When working in the *godowns*, morality went out the window. Some of the Japs were not too bad and even stole along with us but you were always wary of them. You would look them in the eye and smile while your mate was stealing from behind their back.'

Gunner John McEwan agreed: 'We would hide cotton reels in the turn-ups of our shorts or in our long hose, and during the inevitable search, one of the more reasonable guards who spoke good English would joke, "You have very bad varicose veins."'

Those like Pat who had been brought up as strict Roman Catholics could seek understanding from the regular Christian services held in the former beer garden of the Great World by a New Zealand priest, Father Gerard Bourke, who ministered to their needs. Father Bourke, like many of the padres working alongside the POWs, was a great source of comfort and support to the men and was pragmatic and realistic about the unusual circumstances they were in. Stealing from the enemy was fair game; compassion and loyalty to your mates were the Christian ethics that mattered. Later, when on the Death Railway, Pat would

70

carefully carry and look after the crucifix that had been displayed on the makeshift altar in the beer garden at the Great World.

Back at Changi the Regiment had sustained more losses.

Gunner Fred Hoskins died in Roberts Hospital on 14 July 1942, from dysentery.

Fred, from London, was twenty-three years of age.

Lance Sergeant John Halifax died in Roberts Hospital on 20 August 1942, from blood poisoning resulting from a sting from a stingray while on a work party to the beach.

John, a married man from Elie, Fife, was thirty years of age.

The uneasy 'cat and mouse' relationship between POW and guard came to an end in August when the infamous Selerang Incident occurred. Selerang Barracks, which before the invasion had been the base of the 2nd Gordon Highlanders, had accommodation for 800. However, on 30 August 1942, following the recapture of four prisoners who had attempted escape, the Japanese demanded that all POWs sign a 'no escape' pledge. When, not surprisingly, the men refused, the Japs removed the POWs from the various camps and confined them, 17,000 in total, in Selerang. Even with the inevitable hardship and chronic conditions that very quickly ensued – borehole latrines had to be dug in the concrete drill square – the prisoners still refused to comply with the Japanese demands. It was only when threats were made to bring the sick and wounded from Roberts Hospital into the grossly overcrowded barracks that the men agreed to sign the pledge 'under duress'.

Elsewhere, other plans were being devised for the POWs to be used to even greater effect.

Chapter 6

The Drivers' Party Moves Out

The morning of 21 October 1942 was hot, as were most mornings in Singapore. In the shadow of one of the houses at Adam Park, a small group of men clustered around Lieutenant David Ffolkes and Second Lieutenant John Durnford of the 155th (Lanarkshire Yeomanry) Field Regiment RA.

'All the best, Sir!', 'I hope you get on OK wherever you're going', and 'Don't do anything I wouldn't do!' was typical of the banter passed around. Smiling, but solemn, the two officers shook hands with the fifteen Other Ranks from their regiment, including Tom Hannah, Pat McCready and Geordie Shannon, wishing them well for the future. They had been with their men, part of the 'drivers' party' in Adam Park, since April that year and had built up a good rapport with them as their combined labour constructed the roads around the monument to the Japanese dead, which now towered above the surrounding countryside on Bukit Timah.

The warning shout, 'The Japs are on their way' was the signal for the Other Ranks to move away and, giving their officers a last thumbs-up, they returned to their own billets.

David Ffolkes and John 'Dinky' Durnford, as the men had affectionately begun to call him, fell into line with the men from other regiments who were also moving out that day. At a command from the Japanese guards they formed ranks and moved off into the next stage of their captivity as POWs of the Japanese. As the two friends strode along side by side they were aware of sympathetic looks cast towards them by the native population. Here and there the occasional Chinese civilian furtively passed cigarettes, fruit or water to the POWs as they passed, all the while keeping a watchful eye out for the snarling guards who were all too willing to reinforce with their fists the Japanese order of non-fraternization.

As the sun rose higher, the heat became more intense but, having been on the island for more than eight months, the prisoners were more or less accustomed to it. They were all hungry – but hunger pangs were no stranger to them. All of them were thirsty and although they had water in their bottles, they sipped from them sparingly. If their time in the tropics had taught them anything, it was that hunger pangs were easier to cope with than the extreme thirst caused by the perspiration that flowed in streams from their bodies.

The guards had not told them where they were going and no one asked. They had learned long ago that curiosity was met with aggression – and they now waited until the guards deigned to pass on information to them. Enlightenment was a long time coming that day and it was only when the group was ushered into Singapore Railway Station – 6 miles from where they had started out – that they realized that this was going to be a significant move. A few minutes later, their train pulled in – and was viewed with apprehension by all of its waiting passengers. It was nothing more than a line of windowless steel wagons of the type normally used to transport food or cattle.

Immediately the train screeched to a halt the guards pushed and prodded the prisoners into line and hustled them into the waiting wagons. After eight months as POWs, none of them were fat, but it was still a tight squeeze and, alarmed at the lack of space, they hoped that they were not going far. Even when each wagon seemed full, the guards continued to push, kick and beat with rifle butts until all of the 600 prisoners were on board. Eventually, each 20-foot-long, 7-foot-wide wagon held over thirty men!

As soon as the platform was cleared of prisoners, guards moved along the train, shutting the sliding doors and heightening the rising alarm of the POWs. Even with the doors open, the interiors of the wagons had been airless and claustrophobic. With the doors closed, the feeling was akin to being shut in a tomb.

Said Second Lieutenant John Durnford: 'Once on the move, the interior of the truck became a Black Hole of Calcutta on wheels. The tropical sun heated walls and roof to an unbearable degree. ... At nightfall on the first day we reached Seremban and fed like pigs from buckets of rice on the platform.

'On the fourth morning we passed the former defensive positions at Jitra on the frontier, with their ridiculous fields of fire and lack of observation. At least those killed on the first night of the breakthrough could not see us now.'

At times the guards allowed the doors to remain open and a rota was organized that allowed everyone time to stand near the doors and the opportunity to lie down.

The journey was remembered by Stanley S. Pavillard, Medical Officer attached to the Singapore Volunteer Force: 'Eventually my turn came to stretch out and sleep; this was very pleasant indeed, but there are at least two drawbacks to sleeping feet to face like sardines in a tin. One is that feet smell; the other is illustrated by the fact that during my sleeping session my big toe accidentally found its way into the mouth of a fellow sleeper, who bit it sharply.'

The open doors allowed desperate men the opportunity to relieve themselves without fouling either the wagon or those standing beside them. Diarrhoea or dysentery sufferers were held by others while they leaned backwards out of the doors to 'do the necessary'. After a few close shaves with bridge supports or other hazards close to the line, everyone learned to keep a watchful eye up front. During the nights when the doors were shut, unfortunate men, unable to control their bowels, fouled where they stood – to their humiliation and the discomfort of those around them.

After five days, the nightmarish journey finally came to an end and the prisoners were ordered off the train and lined up to be counted. Finally satisfied that no one had escaped, the guards ordered '*Orru men marchu!*' and the men marched, tired and hungry, to the staging camp at Ban Pong, in southern Thailand, where they discovered that they were to help build a railway. The railway would stretch from Ban Pong to Thanbyuzayat, in Burma – a total distance of 415 kilometres – and would pass along flat ground for only 60 kilometres of its length.

In 1910, British engineers had surveyed a proposed railway linking Burma and Thailand but abandoned the project in 1912 because of the difficult terrain. Impenetrable jungle, innumerable ravines, rocky out-crops and mountain slopes were only some of the difficulties and when the varying width of the river, the monsoon rains and the many endemic diseases along the proposed route were added, it was considered impossible. However, the Japanese did not agree.

Owing to the growing presence of Allied submarines in the Gulf of Siam and the Andaman Sea, Japanese merchant shipping was being lost at an alarming rate and it was becoming increasingly difficult to supply its army in Burma. The building of a railway would allow supplies to reach the troops quickly and efficiently and, with over 100,000 POWs taken after the fall of Singapore, a ready labour force was at hand.

For five days and nights the prisoners on the train had been unable to rest properly or to wash and looked forward to arriving at a camp and putting themselves to rights. Sadly, this was unlikely to happen at Ban Pong – the sight of which might have broken the spirit of the strongest

74

man. The monsoon rains had fallen steadily during September and October and the entire camp was flooded. The latrines, positioned close to the huts, had overflowed, and the sight and smell of human filth was everywhere. The bamboo and *attap* huts were in very poor condition; roofs were broken and leaking and, in some of them, the sleeping platforms were sloping down into the flood waters.

With sinking hearts Durnford and Ffolkes waded in the open sewer of Ban Pong, searching for a space on a sleeping platform where they would at least be able to lie down. Having found a place to sleep, they next hoped that they would be able to find the latrines in the flood water, as misjudging the edge or slipping on the mud presented the terrifying prospect of disappearing into 9 feet of sewage – with little hope of ever coming out alive.

Meanwhile, and unbeknown to them, the fifteen men including Tom Hannah, Pat McCready and Geordie Shannon whom they had left behind in Singapore a short time before had also embarked on the same journey and were only days behind them in identical wagons, suffering the same torment. They were part of a large group of POWs that had left Singapore under Lieutenant Colonel Philip Toosey of the 135th Field Regiment on 24 October – destined to build the bridge at Tamarkan – the so-called 'bridge over the river Kwai'.

After an overnight at Ban Pong, Ffolkes and Durnford left with their group and travelled by lorry to Kanchanaburi, better known as Kanburi, where they discovered that they were about to set out on a three-day route march, carrying all of their possessions. That night they went through their packs deciding what they could do without. Essential items, precious photographs, mugs and plates were bundled up together and everything else was given away or sold to natives or Japanese guards. Next morning they set off in the predawn, packs slung across their shoulders.

One of the group, Gunner Arthur Allbury of the 135th Field Regiment, recalled: 'After about 4 miles walking along a wide track, we passed a seething army of brown-skinned, nearly naked Britishers digging, shovelling and listlessly carrying wicker baskets filled with earth. We noticed the complete lack of mechanical aids, the absence of cranes, grabs or excavators. The cranes were weary, aching muscles, the grabs those pitiable little baskets, the excavators, picks and shovels wielded by a dispirited rabble of white coolies. Moving among them, with rifles slung over their shoulders, were the flat-faced Korean guards.'

Within a few hours, the march had degenerated into an exhausted straggle. The ground, after months of continuous rain, was waterlogged, and the packs and clothes of the men likewise. Swiftly-flowing streams had to be waded through. Crude log bridges, the surface wet and their boots slippery, had to be negotiated. By the time they reached the transit camp that was journey's end on the first day, they were almost incoherent with exhaustion.

During the night, an unexpected roll call, 'tenko', was called and the men dragged themselves out of an exhausted sleep to assemble on the parade ground. Unfortunately, John Durnford was so deeply asleep that he was unaware of the tenko until two guards wakened him. He got up quickly – but not quickly enough. 'As I did so, a blow in the chest knocked me down again. Half awake, and none too sure of the situation's prospects, I stood up as smartly as possible, only to receive another flattening blow to the face. ... If this was an attempt to get me onto roll call, then it was largely defeating its own object. ... When they stopped knocking me down I shambled off, trouserless, onto the square.'

The Japanese officer in charge, nicknamed 'The Boy', was drunk and looking for trouble. He ordered the prisoners to number off in Japanese. At this stage of their captivity, this was something that they were unable to do easily but was eventually achieved by the urgent promptings of David Ffolkes, who was proficient in Japanese. The prisoners were then allowed to return to the huts, where they spent the rest of the night uneasily waiting for dawn, keen now to proceed with the march and put distance between them and the unpredictable Boy.

It took three days to reach Tarsau, where they rested for a day before making their way to Tonchan, 8 miles further on. Tonchan camp was positioned on the top of a steep bluff overhanging the river but John Durnford did not plan to be there long. On that black day in Singapore when he had learned of the capitulation, he and a friend went down to the docks to make their escape on the boat of a Portuguese skipper – an arrangement made some days earlier. Unfortunately, the escape bid was unsuccessful as the skipper had mistaken the rendezvous point and the would-be escapees, unable to find him, had to return to their units.

Now, surrounded by jungle at Tonchan and with a map of Siam and a compass in his pocket, and knowing that he was only 50 miles away from the Andaman Sea with its boats and freedom beckoning, he thought that the time was ripe for escape. Leaving camp on a recce, he climbed around 1,000 feet to the top of a nearby hill to survey the area and plan a possible escape route. Slowly he climbed the steep slope, stopping every now and then to watch the line of human ants labouring on the embankment below. But when he pulled himself to the summit, all thoughts of escape were immediately abandoned.

Said John Durnford: 'Turn in whatever direction I would, the country unrolled itself in a succession of knife-backed, rock-tipped ranges, endless in number, similar in character to the uncomfortable razor edge where I was now perched, my long legs dangling over a 1,000-foot drop into prickly bamboos. North-east or north-west, beyond the fold in the trees that betrayed the presence of the river, the dark green mountain landscape showed an infinite number of outcrops, one behind the other. . . . Stronger than barbed wire or moats covered by machine guns, the hills lay between us and freedom. Compasses and a pocketful of rice were not going to get us very far in that country.'

Throughout Thailand, POW camps had been sited along the proposed route of the railway and each camp had a certain section of the line to complete. The Tonchan section began in the middle of a dense patch of jungle, which the POWs had to clear to provide the trace for the line.

At six-thirty every morning, a bugle sounded in the camp at Tonchan, dragging the men out of sleep into the misty chill of dawn. Abandoning their bug-ridden bed slats, they collected a mugful of tasteless rice and, after a quick wash in the river, climbed back up the hill for *tenko*. Once the guards were satisfied that no one had escaped during the night, the work detail collected their tools and set off for the railway.

Said Arthur Allbury: 'Soon the humid air was heavy with the ring of axes, and crashes and earthy thuds reverberated dully as one by one the teak and pinkado trees toppled ponderously to the ground. Teams of half-naked men hauled away at tree trunks and boulders. We slipped and slithered in the mud as, day after day, week after week, the rains beat down on us with pitiless intensity.

'Then, after about a month, the rains died away, the sun rose daily into a cloudless sky, and soon the great swathe we had cut through the jungle became a parched inferno, in whose glare and heat we toiled, sweat-blinded and blistered, week after despairing week.'

Tom Hannah and the others of the 155th who had begun the journey to Thailand along with Lieutenant Colonel Toosey arrived at Ban Pong just as a rainstorm began. All day and all night it poured and the dilapidated huts gave them no protection. The overflow from the latrines burbled and frothed under the sleeping platforms and, with horror driving sleep from them, they perched on the bamboo slats, watching the sewage rise higher by the flickering light of coconut oil lamps.

In any POW camp in Thailand, the chain of command filtered down through the Japanese commandant to Japanese guards often of low rank, then to Koreans who, themselves regularly abused by the Japanese, vented their frustration on the POWs. The final link in the chain of command was the senior Allied officer in the camp and it was his lot to tread a fine line between collaborating with the Japanese and achieving the best conditions for his men. Confronting the Japanese or refusing to obey an order for any reason resulted in, at the very least, a beating. For this reason, many senior officers kept their distance from the Japanese and abandoned their men to the savagery of the guards – to the despair and disgust of the troops under them. The Allied officer in charge at Ban Pong was one of these and, not having the courage to face up to the Japanese, had allowed the camp to fall into the sorry state that the men of this – and subsequent groups – found themselves facing. Toosey was appalled at the officer's failure to look after the men under his command and harangued him with a savage tongue-lashing. However, it had little effect and Ban Pong remained a veritable sewer.

After a few days at Ban Pong, the fifteen men from the 155th were part of a group that moved the 55 kilometres to Tamarkan along with Toosey. The camp, recently built by an advance party of Argylls and Gordons, was above the flood plain and consisted of long bamboo and *attap* huts in good condition. The huts, typical of the accommodation for prisoners working on the railway, were of varying lengths, about 25 feet wide and with the roof sloping down to within a couple of feet of the ground. Sleeping platforms along each side made from bamboo and surfaced with flattened bamboo slats gave each man a space approximately 2 feet wide and 8 feet long on which to sleep and keep any personal belongings. Throughout the railway, the hospital huts were built in exactly the same way and doctors had to climb up onto the sleeping platforms to attend to their patients.

Lieutenant Colonel Toosey took over command of Tamarkan and ensured that the camp was kept clean and tidy and that the huts were maintained in good condition. He laid down strict rules and insisted on discipline to ensure that the camp operated to everyone's benefit and to avoid confrontation with the guards. Officers shared the huts with the men and went out to work with them each day to protect the POWs from excessive demands by the Japanese engineers and to intervene if a guard was handing out excessive punishment. As long as the men obeyed his rules, Toosey stood up for them and argued their case with the guards – even at the cost of being beaten up himself.

Asked about his approach he responded: 'I didn't particularly like being kicked up the arse nor having my head split open with a bamboo cane.' But the men depended on him and he did not let them down.

Toosey's readiness and ability to communicate with the Japanese in order to obtain the best conditions for his men led to the Australian POWs under his command to affectionately refer to him as 'a fucking gentleman', while others of a less generous mind quietly called him 'a Jap-happy bastard'. In many other camps the POWs would have been delighted to have had this particular 'Jap-happy bastard' on board.

The Japanese officer in charge of Tamarkan, Lieutenant Kosakata, refused to speak directly with Philip Toosey. Kosakata is remembered for his assertion that one elephant could do the work of fourteen men – and on this principle he calculated the number of men required for each day's work. His reluctance to speak with Toosey was no bad thing as his second-in-command, Sergeant Major Saito, was more reasonable and was occasionally able to persuade Kosakata to allow some benefits for the prisoners. The opening of a canteen where working POWs could supplement their diet with the purchase of whatever cigarettes or food-stuffs they could afford from their ten cents a day pay was one of these benefits.

The function of the Tamarkan camp was to provide the labour force to build an embankment on which the rail track would run for approximately 2 miles on each side of the river and for the building of two bridges across the Mae Khlong, or Kwai Yai (Big River). By mid April 1943, a temporary wooden bridge roughly 240 yards long, and a permanent steel and concrete bridge, roughly 330 yards long, would rise above the water.

Said Tom Hannah: 'The embankment stretched the whole length of the railway and in some places it could be 30 feet high. The work was brutal. Each man, whether you were sick or not, had to move 1 metre of earth each day. Now, you maybe don't think that's a lot but when you've only got a *chunkel* and a basket and you have to carry the earth maybe 50 or 60 yards, that's one hell of a lot to do.' (The *chunkel* is a common tool throughout Asia, similar to a hoe or mattock.)

Simultaneously with the building of the embankment, construction of the wooden bridge began. Huge teak and deadwood trees that had been felled upcountry were floated downriver to provide the piles for the bridge. Manhandled into position by POWs standing up to their chests in water, they were then driven down into the earth or riverbed, using an ancient system of pile-driving. A heavy metal-capped block with ropes attached was suspended from a pulley and raised by teams of prisoners pulling on ropes attached to the block while singing a chant to keep them pulling in time. On a signal they let go of the ropes and the weight fell on the pile, driving it into the earth.

Said Tom Hannah: 'The wooden bridge was built on piles and the piles were driven by the hammer with men pulling on the ropes on each side of it. The clapper would shout the call and you would sing, "*Ichi, ni, nasaio, nasaio*" – "One two and higher and higher" – and then you would drop the hammer. One day I was the clapper but I lost that job because I didn't realize there was a Japanese officer on site that understood English and my call was "Tojo's a bastard, a bastard". I got a hiding and I lost a good job.'

The hot sun sapped the strength of the men, sharp stones cut into bare feet, thorns from the ever-present bamboo lodged deep into flesh causing it to become infected, and beatings became a regular occurrence for anyone not working fast enough.

Said Second Lieutenant Stephen Alexander, 135th Field Regiment: 'The monotony of the work and the primitive nature of the tools and the sheer numbers of men slaving away – some digging, some in long, snaking queues carrying baskets of earth, some chaining sand and stones from the riverbed – made for a positively biblical scene.'

Towards the end of 1942, the building of the wooden bridge was on schedule, everything was proceeding according to plan and the structure was almost ready for the track-laying gang when, one morning, a large section of the bridge wasn't there any more.

Tom Hannah remembered with amusement: 'The engineer was walking up and down, scratching his head, looking at the bridge. You could almost hear him thinking, "Where is it?"'

It was, in fact, further down river. Nature had intervened and a torrential storm had caused a sudden flood, which had washed part of the structure away overnight. The initial joy of the prisoners at this calamity to the Japanese war effort was tempered by the fact that a team of them had to go downstream and haul the missing pieces back again.

When the flood waters receded, the men had to work doubly hard to bring the project back on schedule and ensure that it was ready for the track-laying gang to put down the sleepers and rails. In February 1943, to the consternation of the POWs who had tried their best to sabotage the bridge by inserting colonies of termites and white ants into cracks in the wood, the bridge was completed. It had been built entirely by hand.

Even before the wooden bridge was completed, work had begun on the concrete and steel bridge. This more substantial structure was required as, during the monsoon season, the Mae Khlong could swell to over 300 metres in width, bringing the possibility that the wooden bridge might, once again, be swept away.

While the men at Tamarkan had been busy building the wooden bridge, David Ffolkes and John Durnford's group had been just as busy clearing the jungle at Tonchan. A strip of land more than 50 yards wide had been cleared in a northerly direction but, just before Christmas 1942, the engineers realized that they had set the prisoners to work in the wrong place. A new strip had to be started in the opposite direction and the prisoners made to increase their efforts to make up for the time that had been lost. The simple tools provided had to be wielded with great displays of energy to avoid unwelcome attention from the guards – always willing to improve a prisoner's performance by administering a sound beating.

By March 1943, the new strip was 4 miles long and work had started on a cutting through a hill. John Durnford later described some of the problems encountered: 'Half the hillside had to be breached by blasting every yard of the ground and carrying away the spoil in wicker baskets. It proved the hardest work of all. ... Blasting often took place without warning. Before the bang in the extreme distance became audible, the air filled with flying splinters, whistling like rifle bullets.

'The heat that now blazed down on us from clear and torrid skies drove all thought from our brains and life from our bodies.'

As life became even more difficult at Tonchan, the same was true for many of the men who had been at Tamarkan. A large group, including the men from the 155th, were moved out at the end of February to work on the embankment further upriver.

Tom Hannah remembered: 'We went on parade one morning and some of us were told that we were moving out. We had about half an hour to get our stuff but none of us needed that long. I had the clothes I was standing up in, half a mess tin and a rice sack that I used as a blanket, so I was ready in two minutes. We were sorry to be leaving Tamarkan – Philip Toosey was a good leader and we knew he would look after us if the Japs started playing funny tricks – but now we didn't know what might happen to us.'

As soon as the group had been counted they moved out, marching behind one of the guards. By now used to the shouts of '*Hurryupu*' they slogged on gamely, oblivious to the sun beating down on their backs, but struggling badly to cope with the dust that swirled all around – the inevitable result of hundreds of men marching on a dirt track in Thailand during the dry season. The dust got into their eyes and up their noses but, worst of all, it dried up throats that were already parched and they were afraid to drink their water because they didn't know when they would get any more.

After just a few miles many of the men were suffering and started to fall behind. Some, too exhausted to continue, collapsed onto the ground and were immediately attacked by the guards. When kicks and rifle butts didn't get someone back onto his feet, rifles would be reversed and bayonets were used. Desperate men pleaded with the guards, 'Please stop. Please stop!' And then they would plead with the men who were watching, 'Please help me! Please make them stop!'

Tom Hannah said: 'It was the hardest thing I saw during the time I was a POW. To have to watch while someone was beaten, sometimes to death, and to listen to them pleading for mercy and to be able to do nothing to help them. It was terrible, terrible.'

After what seemed like an eternity, a *'yasume'* (rest) was called and the prisoners gratefully sank to the ground, glad of the respite from the blows of the guards as much as from the rigours of the march. There was no food and no water but the rest revived them and those who did have water shared it with those who had none. By the time they reached the new camp they were exhausted, hungry and desperate with thirst. From their small stores of rice, the cooks in the camp gave them a meal and some tea, both accepted with gratitude, then, wearily, the men searched around the huts for spaces on the sleeping platforms and laid their aching bodies down to rest.

The camp, Bankau, was on the banks of the Kwai Noi (Little River) close to a native village of about a dozen huts on stilts. 'Bankau' means 'hill house' and the hill house in question was a temple where some Buddhist priests lived. In the mornings the men could hear them beating a drum to call the faithful to prayer. That sound reassured the POWs that there was still a world outside their bleak existence.

Day after day was spent scraping earth into a basket with a *chunkel* and carrying it to the embankment. Any easing-up brought the guards down on them, lashing out with rifle butts or fists. But at the end of each day the men had the consolation of the river, where they could relax in the shallows as the flowing water cleansed the multitude of cuts and sores. Their bodies refreshed, they could relax, for a while at least, in the solitude of the jungle.

Sergeant Major Ronald Hastain, Royal Army Ordinance Corps, said: 'If one was still, the life of the jungle revealed itself. Birds of brilliant plumage emerged from the depths into the clearing of sunlight. Butter-flies basked in the bright sunshine, bigger and brighter than any seen before. Snakes moved with ease across the sun-drenched trunk of a fallen tree. Beetles of gay colours appeared as from nowhere, walking laboriously over one's foot or up one's arm.'

Working on the embankment became worse when the monsoon started. The ground was sodden, the baskets were twice as heavy and climbing up the embankment to empty them was fraught with danger. It wasn't unusual to see barefoot men struggling to the top and, at the last minute, lose their footing and slide all the way back to the bottom, knocking aside anyone who got in the way. Baskets would join the slide, tumbling over and over, strewing their contents all around. Then the unfortunate labourers had to trudge back to the diggings, refill their

The Lanarkshire Yeomanry at Lanark Racecourse, 1939. (*Courtesy of Robert Johnston*)

Newly called-up: Jim Fergusson, Bobby Findlater and John Waugh. (*Courtesy of Findlater family*)

Captain Fraser Stewart with Elizabeth and Lesley. (*Courtesy of Stewart family*)

Lieutenant Colonel Alan Murdoch. (*Courtesy of Gillian Murdoch*)

Lieutenant Colonel James Fasson. (*Courtesy of Anthony Fasson*)

Gunner Tom McKie. (*Authors' collection*)

Bombardier George Mair. (*Courtesy of Anne Mair*)

Lieutenant John Durnford. (*Authors' collection*)

Morris field artillery tractor, limber and field gun. (*Authors' collection*)

Members of Regimental HQ staff – RSM Peter Scullion is in the middle. (*Authors' collection*)

E Troop, C Battery. (*Authors' collection*)

D Troop, B Battery. (*Authors' collection*)

Captain Charles Gordon Brown – at beginning and end of the war. (*Courtesy of Clare Wilkinson*)

Bombardier James Fergusson – at beginning and end of the war. (*Courtesy of John Fergusson*)

Japanese propaganda photograph of POWs working in the docks at Singapore Harbour, Pat Campbell is seventh left, back row. (*Courtesy of Pat Campbell*)

Metal railway wagons of the type used to transport POWs. (*Courtesy of Arthur Lane*)

Bridge-building on the Death Railway. (*Permission of Australian War Museum*)

The wooden bridge at Tamarkan. (*Permission of Australian War Museum*)

The bridge at Songkurai built by POWs of F Force. (*Permission of Australian War Museum*)

A cutting at Chungkai. (*Courtesy of Arthur Lane*)

Cartoon by F. Morris to mark 40th anniversary of VJ-Day. (*Courtesy of Betty Gwillim*)

Major Ian Macdonald, the RAMC doctor who saved many lives on the Death Railway. (*Courtesy of Deidre York*)

The bund at Chungkai. (*Permission of Australian War Museum*)

Another beating from 'Frying Pan' in the copper mine at Kinkaseki. Drawing by John McEwan. (*Authors' collection*)

POW postcard from
Lance Bombardier
Jock Douglas. (*Courtesy
of Audrey Douglas*)

IMPERIAL NIPPON ARMY

DEAR MOTHER AND ALL,   23ᴿᴰ MARCH 1944

                    HOPE THIS FINDS YOU
ALL IN GOOD HEALTH, AND NOT WORRYING TOO
MUCH. MY HEALTH IS GOOD AND ALL I AM
AWAITING NOW IS FREEDOM, WHICH I TRUST
WILL NOT BE LONG. HAVE NOT HAD ANY LETTERS
YET.   LOVE TO ALL
                        JOHN

Rank:- & Name J.C. DOUGLAS L/BDR
Nationality:- BRITISH
P. O. W. Camp of Taiwan.
Date:- 25.6.44

SERVICE DES
PRISONNIERS DE GUERRE
TO:
MRS E.N. DOUGLAS,
WESTWATER,
LANGHOLM,
DUMFRIESSHIRE,
SCOTLAND.

PASSED
P.W. 3647

Japanese propaganda photograph of a Service for Peace, taken at Kinkaseki. (*Authors' collection*)

MRS G.H. MITCHELL
MAIN ST.
MUIRKIRK SCOTLAND
AYRSHIRE

1/4/44.

MY DEAR BELLE

A FEW MORE LINES TO SAY THAT I AM IN GOOD HEALTH HOPING YOU AND THE BOYS ARE THE SAME DEAREST THERE WAS MORE MAIL ARIVED BUT AGAIN NONE FOR ME SO I WILL JUST HAVE TO LIVE IN HOPE FOR THE NEXT LOT HONEY THIS IS MY BIRTHDAY THAT MAKES THREE AWAY FROM HOME AND I HOPE THE NEXT WILL BE AT HOME BESIDE YOU ALL TELL ALL MY FRIENDS I WAS ASKING FOR THEM AND THAT I OFTEN THINK OF THEM ALL. CHEERIO SWEETHEART AND GOD LOOK AFTER YOU ALL YOURS EVER

HODGE

George Mitchell.

POW letter to home. (*Courtesy of Blyth Mitchell*)

Home-made POW birthday card. (*Courtesy of Blyth Mitchell*)

The track to the Kinkaseki Copper Mine: former POWs John Marshall and Benny Gough return, 1999. (*Courtesy of Benny Gough*)

POWs at Shirakawa, Formosa, at the conclusion of the war: Jock Douglas, first right, sitting front. (*Courtesy of Audrey Douglas*)

Steps to the 'death' tunnel at Kinkaseki. (*Courtesy of Michael Hurst*)

Funatsu POW Camp, Japan. (*Courtesy of Anne Mair*)

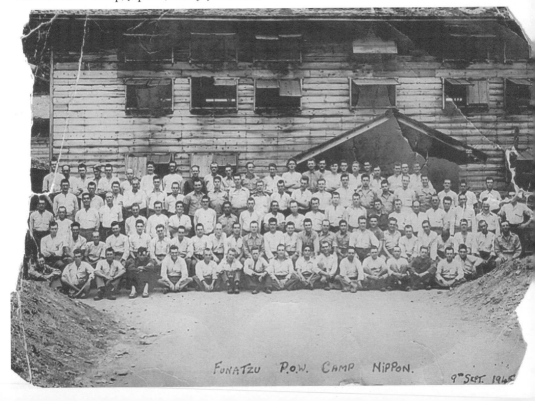

Regimental reunion in Dumfries. From left to right: Willie Brown, Dick Gwillim, Tom Menzies, Andy Hiddleston, Sir Alex Douglas-Home, Jim Fergusson, Robert McGowan, Mrs Macdonald, Bobby Findlater, Bryan Johnston-Fergusson and Dr Ian Macdonald.
(*Courtesy of Findlater family*)

A garden party at Holyrood Palace. From left to right: John McEwan, Alex 'Dusty' Miller and Pat McCready.
(*Authors' collection*)

Old comrades meet again, 1999. From left to right: Jim Watson, Jim Scott, Benny Gough, John Marshall, Jim Brennan and Bill Notley.
(*Courtesy of Carrie Watson*)

Memorial plaque, Alexandra Hospital, Singapore: Jack Edwards and Dick Gwillim.
(*Courtesy of Betty Gwillim*)

Former POWs reminisce, 2010. Tom Hannah and Andy Coogan with a canvas work boot from the Kinkaseki Copper Mine. (*Authors' collection*)

Memorial to the Fallen: asterisks denote those who died as POWs. (*Authors' collection*)

baskets, return to the embankment and attempt the climb once again, but this time with a screaming, kicking guard helping them along.

After Bankau, the group was moved to Kanyu, described by Tom Hannah as the worst camp he was in. There were a lot of sick men at Kanyu and it was difficult for them to get better when there was no medicine. When men in a camp became sick it had an effect on everyone as no food was provided for non-workers. So, to allow all of the POWs to be fed, the available rice had to be divided up accordingly, with everyone in the camp receiving less – which meant that more men became sick and the health of everyone suffered.

As disease and heavy work reduced men to skin and bone rendering them unfit for work, less and less food was provided and many men died from starvation, although this cause of death was not permitted to be recorded. Instead, a variety of alternatives were used – 'debility' and 'post-dysenteric inanition' being just two of them.

Said Tom Hannah: 'Everyone had to appear on the parade ground in the morning, so if someone died during the night we had to keep their body and carry it out in the morning so that the Japs could see that no one had escaped since *tenko* the night before. Death was often our bedmate on that bloody railway.'

From Kanyu the group moved on, through the camps at Hintock, up to Prankassi, clearing the jungle, working on the embankment, building bridges. Through starvation, ill-treatment and the terror of cholera they lived – and they hoped – and they prayed. They yearned for the end to their toil and for that joyous day of deliverance – still more than two years away – although fortunately they were unaware of that.

Tom Hannah later revealed how badly they were affected by hunger: 'To survive we stole out of the Japanese cookhouse – and if you were caught you knew you were in for a bad time. Whatever you were caught with you had to hold above your head standing at attention – and you had to hope that it wasn't heavy. There was a guard standing beside you and if you dared relax he was into you with his feet and his rifle. You could be standing there a day or a week – whatever they decided.

'There was one time Paddy [McCready], Geordie [Shannon] and I were so hungry that we decided to steal the Jap commandant's chickens, which were always tied to the legs of his bed. During the night, we crept in on our stomachs, chook-chooking away to lull them into a false sense of security, and then we grabbed them round the head to keep their beaks shut and stop them from squawking while we smothered them. We were absolutely terrified that we would get caught because the Japs wouldn't have wasted time asking questions – they would have beheaded us as a warning to everyone else. We got clean away with it but it was terrifying the next day when the guards were looking for the birds. People have asked me if we weren't scared we'd get caught and all I say to them is, "Have you ever been hungry?"'

During August, John Durnford ran into trouble at Tonchan when he accidentally tipped a container of boiling water over his left foot. The wound quickly became ulcerated and he was included in a large consignment of sick men sent downriver by barge to the hospital camp at Tarsau. The unfortunate souls on the barge were in a pitiful state, with faces so thin that they looked little more than pieces of grey gristle. Without the strength to sit upright, they lolled against each other and, as the barge pulled away from the shore, one man died and lay there, a skeleton covered in dried skin and rags. When the barge arrived at Tarsau, the men were unloaded onto the riverbank and anyone unable to walk to the camp had to lie in the rain until stretcher parties arrived.

After a period in the hospital at Tarsau, John was moved further downriver to Chungkai, a former working camp but now a hospital camp set on a broad, sandy strip at the edge of the river. Here, he describes how close to death he came: 'By now I had very little strength left, and was indeed at the point of dying. One morning I was moved to the other side of the hut next to an elderly Dutch officer and we lay beside each other, supporting our lolling heads on lumps of wood. For many hours I felt that I had no contact with the world of reality. Indeed, but for one human being, the face and eyes of the Dutch officer might well have been the last sight I saw on earth. This was the appearance of the British colonel on his morning rounds.

'"Come on John," he said. "There are people at home waiting for you." Then he told me that one of my own men was to be buried that afternoon. He had reminded me that there was someone to live for and filled me with a determination not to be shovelled feet first into a hole in the ground in Siam in an old army blanket like Johnson, whatever else happened. And I owe him my life.

'With a great effort I attended the funeral that afternoon, standing at the graveside like a clothed skeleton, with boots that seemed several sizes too big. It was terrifyingly hot, and I could scarcely stand there. But when I returned, it was to get well.'

In April 1943, the steel and concrete bridge at Tamarkan was completed and the POWs moved on to work elsewhere on the railway. Between October 1942 and May 1943, there had been only nine deaths out of a workforce of 3,500 at the camp – a tribute to Lieutenant Colonel Toosey's stewardship and his willingness to provide what protection he could for the men in his care.

No longer needed to service the railway, Tamarkan was designated a base hospital and the full horror of conditions further north immediately became apparent. On 3 May 1943, the first party of sick men arrived at Tamarkan by barge. Philip Toosey and Dr Moon, who had been transferred from Hintock, met them and were shocked at what they saw.

Said Lieutenant Colonel Toosey: 'Parties of approximately 100 arrived nightly and the camp reached its maximum strength by July. The sick were in appalling condition, approximately 75 per cent of the parties were stretcher cases and men frequently arrived dead. ... During this time we saw scenes of misery that will live forever in the memories of all of us.

'I remember one man who was so thin that he could be lifted easily on one arm. His hair was growing down his back and was full of maggots. He was lousy and covered in flies all the time, which he was too weak to brush away from his face and his eyes and the sore places on his body.

'I watched the doctor in my camp – a certain A.A. Moon, an Australian gynaecologist – cut off a leg underneath a mosquito net with a local anaesthetic, his main tool was the cookhouse saw, admittedly sterilized and sharpened up for the occasion.'

It should be remembered that the sick men who were sent down to the base camps were considered by the doctors to be well enough to stand the hardships of the journey. The worst cases remained in the upriver hospitals.

Chapter 7

The Track-Laying Gang

During October 1942, more than half of the men of the 155th who had been based at the Great World Amusement Park in Singapore were moved out. They were there one day and gone the next and not even the officers knew where they had gone. A few weeks later, on 9 November, a further 153 men from the regiment discovered that they, too, were moving on. No one told them where but they expected that it would be to Changi. They were looking forward to it – maybe the work wouldn't be so hard there.

However, experience often proves that the grass is not always greener on the other side and these young men were about to find that out the hard way, their first clue being the sight of the goods wagons that awaited them in Singapore Railway Station. The next clue was the sight of the Japanese guards brandishing rifle butts and bayonets. Wisely they decided not to look around for a third clue and obligingly scrambled aboard the wagons; rucksacks, blankets, groundsheets and all.

Anyone still unaware that they were in a sticky situation quickly realized otherwise when the guards shut the sliding doors of the wagons. More than thirty men, plus kit, enclosed in a steel box 20 feet long and 7 feet wide, did not make for a comfortable situation.

Just a few hours later, they were slumped in the wagons, eyes half shut, chests heaving with the effort of trying to breathe in an atmosphere that was almost liquid. Bill Clark, a Gunner with the 155th and former mill worker from Kilmarnock, tried to ease his aching body, stiff from the strain of sitting on his pack with his knees up to his chin. He needed to move, but didn't want to disturb the men around him who were suffering just as he was – but thankfully he didn't need to. Just as he began to tentatively stretch out an ankle, the train slowed down and stopped. The door was opened and, at the shout, 'Orru mei oriro!' (All men get off!), the POWs surged forward, towards the light, towards the fresh air, relieved that the terrible journey was over.

'Mizu' (water), said the guards gruffly, pointing to the engine of the train, followed by *'Meshi'*, indicating buckets of rice lined up along the track.

For an instant, the men found themselves in a dilemma as to what to do first – answer the calls of nature? Fill their water bottles? Collect their rice? The resulting scene would have done credit to any racetrack as bodies, paralysed with immobility only minutes before, ran madly up and down the full length of the train, attending to their various needs.

That done, they stood around, wondering what they were going to be doing in this part of Malaya – only to find that the answer to that was 'nothing', because the shout of *'Orru mei nore!'* (All men back on!) was heard and, with sinking hearts, the men climbed back into their steel boxes. But at least this time the guards left the doors open. It didn't make the overcrowding any less but a slight draught of air circulated in the wagons and men were able to use the open doors to relieve tortured bowels and bladders.

As night approached, the train stopped briefly to allow the guards to close the wagon doors, thus thwarting the plans of any who thought they might escape in the darkness. Where they might have gone if they survived the jump from the train was anyone's guess. Whether they would survive at all would have been an easier question to answer with thick jungle, lack of food and water and inhospitable natives all counting against them, but the main drawback to a successful escape was their white skin and European features. The Japanese had announced a bounty for anyone turning in an escaped POW and the natives were more than willing to take up this offer of easy money.

When morning came the pattern of the previous day repeated itself, then another night and another day. Three days after leaving Singapore, the POWs could see that they were moving along a flat plain that showed signs of flooding. Shortly afterwards, the rail track disappeared under water and, a few miles further on, the train jumped the track. Appalled, the POWs held their breath as it ploughed on, drawing ever closer to the edge of the embankment. Urgent petitions to heaven were answered, however, and the train stopped just before the engine began the plunge down the steep slope, taking them all with it.

Gingerly they stepped down from the steel boxes and walked away from the teetering engine. Immediately, the guards were around the prisoners, indicating that they should push the engine back onto the track. 'You've got to be bloody joking!' was heard all around, but was uttered only once as guards lashed out with rifle butts and fists. Incredible as it may seem, by dint of much pushing and shoving, yelling and hauling, the 600 men managed to get the train back on the track and the prisoners climbed back on board, wet, muddy and exhausted. For another few miles the journey continued, the engine forcing its way through the water until it came to a halt at a railway station, unable to continue because of the worsening floods.

The men remained at the station for more than a week waiting for the water to recede, their rations consisting of a handful of rice twice a day. At night-time, they slept wherever they could – in the wagons, in the puddles under the wagons or in the puddles elsewhere. They slept in the puddles, washed in the puddles and drank from the same puddles.

When the waters had receded sufficiently, the train moved on again until, a few miles up the track, the engine driver discovered that the 20-foot high embankment had been washed away. Many of the sleepers had disappeared and long stretches of track were suspended in mid-air. The prisoners spent the next two weeks repairing the damage. Knee-deep in mire, tormented by insects that attacked them both day and night, they thought that they were having a really bad time. They were to discover what 'having a bad time' really meant when they arrived at Ban Pong. Appropriately, Ban Pong had, in former times, been the site of a slave-trading camp. Nothing much had changed.

Said Lance Sergeant Bobby Findlater of the 155th: 'I had never seen anything like it before. The place was hoaching with rats and flies, and mosquitoes were swarming in their millions. The stink was unbelievable.'

It was at Ban Pong that they discovered they had been brought to Thailand to help build a railway that would transport Japanese troops north to Burma. They were to be the 'track-laying gang' and their efforts would bring the conclusion to this mammoth undertaking.

The track-laying gang was divided into three teams. The 'sleeper' team, two men to a sleeper, carried the timbers and positioned them on the trace. The 'rails' team placed the rails on the sleepers and linked them together with the fish plates, and the 'spiking' gang hammered in the dog spikes that secured the rails to the sleepers. This was probably the most hazardous work as there was always the danger of the dog spike jumping up and hitting someone.

Two officers from the 155th, Lieutenants Peter Legard and John Tinsley, were with this group and went out with the men each day to intervene when guards were unreasonable in their demands, or when someone was being beaten.

Said Bobby Findlater: 'When the Japs hit us we used to pretend that it was really sore and we'd fall down and look as if we were stunned –

and sometimes they would leave you alone then. One day, Glen Young was getting battered but every time he fell down he'd be rolling about and jumping back up again. We were all shouting at him, "For God's sake lie still!" But he shouted back: "I can't – the ground's that bloody warm!"'

For three weeks, while the men of the 155th laid their first section of rail track they lived at Ban Pong before moving to Non Pladuk – the start of the railway. It was here that they met up again with Lieutenants John Brocklehurst and Joseph Wilmer. The two officers had not been seen since the Battle of Slim River on 7 January 1942, and it was feared that they had died. In fact, they had been captured near Segamat and had been held in the notorious Pudu Gaol in Kuala Lumpur. Gunner Bobby Warwick, who had been seriously wounded when Colonel Murdoch was killed at Slim River, had also been held there but was later sent to Roberts Hospital in Changi. In April 1943, he was to be part of the ill-fated F Force sent to work on the railway.

The flood waters that had earlier caused such inconvenience had dried up, but the dry ground caused a new problem – dust! Dust was everywhere; it hung in the air, it got into the eyes, it lay on the skin, and it was not easily got rid of. Non Pladuk was not beside the river so water was in short supply.

Said Gunner Tom McKie of the 155th: 'There was so little water at Non Pladuk that what we had was needed for drinking and cooking. We were there for two weeks and, by the end of it, we all looked like tramps because we couldn't shave or wash and we had all started to grow beards.'

The track-laying progressed at a tremendous rate as the need for ballast was overlooked by the guards in the attempt to speed up progress in pushing the railway through to its joining point with the line that was being laid southwards from Burma by the middle of August 1943. The prisoners suspected that this lack of ballast would later cause sections of the line to become unstable and even unusable but, by doing what they were told, they hoped to frustrate the enemy's war effort. However, in helping create the problem, the men made another one for themselves as it was they who had to rectify things when the monsoon rains caused the track and embankments to slide and collapse.

Said Gunner David Paton of the 155th: 'The guards would get you up in the middle of the night. If there had been too much rain the embankment was soaked and sometimes slid away and you had to build it up again. They were ruthless!'

On 7 January, the men moved on to Tahrua and then on again to Kanburi. This camp was not near the river and, once again, water was a consideration. To make matters worse, the latrines were insufficient for the number of prisoners and the guards would not release men to dig more during the day. So the POWs had to dig them when they returned to camp in the evening, exhausted and hungry.

Until now the track-laying had been on the flat plains but the sight of the hills, which were coming ever closer, caused apprehension. Working in the blistering hot sun had been hard enough with many having no footwear, shirts or hats. What was ahead of them now, they wondered? What was ahead was the nightmare of the wooden bridge at Tamarkan.

From a distance, the bridge looked like a child's toy made from matchsticks, criss-crossed and balanced on top of each other. Up close it was a precarious-looking structure made from timber and bamboo. It loomed above them, this giant structure, waiting for the sleepers and rails that they were going to lay across it.

The track-layers had difficulty believing that men had actually built this basic, yet complicated, structure – and now it was time for them to play their part and finish it. Hopes that the top of the bridge would be covered over were dashed. A narrow catwalk was all that separated the workers from falling into the river far below. Cautiously, the sleeper team inched across the catwalk, balancing the timber on their shoulders. Concentrating on looking ahead and not down, they fought the nausea and dizziness that the height of the structure induced.

Seeing the terror on their faces, guards would deliberately get in the way – forcing the prisoners to gingerly inch their way around the intimidating obstacle. Some brave souls muttered about 'pushing the bastard off', but resisted the temptation, knowing what the outcome would be. Great would be the satisfaction but it would be only momentary as the offending POW – and probably many more – would follow the guard over the edge. Once the sleepers were laid, the task became easier for the men who laid the rails and for those who spiked them in – at least they had the width of the sleepers to protect them from the beckoning depths.

After Tamarkan there was a short stay at Bankau, before they moved to Wampo on 24 April, where they remained for six weeks. The scale of the bridge and viaduct there caused many an intake of breath. Unfortunately for the track-laying gang, sickness in the camp had caused the work to fall behind schedule and they had to join with the prisoners already there in cutting the trace down from the overhanging cliff.

Bobby Findlater later said: 'We could see it [the Wampo section] when we were working near the Mae Khlong. The cliff went right round a corner and we thought, "They'll never get a railway round there." But they did. We had to cut the rock in from the top of the cliff. One of the engineers, Ukemi, was a right so-and-so – he'd have pushed you over the edge if you weren't careful. Then one day a tree fell down from the top of the cliff and knocked him over the edge of the embankment. When the guards lifted him back up he was so battered you wouldn't have recognized him. The Japs put out biscuits for his spirit but they got eaten by the prisoners.'

Gunsuko Ukemi was a civilian engineer in uniform and had been the most dreaded Japanese in the camp. He was not missed by the POWs.

When the monsoon arrived in early May, the ground became a churned-up mass of mud, and laying the track became a much more perilous undertaking. Many of the men were barefoot as their boots had long since worn out and the ground, the sleepers and the rails were very slippery. Levels of sickness and death among the POWs had decimated the numbers who were fit to work and, under pressure to forge ahead with the railway, the engineers decided that the POWs deemed fit to work would have to work harder. Thus, the *'Speedo!'* period was born.

The guards became harsher and the hours became longer. Men left the camp in the morning while it was still dark and it was dark again before they returned. And there was no comfort for them when they did get back to camp because the monsoon rain came pouring through whatever shelters they had. During this time the men on the railway were never dry. Expected food supplies often failed to arrive and the POWs, already suffering from disease, starvation and vitamin deficiencies, began to deteriorate further.

Gunner Henry Baillie died at Wampo on 27 May 1943 from beriberi and dysentery.
Henry, from Streatham Vale, was twenty-five years of age.

The monsoon rains brought the comeuppance for the lack of ballast on the line. The sleepers sank into the mud and the track moved and sometimes even separated from the sleepers. An emergency ballasting programme had to be carried out and lorryloads of stones for use as ballast were piled at intervals along the track. Teams of four did the ballasting: two men levered up the sleepers and the other two used packers, poles with a half-moon shape on the end, to push the stones in. Severe beatings were administered by the guards if an even surface was not achieved or if sleepers were broken. Having been 'acquired' from rail tracks in Java and Sumatra, many of the sleepers were old and rotten and splintered easily in spite of the great care taken by the prisoners. However, there was an occasional moment of light relief in the tedium of the job.

Bombardier Pat Campbell of the 155th speaks of a 'close shave': 'Back in Lanark I used to box for the regiment and one time I was matched against Johnny Kane. Before the war he was a coal man, but he was also an amateur boxer and was so good that he had gained the nickname 'Dempsey' Kane after the well-known world champion boxer.

'One day the guards were taking us on the bogies to do the packing. I was sitting trying to catch up on some sleep and yawning away. Tommy Douglas was sitting beside a Jap and they were talking about boxing. Tommy was kidding him on that I had fought the World Boxing Champion, Jack Dempsey [from John 'Dempsey' Kane]. I thought I'd better make it sound real and I said, "Yes – I drew with him but I couldn't beat him." The Jap's little eyes were like saucers. He wasn't sure whether we were telling the truth or not.

'That same day we were building up an embankment that had gone. I was working away with the packer when suddenly I could hear a noise like an enraged bull coming from beneath me and someone said, "He thinks you're not working hard enough." This Jap was rushing towards me ready to give me a thrashing and my heart sank. I just stood there, waiting for him to lash out, but he turned and went away and all I could hear was his voice muttering "Dempsey, Dempsey!" and he kept his distance from me for the rest of the day. It was the same Jap that Tommy had been talking to earlier.'

On 13 June, the men moved on, some to Wun Yeh and some to Tarsau, before both groups moved on to Tonchan South a week later. By now the flat land was well behind them. The main camp at Tonchan was close to another at Tonchan South, as was a large camp of native workers. Over 100,000 Asians, mainly Tamils, Malays and Chinese, collectively referred to as the 'Romusha', had been enticed or conscripted to work on the railway or on building the service road for the railway. Lacking the discipline or organization of the POWs, this workforce quickly degenerated into a sad and pitiful rabble. Further upriver, they had been stricken with cholera and this dreaded disease had swiftly spread to the downriver camps.

At Tonchan South, cholera and death stalked the camp hand-in-hand, seeking out the unwary and the careless. By the time the track-layers arrived, many men had already died.

Bill Clark later recalled: 'Doctor Macdonald told us, "You can only get cholera if the germ enters your body through your mouth or through your nose. You can't catch it through your ears or through your skin. But you can catch it from contaminated water. All water must be boiled – whether you're going to drink it or wash in it. Remember, cholera kills – not many people survive it!"

'He made sure that a big container of boiling water was kept at the entrance to the camp and we all had to dip our dixies in it to get rid of any contamination.'

Major Ian Macdonald from Carlisle, a married man with two children, was a doctor from the Royal Army Medical Corps assigned to the track-layers' group.

Cholera is a waterborne disease and can kill within a few hours. The sufferer suddenly begins to vomit and to excrete a watery fluid and the body becomes extremely dehydrated, causing agonizing muscle cramps. If rehydration treatment is started quickly, the victim has a fair chance of recovery. If not, then a speedy death is the usual outcome. Within a matter of hours of contracting the disease, the sufferer loses all body mass and the skin becomes so wrinkled that the victim becomes unrecognizable.

In camps up and down the river, doctors improvised equipment in an attempt to combat the dehydration brought on by the disease. Stethoscopes were cut up to provide tubing and needles were fashioned from bamboo, which allowed transfusions of life-saving saline into the veins of cholera sufferers. Courageous POWs risked their lives to steal items from the Japanese that the doctors desperately needed and officers sat up all night, keeping fires stoked to boil the water for the saline solution.

An area of ground outside the camp was cleared for use as a cholera compound and some tents were given by the Japanese in which to lay the sufferers.

Said Doctor Stanley S. Pavillard: 'One of the worst things about cholera was the painfulness of the muscle cramps ... and from the compound there arose, continually, a faint, desperate moaning accompanied by appalling shrieks as some unfortunate's muscles snapped.

'The stench from the burial pit was everywhere. When one approached the pit to use it, one saw bubbling millions of maggots. There was no one to look after the cholera victims from the Asian camp and the guards used to dump them in the compound.

'Once I saw an Asian sit up just before he was pushed into the pit. A look of horror came on his face and he roared out that he was not dead. Before I could intervene, a Jap killed him with a shovel.'

When they returned to camp after work, the men had to bury those who had died. Naked bodies were carried on stretchers made from rice bags and bamboo poles and placed in burial pits or on funeral pyres. Men stood with sadness in their hearts watching the last visible signs of their comrades disappear.

Said Tom McKie: 'The men who had died of cholera were poor-looking creatures – all wrinkled up – you wouldn't have recognized them from what they were before. Sometimes we had to put the bodies into a pit together and cover them with lime. Other times you would put the bodies on a big pyre and burn them. That's when some of the lads' heads went down. They would say, "What's the point of battling on if you're going to end up like that?"

'You tried to encourage them but once a man's head went down it was hard to get him back up again.'

Hunger was a major problem in all of the Tonchan camps. Because of the high number of sick men, rations provided by the Japanese were well short of what was required. They did not accept that food should be made available to the sick – only those who worked should be fed.

Said Bobby Findlater: 'If we came across any food at all, we ate it. You might eat twenty bananas a day if you were lucky enough to find them. I ate a lot of snakes and we used to snare lizards – they were only a few inches long but they helped keep us alive. One time we were so hungry that we collected leaves off the bushes and boiled them up in our dixies. It was great to get something to eat – there's nothing so bad as real hunger. Another time we thought we had found the same leaves again and boiled them up. But then we were all running to the latrines and we discovered they had been castor oil plants.'

The track-layers of the 155th moved to Kinsaiyok at the beginning of August. Situated on the banks of the Kwai, it was in a natural basin, which retained the incessant downpours of the monsoon rain, and the entire camp became a huge, stagnant pool. The prisoners already there were a pathetic sight, mere skeletons staggering down the track to work on the railway. The huts were falling to pieces because of a lack of fit men with time to repair them. Even the camp hospital seemed about to fall down around its occupants – emaciated wrecks suffering from dysentery, malaria, beriberi, tropical ulcers and innumerable other conditions. Some poor souls could be heard screaming in the agony of cerebral malaria – an affliction that would send them mad before death provided a merciful release. These POWs in the hospital were the sad remnants of what had been fine young men only a few months before.

Said Second Lieutenant Geoffrey Pharaoh Adams, Royal Army Service Corps: 'A large burial ground testified to the death roll; of

900 [POWs] in Kinsaiyok, 300 were to die inside six months. The first, last and indelible impression of the camp was the stench, a miasma of dysentery, excrement, decay and death.'

For some time the engineers had known that the August deadline for completion of the railway was an impossibility (it was later put back to mid-October) but that had not deterred them from brutalizing the prisoners in the attempt to meet the target date. The men in these upriver camps had been starved and beaten until they were mere shadows of what they had been, yet every day the engineers came into camp demanding a full quota of workers.

Doctors tried, often in vain, to protect their patients but sick men were carried out to work and, if they died, had to be carried back to the camp for the night-time roll call before burial. Exhausted men who had worked all day then buried the naked bodies of the dead – all clothing, even a 'jap-happy' (loincloth), being removed for the use of others.

Because the river had been in flood, no provisions had reached Kinsaiyok for weeks and the rice in store had gone sour because of the dampness.

Tom McKie remembered: 'A lot of the rations came up by river and most of it was rotten by the time it got to you. The Japs took out anything that was good and you were left with the rest.'

At Kinsaiyok, progress on a cutting had been so painfully slow that the track-laying gang had to help out with 'hammer and tap' before it was possible to lay the track. Working in pairs, one man held a long drill while the other hit it with a large hammer. The man holding the drill turned it after each clout and hoped that the man with the hammer hit the drill and not his hand. Water was poured into the hole at regular intervals so that the dust could be poked out with a wire probe, allowing the required depth of 1 metre to be reached. The engineers gave each pair of men a 1-metre length of bamboo and this was inserted into the completed hole to show the engineers that it was drilled to the necessary depth. To make the task a bit easier for themselves, if the guard's attention was elsewhere, the men would break a bit off the end of the bamboo so that when it was left in the hole for the engineers to check, they would assume that the hole was the correct depth.

But, as Tom McKie said: 'Sometimes they caught us cheating and they would give us a good clout!'

While at work in the cutting at Hintock, Battery Quarter Master Sergeant Alfred Bartlett, the popular 'Wee Q' who had escaped the ambush at Nee Soon on Singapore just before the surrender, began to show symptoms of cholera. In an act of great kindness, and disregarding the risk to himself, a Dutch doctor carried him on his back from the cutting to the camp hospital hut.

Battery Quarter Master Sergeant Alfred Charles Bartlett died at Hintock on 16 August 1943 from cholera.
Alfred, a married man from Bromley, Kent, was forty-one years of age.

Two days after the death of BQMS Bartlett, the track-laying gang moved on to Prankassi. Like Kinsaiyok, this was a 'mixed' camp, with British, Australian and Dutch prisoners. Dutch mess tins were considered to be superior to those provided to British troops and it was in one of these camps that Lance Bombardier Robert Hudson of the 155th obtained two Dutch mess tins on which he skilfully inscribed the badge of the Lanarkshire Yeomanry using only a nail and a stone. The tins were found in Robert's home in 2009, after his death.

While at Prankassi, Bombardier Pat Campbell received a cut to his leg, which quickly developed into a serious tropical ulcer. The usual treatment of scraping the diseased flesh away with a sharpened spoon was tried but the ulcer refused to heal and eventually Dr Macdonald sent him down to the hospital camp at Chungkai. During the resultant surgery, flesh and bone were removed to a depth sufficient to remove all of the decayed material. Anaesthetic was in short supply and Pat awoke while the doctors were still working on his leg.

Said Pat Campbell: 'A *Book of Commonwealth Law* had been given to me while I was in Singapore and I kept it because I thought it would be useful after the war as I was studying to be a solicitor. After my operation at Chungkai I needed to use pages from it to bandage my leg. Someone asked me for some sheets from it to go to the toilet. I said "No! If you want it to bandage your leg, OK, but not for wiping your backside." '

'I was wearing ragged short trousers but I burned them later because they were full of bugs. I had had a good pair of long trousers at one point but I sold them for a couple of dollars to buy food. I should have kept them because I ended up with just a jap-happy and that was the only clothing I possessed till the end of the war. When I arrived at Chungkai I had an old sheet that I covered myself with at night but it was filthy and I washed it and hung it outside to dry. I would have been better leaving it dirty because someone stole it and I never saw it again.'

Eventually, Pat Campbell was well enough to be moved down the line to Kanburi and then to Nakon Pathon, a brighter, better-equipped camp where he saw out the remainder of the war. While at Nakon

Pathon he renewed acquaintanceship with Gunner George 'Butcher' Smith, from his home town of Dumfries. George had gained the nickname 'Butcher' as he had worked as a butcher in Dumfries, a trade to which he returned after the war. George was gravely ill at this time and, although he survived and returned home, he never completely recovered from his time as a POW.

Pat Campbell later said: 'As a prisoner of war I had very few possessions – the remains of my book, something to eat from, my jap-happy and a hollowed-out piece of bamboo to use as a cup. I had no shirt, no hat – all year round my clothing was a jap-happy. But I had a few very precious things, which I guarded carefully. They were my prayer book and a crucifix, which Father Bourke, a New Zealander, had on the altar when saying Mass at the Great World camp in Singapore. An Australian, Jack Heyden, removed the crucifix when the camp closed and took care of it. I met him later in one of the camps on the railway and he gave it to me. I also met Father Bourke when I was at Kanyu. He carried out his duties as a padre and laboured on the railway as well.'

Pat managed to keep and bring home the crucifix and in 2012, after having re-discovered it in his garage at his home in Dumfries, it was sent back to Thailand, where it is now displayed in the Death Railway Museum.

The track-laying gang moved on up the line to the end of the Thai section at Konkuita, where, on 17 October 1943, it joined up with the Burma section. In a final push to meet the deadline, some men had been sent even further north and worked non-stop for over thirty hours.

On the night of 6/7 September 1944, the prisoners at Non Pladuk experienced the terrifying bombing of the camp by American planes during a raid on the railway sidings. Tragically, ninety-eight men were killed. Having survived the worst that the Japanese could throw at them, they had been killed by their own people. Similarly, at the end of November 1944, a bombing raid on the concrete bridge at Tamarkan caused the deaths of seventeen POWs and injured another sixty.

After the bombing of Non Pladuk camp, the 330 injured were transferred to Nakon Pathon hospital camp. There, the POWs had to dig a moat approximately 8 feet wide and 9 feet deep all around the camp, throwing the excavated soil to the inside, creating a high earthen screen around it. Machine-gun nests were positioned at the four corners of the moat and, with heavy hearts, the men realized that the Japanese had no intention of ever allowing them to go home. One day they would be lined up along the edges of the moat and machine-gunned. The earth stacked along the edges would be pushed in on top of them, leaving no trace that they had ever been there!

'What kind of people are these?' the men asked each other.

And then they wondered why they were asking such a stupid question. They knew what kind of people the Japanese were. They had seen it over and over again when they were working on the railway when the sick were forced out to work and when men were beaten for not working hard enough or fast enough.

But most of all, they had seen what kind of people the Japanese were when a goods trains of the type that had carried the POWs from Singapore had stopped at a railway siding. The wagon doors opened slowly and sick and wounded Japanese soldiers fell out onto the platform. Some remained on the train, too ill to move, lying in the filth that covered the floors. Immediately, the POWs rushed forward to help, common decency overriding the fact that they were enemy soldiers. The POWs washed them, gave them water to drink, gave them cigarettes if they had them – and the Japanese guards turned their backs. Turned their backs on their own comrades because they were now useless to the Japanese War Machine.

So why should prisoners of war expect to be treated any better?

By the time they were moved back down the line to the base camps, many of the POWs had reached the limits of their endurance and, their bodies weakened by the privations that they had suffered during the previous months, they succumbed easily to illness.

Gunner William Cunningham died at Non Pladuk No. 1 camp on
4 December 1943 from dysentery.
William, from Glasgow, was twenty-eight years of age.

Gunner John Hendry died at Kanchanaburi Aerodrome Camp on
10 December 1943 from dysentery.
John, from Coatbridge, Lanarkshire, was twenty-three years
of age.

On principle John would have preferred not to have joined up, following the example of his father, who had been a conscientious objector during the First World War. But, remembering the animosity that had been directed at the family, his mother had persuaded him to accept his call-up – and John's fate was sealed.

Gunner Ernest Steward died at Non Pladuk No. 1 camp on
21 December 1943 from dysentery.
Ernest, from Staffordshire, was twenty-four years of age.

Lance Sergeant Edward Barnes died at Non Pladuk No. 1 camp on 23 December 1943 from bacillary dysentery.

Edward, a married man from Nottingham, was thirty-five years of age.

Gunner William John Grierson died at Non Pladuk No. 1 camp on 1 February 1944 from beriberi and tropical ulcers.

William was a married man from New Lanark.

Gunner John M. Patterson died at Non Pladuk No. 2 camp on 26 March 1944 from pleurisy.

John, a married man from Glasgow, was thirty-five years of age.

Gunner Thomas Crawford died at Non Pladuk No. 2 camp on 21 April 1944 from malaria.

Thomas, a married man from Paisley, was thirty-four years of age.

Captain Guy Roger Coles died at Nakon Pathon camp on 5 September 1944 from Huntingdon's Chorea.

Guy was a married man from New Abbey, Dumfriesshire.

Chapter 8

'D' for Damned – Hellfire Pass

Under the joint command of the British Lieutenant Colonel G.G. Carpenter and the Australian Lieutenant Colonel McEachern, a group of some 5,000 POWs (2,780 British and 2,220 Australians) made up what was known as D Force. Twenty-two of them were from the 155th (Lanarkshire Yeomanry).

The men of D Force left Changi in groups of roughly 600 over several days towards the end of March 1943. The turn of the men of the 155th came at dawn on 22 March 1943, when they were packed into lorries and driven at breakneck speed through the streets. Flung against each other at every corner, they were glad to reach Singapore Railway Station and clamber down, bruised and battered, onto solid ground. Heads spinning from the journey, they entered the station and, like the groups who had gone before them, pulled up in disbelief at the sight of the long line of metal goods wagons that the guards were gesturing them towards. The POWs quickly discovered that hesitation was a mistake corrected by the point of a bayonet. Friends trying to stick together were separated, pushed unceremoniously into whatever wagon was nearest.

Said Sergeant Jack Shuttle, 2nd East Surrey Regiment: 'Jammed into the wagons like sardines it was most uncomfortable and, with the sun beating down unmercifully on the metal roof, so very, very hot. Just the one haversack carried all of my kit but some officers who had remained in Singapore during the campaign came with more bulk, including a number of bedrolls. Room also had to be found for medical and cooking equipment. ... So we set forth, with no water or food to sustain us.'

The train moved north through Malaya and, on the occasions when the guards allowed the wagon doors to be open, the sight of abandoned gun emplacements and shattered rubber trees reminded them of the time, fifteen months before, when they had attempted to halt wave upon wave of Japanese troops – so much more experienced in battle than they themselves – who came at them from every side.

100

With bitterness, the prisoners recalled the message about Japanese fighting ability that their officers had relayed to them from the official document entitled *Raids Behind Enemy Lines*:

His worst natural weakness is that when abroad he is perpetually homesick, and the one thing that will make the Japanese private soldier falter is the feeling that his link with home is broken.

Another weakness is that the uneducated Japanese soldier is frightened of the dark. In his own home, in a tropical summer he sleeps among all his family with the windows shuttered and under a naked electric light for fear of burglars.

It had not taken the Imperial Japanese Army long to blow holes, not only in those hollow words, but also in the battle plans of those Allied commanders who had readied their troops to fight in the 'traditional' way with battle tactics more akin to the First World War. Now, officers and men alike were suffering the consequences of the flawed battle preparations of their leaders.

By the time D Force arrived in Thailand, the large wooden bridge at Tamarkan had been completed and the rail track laid as far as Kanburi. This area, on the flat plains of Southern Thailand, was the more 'straightforward' part of the railway construction and had progressed more or less according to plan.

However, beyond Tamarkan, the railway line followed the left bank of the Kwai Noi before turning north into thick jungle and massive clumps of bamboo. Going towards Wampo it became hill country and, beyond Tarsau, rugged mountains covered with dense jungle and bamboo. The work in this section required the clearing of virgin, primary jungle, felling trees, cutting through outcrops of rock, constructing bridges and building embankments. This section of the railway was technically the most difficult of all. This was what awaited the men of D Force.

After an overnight stop at the malodorous Ban Pong, the men were relieved to clamber aboard a train of flat, open rail cars and be transported away from there to Kanburi. The following morning, in semi-darkness, they continued their journey.

Having travelled part of the distance by river barge, they continued on foot, struggling onwards and upwards on the steeply inclined track, the sun beating down on them from a clear blue sky. Past the cutting at Wampo they went, and into the dense jungle where Tarsau was, following the track hacked out of the jungle by others before them. For some of D Force, Tarsau was their destination.

Located 130 kilometres from Ban Pong, Tarsau was the headquarters camp for D Force and a hospital camp for the many sick from further up the line. It was a hospital in name only as, in common with the other 'hospital' camps for Far East POWs, patients lay on split bamboo platforms without medicine or bandages.

That same day, the new men met the other occupants of Tarsau – POWs from previous groups who had been there for weeks clearing the jungle.

They were described by Donald Smith as 'indescribably gaunt British and Dutch prisoners, some with blood from dysentery running down their legs, and most mottled with filthy sores.'

Regularly working a sixteen-hour day, the men at Tarsau left the camp and returned to it in darkness. By day, the canopy of the dense jungle shut them away from the sun and they lived their lives in a twilight world. Thick clumps of bamboo and massive trees stretched upwards, competing for the light, twisted and twined together into an impenetrable roof, which denied efforts to remove any single part of it. Sweat streamed off bodies as men hacked through compacted clumps of bamboo that refused to fall. Muscles strained and faces grimaced as they hauled on ropes attached to the defiant vegetation. '*Ichi, ni, san, shee! Ichi, ni, san, shee!*' echoed eerily around as they pitted their strength against nature's until the prisoners won and the bamboo fell. But not before it had wreaked its revenge with its needle-sharp thorns, which scratched and lacerated unprotected skin and caused ulcers that ate into flesh and exposed bone.

Bites and stings from flying and creeping creatures, enraged at their home being pulled away from under them, injured the men, but so intent were they on obeying the commands of the bellowing guards that they scarcely noticed these irritating, buzzing, annoying things.

Even the giant, heavy teak trees entwined in the overhead canopy could remain upright, even when sawn completely through at the base.

Second Lieutenant John Durnford, who had been in the first group of the 155th to come up to the railway, described the problem: 'The great boles of teak and deadwood trees, high as a giant clump of bamboo, required hours of work with a cross-cut or 'two-man' saw. They were often brought down at any angle, without warning, by men who had no experience in lumberjacking, and in most cases had to be finished off with wedges and felling axes. It was while thus engaged that I learned of the death of one of my drivers. He had been crushed by a tree falling the wrong way without warning.'

Just twenty days after leaving Singapore with D Force, Gunner William Dalziel, the man referred to by John Durnford, was trapped under a falling tree in the jungle at Tarsau. Hearing the commotion from the POWs who were trying to free him, the guard came over to investigate. Displeased that work had come to a halt, he demanded that someone hit William on the head and put him out of his misery so that everyone could get back to work. Enraged, the prisoners confronted him until he backed away and then, with the strength born out of desperation, the men managed to lift the tree sufficiently to allow William to be pulled clear. He was carefully manoeuvred onto a rough stretcher made from bamboo and rice sacks and carried back to camp, placed on a hard bamboo sleeping platform and covered with a blanket. The medical officer in charge, Doctor Marsden, sent a message to the camp at Kanyu asking the Australian doctor, 'Weary' Dunlop, for help.

Said Lieutenant Colonel Edward 'Weary' Dunlop, Australian Army Medical Corps: 'At this stage I was asked to see Dalziel, a young man with scalp lesions, said to have a fractured skull from a falling tree. I found a fractured neck and quadriplegia. [Dr] Marsden did not show any particular concern for the fact that the chap was still lying on hard bamboo slats just covered by a blanket and that the diagnosis was alarming. In fact, he felt he couldn't cope. ... I asked for a mattress and when by six hours it had not arrived, Colonel Warren gave me authority to confiscate one from an elderly officer who had otherwise no bedding, poor chap. .... Dalziel was placed on the mattress and I had to leave.'

Sadly, 'Weary' Dunlop's help was not sufficient to save William and he died the following day.

Gunner William Dalziel died at Tarsau on 12 April 1943 from
extensive injuries caused by a falling tree.
William, from Glasgow, was twenty-six years of age.

In May, the monsoon broke. Work that had been hard enough with the sun shining down became even more arduous with the rain teeming down, turning the dusty ground into a muddy sludge. On the embankment, baskets of earth that had been heavy before now seemed double their weight. The hours of work demanded of the men left them little time for rest and gradually, overwork, starvation and disease began to take their toll.

Gunner William Daly died at Tarsau on 12 July 1943 from
dysentery.
William was thirty-four years of age.

Gunner Alex Christie died at Tarsau on 10 August 1943 from
malnutrition and dysentery.
Alex was twenty-seven years of age.

While some of D Force remained at Tarsau, others, including some of the 155th, were sent 36 kilometres further on to Kanyu, or to Hintock.

There were several camps at different locations at Kanyu and the men were dispersed from one camp to another according to the demands of the railway engineers. Kanyu River camp was situated on the banks of the Kwai Noi, at the foot of a steep slope and, but for the demands of the engineers and the misery of the monsoon, might have been considered a better location than the norm, with a ready supply of water and the possibility of bathing when the day's work was over.

But each morning the men had to climb up the slope to get to work, and every night they had to climb back down again. Then, with the arrival of the monsoon, the level of the river rose, the camp became flooded and the latrines overflowed. Cholera arrived and the river became out of bounds and flies, attracted by the sewage, arrived in their millions.

Mealtimes became a nightmare because as soon as the cooks arrived with the rice buckets, the flies arose from the ground, where they had been feasting on the contents of the latrines, and formed a thick, black buzzing ceiling over the eating area. The very second that the cooks removed the matting covering the rice, the flies zoomed in, polluting the food. Men covered their mess tins with hands, hats, anything, but still the insects managed to get into the rice. There were many sick men here and, with workers having to share their daily rations with the sick who received nothing, it was a 'hungry' camp with mealtimes consisting of just a quarter of a pint of rice per man. The rice, therefore, had to be eaten – and the flies were, as well.

Said Lance Bombardier Ernest S. Benford, 137 Field Regiment RA: 'Coinciding with the *Speedo*, the monsoon proper broke. ... The river rose in flood and swamped the lower camp at Kanyu, every unmade road and track that we daily used became a watercourse and a layer of thick, glutinous mud lay on the surface of the higher camp. ... Drainage in the camp was non-existent and water lay in great stagnant pools. We were never dry; after a rain-soaked day's work on the line, we would return to a meal of watery rice, which the rain further diluted as we ate it. ... When the monsoon was at its height, food supplies dwindled and fell perilously low.'

104

Gunner John James died at Kanyu River camp on 9 May 1943 from malnutrition.

John, a married man from Nottingham, was twenty-five years of age.

One day, towards the end of July 1943, the prisoners at Kanyu River camp became aware of a strange squealing noise when they returned from work. Trudging through the sea of mud that the camp had become, some men set out to find the source of the noise. Ian Denys Peek later told that a dozen pigs had been delivered by boat – the monthly meat ration for the Kanyu camps. The animals were stranded belly-deep in thick mud and unable to move. Seizing the opportunity for an easy meal, rats had begun feasting on the helpless animals, eating into their backs and faces and tearing the cheeks from them. Unfazed by the arrival of the prisoners, the rats continued gorging on the pigs in spite of the efforts of the men to knock them off with stones or bamboo. When the prisoners pleaded with the guards to shoot the screaming animals to save them further agony, the guards threatened to shoot the prisoners and they had to walk away, leaving the pigs to die a slow, agonising death.

The Kanyu/Hintock section of the railway presented considerable problems for the progress of the railway. Huge rocky outcrops had to be cut through and in many places deep ravines through which the monsoon water hurtled had to be bridged.

The cutting to be excavated at Kanyu was in two sections, one 500 metres long by 8 metres high and the other 80 metres long and more than 26 metres high. On realizing the work that they were to under-take, the prisoners looked around for the machinery that would help excavate the cuttings and were appalled to discover that *they* were the machinery and their tools would be simply *chunkels* and baskets, picks and shovels, and hammers and drills.

They were divided into three 'gangs' to excavate the cutting. One gang scraped away the topsoil to reveal the rock and then carried the soil to where the embankment was being built up. Another gang did the 'hammer and tap' work, providing the holes for the explosive charges and then, when the charges had been detonated, the third gang would clear away the debris. Meanwhile, the soil shifters and the 'hammer and tap' men would move on to another section to move more soil and drill more holes – and so it went on, day after day, after day, with the demands of the guards becoming more and more onerous. The daily task of one hole to be drilled by each pair of men was increased to two holes and sometimes three holes per day. Anyone considered to be not working hard enough would find rocks thrown at them by the engineers, and injuries caused in this way were not considered sufficient for a man to be excused work.

Said Ian Denys Peek of the Singapore Volunteer Corps: 'The Nips scream for faster work and throw more rocks at us. One of these missiles hits my brother just below his right knee, splitting the skin through to the muscle. He is not allowed to return to camp and the wound is soon covered in sweat and mud. The medical officer has no treatment and, by Nip standards, the injury is not enough to keep him in camp. In two days, Ron has a full-blown tropical ulcer, 2 inches across and filled with yellow ooze.'

Ron Peek was eventually removed to a hospital camp downriver, where his leg had to be amputated as the ulcer had turned gangrenous.

Guards would often punish a 'lazy' worker by making him stand holding a large boulder above his head. Any attempt by the man to lower his arms would result in a beating followed by the order to raise the boulder above his head again. This treatment would continue until the guard became tired of the 'sport'.

Then, on 16 June 1943, cholera came into the camp, killing men in a matter of hours. The doctors performed miracles with their home-made equipment to halt the dehydration of the disease but it still decimated the number of men in the camps – a careless drink of water from a contaminated source; an unfortunate proximity to a suddenly stricken victim – that was all it took and POWs and native workers alike died in their hundreds.

A cholera compound outwith the camp boundaries was organized and the bodies of sufferers carried to the tents there. Little could be done for them and, in their agony, they wished for death to take them swiftly. And in the nearby camp, native workers died in their hundreds.

Said Ernest Benford: 'One morning, our group of twenty-four was taken out of camp carrying picks and shovels. When we reached a Tamil coolie camp we could see that it was strewn with dead bodies. We were ordered to dig pits and bury the dead, while the Japs stayed at some distance outside the camp. The Tamils had succumbed to cholera. ... Each body was lying in a pool of grey liquid vomit and excreta. Flies swarmed over the bodies in their millions and set up a continuous humming.'

During the infamous *Speedo* period, so-called fit men regularly worked eighteen-hour shifts. The 'light sick' were also required to work and men regarded as sick even by the engineers were carried to the workplace to do jobs that could be done while lying down – breaking rocks or holding drills. Daily, the demands of the engineers increased and the beatings intensified.

Jackhammers were issued to speed up the work but, at the same time, the monsoon slowed down progress. As the cutting deepened, ladders were set into the walls to facilitate the removal of rock that had been blasted. Fires and carbide lamps were used to illuminate the area sufficiently to enable the prisoners to work after dark. During the hours of darkness, the sight of shadowy figures scraping, lifting and carrying rocks in the flickering light of the fires resembled a scene from Dante's *Inferno* and the cutting became known as 'Hellfire Pass'.

Emaciated, gaunt figures laboured, scraping rocks into baskets before staggering towards the ladders, footsore, bruised and weary. Desperately they climbed upwards, clutching the rungs of the ladder with one hand while balancing the basket on their hip with the other. Reaching the top, tipping the rock over the edge, climbing back down again – and beginning all over again – that was their life now. And if they fell, they picked themselves up quickly before a guard could reach them and beat them.

One night, a man felt ill while working and collapsed, unconscious. Seeing him, a guard came over and began kicking him. The man remained on the ground, eyes closed, silent and unmoving. Deciding that he was feigning illness and merely taking a rest, the guard took a piece of wire and put the tip into one of the fires. When the tip glowed red hot, he pushed it into the foot of the sick man who remained unconscious, his foot twitching at the cruel violence being delivered to it. Eventually, the guard became fed up, kicked the prisoner a few more times and walked away. The unconscious man remained where he had fallen, the rain beating down on him. He died later that night.

And the rain continued to fall, and the engineers continued to shout, and the guards continued to beat the prisoners.

Gunner John (Tony) Greig died at Kanyu No. 1 camp on 25 June 1943 from dysentery.

John, a married man from Glasgow, was twenty-seven years of age.

After work, Tony's friends visited his grave and, on the wooden cross that marked it, they attached a metal plaque on which they had scraped his name and regiment. This enabled the Commonwealth War Graves Commission to locate, not only Tony's grave, but also the cemetery there.

As the cutting grew deeper and longer, the engineers laid railway lines at the bottom and brought in bogies to speed up the removal of the blasted material. The pile of debris lifted out of this cutting can still be seen today – as can the remains of the holes that were drilled in the sides of the cutting to hold the ladders.

Elephants were brought in to help with the heavy work but their mahouts died from cholera. No matter how hard the Japanese beat these gentle animals, they refused to work without their mahout and one day, when a guard had beaten an elephant repeatedly, it decided that it had had enough. It picked up the guard in its trunk and threw him against a tree, bellowing furiously all the while. Terrified, the guard scrambled to his feet and ran into the jungle before the animal could attack him again. The guard survived – and so did the elephants, wandering off into the jungle and freedom. Only the POWs could not escape – unless through death. The cutting, which was started in May, took until 24 August to complete. It cost the lives of hundreds of men.

As sickness in the camps increased, some sick men were sent downriver by barge to the hospital camps at Tarsau and Chungkai. This 'merciful' move was, in itself, a sore trial for them. Firstly, there was the scramble down the steep slope, hearts thumping with fear and exhaustion, ignoring the pain from scraped elbows and knees to reach the river, which beckoned to them from far below. Men swollen with beriberi might perhaps be guided down by the trembling hands of men suffering the rigours of malaria. Others would lend a hand to those who were terrified that they might fall.

Then, having arrived on the beach, the desperately ill men were stacked upright, more than 100 at a time, into the waiting barges. The swiftly-flowing river threw the boats from side to side, alarming everyone, making them afraid that they would be thrown into the water and would drown. And when their destination was reached they staggered or crawled off the barges, onto dry land and into the hospital – which really was no such thing as there was no medicine, no bandages and no proper beds. But there *were* doctors, devoted men who would always do their best for the hundreds of sick men under their care. For some men, the journey to a hospital camp saved their lives but for others their bodies had suffered too much punishment and they were beyond recovery.

Among those in the hospital at Chungkai was Bombardier Pat Campbell, who had been moved down from Prankassi in September 1943 after his leg injury turned into a large ulcer. Also at Chungkai at that time was Sergeant 'Big Bill' Robertson, who, also suffering from a serious ulcer, had been brought downriver as he was no longer fit to work on the line. Sufficiently recovered from his own ulcer to be able to walk around the camp, he was in the habit of visiting another of the

155th, William 'Jimmy' Byers from Canonbie, in Dumfries, who lay very close to death in one of the huts.

Big Bill had just left Jimmy one day and was returning to his own hut when he chanced upon Pat Campbell and told him about Jimmy. Pat had known Jimmy since before the war and immediately went to visit him but, on entering the hut, he couldn't see him. Hearing a voice whisper 'Hello Pat', he turned round and saw a cadaverous-looking figure beckoning to him from a sleeping platform. It was Jimmy – the man he had come into the hut to find. When Pat had last seen him back at Changi, Jimmy had been a strong-looking man with plenty of flesh on him. Now he was a shrunken wreck, literally skin and bone. This was what six months slaving on the railway had done to him.

Gunner William (Jimmy) Byers died at Chungkai on 5 October 1943 from debility.

William was from Canonbie, in Dumfries.

Gunner Edward Johnson died at Chungkai on 7 October 1943 from pneumonia.

Edward, a married man from West Bromwich, was thirty-four years of age.

Second Lieutenant John Durnford, who was also at Chungkai at that time, was present at Edward's funeral.

The remainder of D Force continued working in the Kanyu/Hintock area until the railway was completed in October 1943. After that, the sick were transported downriver to one of the hospital camps, although many of them were too ill to survive.

Gunner Thomas Emery died at Chungkai on 19 January 1944 from amoebic dysentery.

Thomas, from Lambeth, was twenty-three years of age.

Some of the POWs were brought back down the line to a new camp at Tamuang, where many of them remained till the end of the war.

Others were retained in camps along the railway to perform general maintenance work, cut down trees to provide fuel for the engines or to repair track or bridges damaged during Allied bombing raids. Conditions in these camps were no better than they had been while the railway was under construction. The prisoners were still beaten, starved and deprived of medical care.

A group of men from the 155th was sent to Tha Mayo camp, also known as Tamajo, to cut wood for the engines.

Lance Bombardier John Graham died at Tha Mayo on
11 November 1944 from malaria.
John, a married man from Glasgow, was twenty-nine years of age.

Lieutenant Colonel McEachern, Commander of D Force Australians, remarked on the attitude of the Japanese to POWs working on the railway: 'The Japanese did not consider human life of any value when viewed in the light that the railway must be pushed on regardless of cost. This attitude was openly professed by Japanese camp commandants who have stated that "Even if men die, they should do so gladly as they are working for the Emperor and the railway must go on."'

Chapter 9

F Force – Lies and Deceit

At the beginning of April 1943, rumours swept the POW camps at Changi that a large number of troops were to be moved out because of the shortage of food on the island. The prisoners could identify with this; there was never rice enough to satisfy them in spite of their rations being occasionally augmented by the produce of the camp gardens, so the thought of a move to a place where food would be more plentiful was very appealing. There were still around 13,000 men crammed into the camps and everyone's health was suffering through inadequate food and the shortage of medicine.

Some of the POWs were glad to hear of the move: 'Not before time. I'm fed up looking at rice. If I get the chance I'm off!'

Others were more cautious: 'I wouldn't trust them as far as I could throw them. At least here our own officers are in charge and we don't see much of the Japs. I remember what it was like in the work parties in Singapore last year. Some of the guards were brutal. No! I'd rather stay here. At least we know what we're up against.'

The rumours soon became fact and the Japanese demanded 7,000 men for a move to a new place in the north. When confronted with protests from the officers that there were not 7,000 fit prisoners left at Changi, the Japanese resorted to their usual tactics of lies and deceit. They gave assurances that this was NOT a working party. The movement of prisoners was simply to help alleviate the food shortage in Singapore and, since the new camps were to be in pleasant, hilly areas with opportunities for recreation, a move would greatly benefit sick or convalescent prisoners.

They said: 'Send your sick. We will provide transport for them. There will be no marching apart from a short distance from the train to the first camp. Heavy baggage will be taken to the camps by lorry. Bring bands and tools and cooking equipment and whatever equipment you need to provide electric light.'

111

And they promised: 'We will provide gramophones, blankets, clothing and mosquito nets at the new location. There will be a good canteen at each camp after three weeks – you can bring your own canteen supplies to last until then.'

And, best of all: 'The group will include a medical party of 350 and there will be equipment for a central hospital of 400 patients, and medical supplies for three months.'

And they smiled, and bowed, as their custom demanded – and the officers believed them and the lists were drawn up. Books, musical instruments, anything that might be remotely useful in a new camp, were gathered together and crammed into overflowing haversacks by POWs looking forward to a better life.

In early April, Lance Corporal Bill Smith of the Norfolks, who had been suffering from diphtheria, became caught up in the excited preparations of those who were to be moving to the new camps and wrote in his diary:

8 April: Told officially that all H.Q. is moving upcountry.
11 April: As yet I don't know if I am going but I am going to the hospital to ask if I can go.
12 April: I'm going. In fact, all Div. H.Q. are going, we can take all the stage props and band instruments.

Lance Corporal Smith's daughter, Carol Cooper, the founder of COFEPOW (The Children of Far East Prisoners of War) group later commented: 'If only he had requested to stay on at Changi, he would have stood a chance, he might have lived. Instead, by asking if he could go he signed his own death warrant.'

The British contingent of 3,334 included 1,000 sick or convalescent men, as suggested by the Japanese. The Australians were more cautious and included only 125 sick in their quota of 3,666. The numbers in each group included volunteers bored with the tedium of Changi and the petty rules and military discipline enforced by the Allied officers. And they were convinced that there must be more to eat in other parts of the Imperial Japanese Empire. Their imagination worked overtime, thinking of the good food that they would soon be enjoying. In fact, although they had no way of knowing it at the time, conditions and food at Changi were infinitely better than in the vast majority of Japanese POW camps throughout the Far East – and in particular in the camps where they were destined to spend the next six or seven months.

The men in this group, known as F Force, were to be the victims of the cruellest of deceptions. Of the 7,000 who left Singapore that April, only 3,904 would survive.

112

F Force, including nineteen men from the 155th (Lanarkshire Yeomanry), began leaving Singapore on 18 April 1943. The first six trainloads carried the Australian troops and the final seven the British and main Japanese party. Some Tamil coolies were also squeezed on board at Ipoh, in Northern Malaya. Each journey mirrored the previous transportations – the panic, the crowding, the furnace-like heat, the hunger, the thirst, the brutality of the guards.

Many of the men had only recently come out of hospital and most had diarrhoea or dysentery. On the few and infrequent stops they would tumble out of the wagons to relieve themselves at the side of the tracks, adding to the piles of excrement left by earlier trainloads, their need too urgent to allow them to seek a private or secluded place. Flies swarmed around, settling on men and ordure alike. Their first urgent necessity attended to, the men swarmed around the engine in the hope of refilling their water bottles before the guards swarmed around them, kicking and beating them back on board the train.

Said Regimental Nursing Orderly Idris James Barwick, Royal Army Service Corps: 'The scenery, the teeming life of insects, animals and humans, the jungles, the paddy fields, the native boys on the elephants and the natives working up to their knees in water. ... I think I could write for a week on what I saw of interest on that journey, but although it was so interesting, it brings back the most painful memories of the appalling suffering endured by so many.'

By the time the journey came to an end, all of the prisoners were in a sorry state, exhausted, dehydrated and with their clothing fouled. However, the thought of the promised 'rest camp with good food' that lay ahead, boosted and encouraged them so that they climbed from the wagons in a light-hearted mood when they arrived at Ban Pong.

This mood vanished in an instant when they were confronted with the reality of their situation; the journey to a holiday camp with no marching was, in fact, a cruel hoax. Instead it was to be a march of 300 kilometres to work camps near the Burmese border to build a railway. To add to their troubles, F Force (and H Force, which would leave Changi the following month) had not been transferred from the Singapore to the Thailand POW administration, hence the reason that no transport was provided for them and, later on, a food shortage for the same reason would help decimate their numbers. During the journey, many of the trainloads received no food or water for the final twenty-four hours.

Those who had volunteered for the move cursed themselves for having believed the Japanese; they should have known better, having seen sufficient instances of Jap dishonesty and deceit in the past to have believed them this time. Now they were trapped in this terrible situation. They looked at the sick, some weeping openly, knowing that they would have difficulty walking 3 kilometres, never mind 300. But Colonel Banno, the Japanese officer commanding F Force, reassured them, and suggested that they leave heavy items behind, promising that everything would be brought up to the camps later on. Once again, the prisoners believed and were deceived. Vital supplies and medical kit were left behind and never seen again.

As each trainload arrived at Ban Pong, the officers complained at length about the situation but were met with the usual impassive faces and threats of violence. No exceptions would be allowed, no leniency permitted. Only the very sickest of men were allowed to be left behind, all others would march and if men died, that was unfortunate! It was only a short march to begin with, to the camp at Ban Pong, and they could rest there for the night.

At Ban Pong, a quick look revealed that the huts still sagged, the sleeping platforms were still broken, the latrines still overflowed but, so exhausted were the men that, after a meal of rice and vegetable stew, everyone found a place to lie down – the first time for five days that they had been able to do so – and fell asleep.

Wrote Lance Corporal Bill Smith:

29 April: Left Ban Pong at about 9.00 pm to start a march up-country. We did approx. 20 miles, it was like hell had arrived.

Each trainload, after rice pap for breakfast, prepared for the first stage of the march, which was to begin that night. Packs were adjusted; items deemed desirable but unnecessary were removed and given away or sold. Small piles of things that men decided they no longer needed could be seen all over the camp.

Said Idris James Barwick: 'I checked and rechecked my kit, sorting it out and reluctantly placing things on one side that I thought might make my load too heavy for the march. Many treasures were sacrificed. Books, we could do without; out they all went and, as many others thought the same, our plans for a library were doomed.... The difficulty of making up one's mind about what to part with was really painful. Even a small tin was of great value as a container for boiling water and many other uses.'

During the day, the POWs made the most of the opportunity to rest and when, at 2100 hours, the order to assemble was given, they gathered together complete with packs and cooking equipment and

114

waited through the interminable Japanese process of counting. An hour later, the order to march was given and the men moved out, taking turns to carry the big metal *kwalis*, the shallow pots used for cooking rice.

Although this first stage was over level ground, things soon became difficult. The British trainloads had begun arriving just as the monsoon started to break and the ground rapidly became a quagmire of slippery mud. All of them were suffering from malnutrition and after the dreadful train journey, were in no condition to march. The sick, in particular, had reached the limits of their strength. Men, their bodies heavy with the fluid of beriberi, dragged one weary foot after the other. Some, who had just recovered from diphtheria, gasped and struggled for breath, their weakened hearts unable to cope with the effort demanded of them. Dysentery sufferers lagged further and further behind, their frequent excursions off the path to relieve themselves causing sudden furies from the guards. Even the fit men began to suffer from the constant, unremitting pace. When, in the middle of the night, the shout of 'Yasume' was heard from the guards, the POWs sank to the ground, dragging off their packs as they did so. Spare socks and other items of clothing were used as padding for their shoulders and haversacks were rearranged to make sure that nothing sharp was sticking out to cause irritation or injury. A meal of rice was provided around 0300 hours, and the march continued until the first staging camp at Tahrua was reached later that morning.

No arrangements for accommodation had been made and the men had to find what shelter they could in order to rest. Many of them made their way to the nearby river, its cooling waters easing their pains and soothing their blistered feet before they crawled into the undergrowth to shelter and sleep.

That night they again gathered and wearily responded to the order to move out. The ground was still level and the track not too bad but men quickly began to suffer from exhaustion. To fall behind was a major problem in the darkness because in some places Thai bandits shadowed the marchers, picking off the weak and unwary. Twenty men from F Force simply disappeared on the march and it is thought that they were probably murdered and disposed of by the bandits.

Major Cyril Wild later wrote in a report about conditions for the men of F Force:

> Men toiled through the pitch blackness and torrential rain, sometimes knee-deep in water, sometimes staggering off bridges in the dark. Sprains and bruises were common, fractures of arms and legs

115

occurred and stragglers were set upon and looted by marauding Thais. Of the large and growing number of sick, many fell by the wayside and they and their kit had to be carried by their comrades.

Each night, by the halfway point when they stopped for their 'meal', most of the prisoners had felt the wrath of the guards and bore the bruises to prove it. Falling behind was not permitted, falling down was not permitted and these instructions were reinforced by stinging blows from bamboo sticks or from rifle butts.

But if the guards were unrelenting in their punishment of the prisoners, the British and Australian medical officers were selfless, constantly doubling back along the line to check on the sick or injured, giving out water and whatever help they could. The padres, with no thought to their own exhaustion, also walked up and down the column of marchers, encouraging those who felt they could not take another step and organizing supporting shoulders for men who were struggling. Often they themselves supported men or carried their packs for them. One of them, Padre John Foster Haigh, who had helped relieve the tedium at Changi by singing at camp concerts, later died at Songkurai in September 1943. Another, Padre Noel Duckworth, who had remained with the wounded at Batu Pahat, and who was affectionately remembered for distributing pages from a bible to the smokers at Changi, survived. On his way home on the MS *Sobieski*, he delivered a stinging rebuke to the Japanese in a radio broadcast telling the story of F Force.

When the marchers reached the next staging camp at Kanburi they were greatly concerned about the future. Hunger, thirst, exhaustion – which was worst? They could not decide – and that was the fit men! Those who had started out convalescent were in desperation. But worst were those who were already sick when they left Changi. They were frantic, knowing that they could not survive this march. Like wounded animals they searched for shelter but, finding none, they lay on the ground, raising their heads only when friends brought food, which mostly was left uneaten. Kanburi was not near the river, and water – that necessity of life – was unavailable unless bought from a privately owned well. Officers complained vehemently to the Japanese but they shrugged their shoulders and turned away. Anyone wanting drinking water would have to pay for it – or go without! A night's rest was allowed at Kanburi but, on the following night, they had to march again.

Said Private George Aspinall, a driver with the 2/30th Battalion Ambulance Unit, Australian Infantry Force: 'After a while, we realized we were marching alongside the railway line and that made us pretty savage. There was nothing much in the way of huts in the staging camps, and we used to try and snatch a few hours' sleep under a bush or anything with a bit of shade.'

It was particularly unfortunate that the sick included in the British numbers arrived in the last trainloads and suffered the worst of the marching conditions. In places, the track was completely underwater and many of the men discovered on pulling their feet free from the knee-deep mud that their boots were gone, and for the remainder of their time in Thailand, went barefoot.

Each night, around 2100 hours, the Japanese called a *tenko*. The men assembled, counted themselves and waited while the guards counted them again until they were satisfied that the numbers were correct, making allowance for those who had died during the day. Then they would move off into the dark, dripping, stinking jungle.

Gunner Tom Hannah of the 155th witnessed F Force on the march: 'Sometimes we would see these men lying in the scrub near our camp. They were poor-looking creatures and there wasn't a thing we could do to help them.'

Following the pattern of 'march two nights, rest one night', even POWs who had been fit at the start began to struggle. More and more often, men fell or slipped or tripped and were beaten back to their feet by the merciless guards. Where the track allowed, they tried to walk in threes so that those on the outside could support the man in the middle, often carrying him between them. But for long distances the track was through thick jungle and they had to move in single file while the unfamiliar vegetation waited to attack them.

Said Nursing Orderly Stanley Wood-Higgs: 'The bare portions of the body, and even those covered by clothes, would often be whipped with sharp and scratchy or pointed thorns, twigs or branches because young bamboo cuts like a knife and many a bamboo cut killed a man by becoming infected.'

Packs were thrown away, exhausted men no longer caring that their only clothes were those that they were wearing. At the rest stops, men could sometimes be seen crawling into the jungle to die in peace, away from the frenzy of the guards. Men from earlier parties who had died at the trackside were buried by men who did not know them, but cared for them nevertheless.

Said Idris James Barwick: 'After collecting my haversack rations I visited the sick and found that they had been placed in the bushes, where they had to fend for themselves. Some had been there since the early parties had passed through and were in an awful state. They were too weak and ill to walk into the bushes so had messed themselves and were lying in filth with no one to care for them. They were simply left to die. ... The next party to come through would probably find these fellows dead and would bury them. The poor devils were at the end of their tether.'

These poor souls were men who had stopped behind to rest, in the hope of being able to march with a later party. But they were too weary to collect food or water and became weaker and weaker until, mercifully, death claimed them.

At times the rain doused the flames of the guards' torches and in the pitch darkness the men struggled along, unable to see where they were going. Many walked with a hand on the shoulder of the man in front; others called to each other every few paces, fearful of losing touch with the party and finding themselves lost in the jungle. With the unrelenting pace and the effort of trudging along, soaking wet and knee-deep in mud, the sound of sobbing could sometimes be heard from men overcome with exhaustion or hopelessness, or from others who had accepted that they did not have long for this world and would never see those at home again. The name of a wife or sweetheart or, simply, 'Someone help me!' could be heard as a man fell on the ground and lay there flinching at the savagery of the guards as they rained blows upon him, demanding that he get up. But resignation had taken over from desperation and these men sank into oblivion – not peacefully or quickly – but thankfully. Death had allowed them to escape and there were times when others envied them that!

As the nights wore on, more men had to be left behind at the staging camps, on the ground, in the rain. Sometimes the guards in charge of these camps would refuse to allow men to be left there.

It took seventeen nights for the prisoners to reach their camps near the Burmese border, by which time their numbers were sadly depleted from the 7,000 who had set out from Singapore with such high hopes of a better life. One thousand men had been left behind at staging camps or had died en route.

There were five main camps in which F Force was congregated – Nikki (the headquarters and hospital camp), 282 kilometres from Ban Pong; Shimo Songkurai; Songkurai; Kami Songkurai and Changaraya. The British troops were congregated mainly at Songkurai and Changaraya.

It would be natural to expect that a period of rest might have been granted to allow the exhausted men to regain their strength but in each of the camps they were allowed only one day – and that day had to be spent trying to make the place habitable. A cookhouse with a covering over the rice boilers had to be built, latrines had to be dug, paths had to be cleared through the jungle and wood and water had to be collected

118

for the cookhouse. In spite of their fatigue, rapidly-developing ulcers, dysentery, malaria and the multitude of other health problems present in all camps, they were then forced out to work.

Songkurai was home to 1,600 British POWs. Situated 294 kilometres from Ban Pong, it was to become known as 'the Horror Camp of the Thai Jungle'. Accommodation consisted of three huts on the side of a hill between two gullies, down which ran fast-flowing streams. Only one of the huts had a roof – it was shared by the guards and the men's own officers. The other huts remained roofless for weeks. Each of them, measuring approximately 300 feet by 24 feet, had the usual sleeping platforms running down each side, allowing each man a sleeping space around 18 inches wide.

Looking at the terrain around them, the POWs were incredulous that a railway was to be constructed. A swiftly-flowing river would have to be bridged, as would a number of deep ravines that slashed the countryside. A road had to be laid, and that would require another bridge.

'It's impossible!' they said to each other. 'It can't be done.'

But it *was* done and it cost the lives of almost half of the men in F Force.

At Changaraya, 301 kilometres from Ban Pong and home to 700 British prisoners, conditions were no better than at Songkurai. Sited on a very steep slope in relatively light jungle, the huts were also without roofs and tigers could often be heard prowling around in the night.

Within a few days of arriving at the camps, men began to fall ill with cholera. They lay on sleeping platforms, their faces drawn with pain and fatigue, eyes sunk deep into their sockets, screaming as cramps contracted and snapped muscles. They groaned as the uncontrollable outpouring of bodily fluids dehydrated them till they resembled skeletons covered with wrinkled parchment.

Bombardier Alex Cavers died at Changaraya on 29 May 1943 from cholera.

Alex was thirty-seven years of age.

There was no treatment for these men. No rehydration equipment, no saline drips, no clean water. Through time the doctors improvised rough and ready saline drips and some men were saved. But at every turn the doctors were frustrated by the Japanese. Only the cooks were allowed to take water from the river, so doctors and prisoners had to collect rainwater for their needs. There were no drugs, no medical equipment and certainly no quarantine measures; after all, that would reduce the number of men available for work. And the equipment and medicines that could have helped lay piled up at Ban Pong.

Gunner David Cadell died at Changaraya on 5 June 1943 from cholera.

David, a married man from Govan, Glasgow, was thirty-five years of age.

During the epidemic Songkurai lost 232 men, about 14 per cent of the camp strength, to cholera. Changaraya lost 23 per cent – 160 men out of the 700 who had arrived less than one month earlier.

At 0500 hours each morning the men of F Force were roused to collect a pint of rice for breakfast and another pint for later. Then, in the cold light of dawn, they set out, scantily-clad because most of them no longer had any clothes other than a jap-happy. Anyone who still had a ground-sheet was fortunate. Wrapped around the body it offered protection from the rain and helped preserve body heat – this was the highest point of the railway line and it was often cold. The clothing, blankets and mosquito nets that had been promised before the force left Singapore never appeared.

Men detailed for the embankment filled baskets with soil from one place and, staggering from weariness, carried it to the steadily lengthening banking. Tree-felling parties covered a considerable distance searching for suitable trees (as near as possible to 15 feet long and 12 inches thick) and cut them down, the blunt axes and saws making the job harder than it needed to be. And the ever-present insects, enraged at having been disturbed, took their revenge, biting and sting-ing viciously. The further the men walked to find suitable trees, the further they had to carry them back through the wet, marshy ground, with leeches that fastened and snakes that bit and rain that poured.

Logs were shaped and cut with blunt tools, difficult to use properly, made slippery with the rain. Stone-cutters and blasting teams worked barefoot on sharp rocks, lifting boulders, carrying them, dumping them and sometimes dropping them, with a beating from the guards as a reward for having broken a foot or a leg. Lines of men moved back-wards and forwards in the quarry, two to a basket, working from early morning till late at night, cutting and carrying stone for the foundations of a road – each man dying a little bit more with every minute that passed.

At midday, work stopped for a short time and the prisoners ate the rice – now sour – which would inevitably cause dysentery. And when the dysentery became so bad that they could no longer work,

120

they would be laid on the floor of the 'hospital' so that an overworked orderly could use a bamboo shovel to clean up the mess instead of having to clean the sleeping platform. And when men died they were carried outside naked, with a piece of cloth to cover their face, there being no blankets to spare.

The rain dominated everything and the end of work brought no relief from the misery. Men stood in the mud in the cookhouse queue, and then slipped and slithered back to the roofless huts, trying to stop the rain pouring into their rice. Having eaten it, they would lie down on the rain-soaked, rough bamboo sleeping platforms, cover themselves with their soaking wet blanket – if they had one – and shiver themselves to sleep. And next day it would be the same.

If the rain was unremitting, so also was the behaviour of the guards. Savage brutality was the norm. A railway had to be built and it *would* be built. Engineers lashed the prisoners with wire whips and bamboo sticks to force them to efforts beyond their strength. Ant-like, men scurried around, frantically obeying the commands of the engineers. *'Speedo! Speedo! Speedo!'* was the screaming instruction day after day, hour after hour, minute after minute until it flooded the brains of the workers even as they lay in exhausted sleep.

The loneliness and isolation in the jungle and the constant savage treatment of the guards weighed heavily on the men of F Force. And the news of the outside world, which they sometimes received by secret radio, often increased the sense of melancholy that they felt.

Said Stanley Wood-Higgs: 'The news we hear, mostly from the pirate radios we operate, suggests a great preoccupation in England with the problems of the Hitler war. The Far East seems to have been forgotten. Do they know, we wonder, about the march, through seventeen nights from a village north of Bangkok to the camp in the jungle below the river? Do they know we carried what we could and jettisoned the rest? That we had only one meal by night and one by day and that the jungle path was often knee-deep in mud and if you fell you probably stayed there? Do they know what it feels like to have a rifle butt brought across your shoulders because you lag behind? No. They will never know.'

By the middle of May, the men of F Force were in the unenviable position of being, to all intents and purposes, cut off from the rest of the world. The service road had very quickly turned into a quagmire, making motorized transport impossible, and despite the monsoon rains, the river was not yet high enough to allow travel by boat.

From the end of May, Lieutenant Colonel Harris, seeing the rapid deterioration of the men and the prevalence of sickness among them, began pressing the Japanese to send seriously ill men downriver by boat as soon as was practicable. But the Japanese steadfastly refused. There would be no movement of the sick downriver. A new hospital camp at Thanbaya in Burma was being constructed and when it was finished the sick could move there. In the meantime, men died – but there were always plenty more men.

By the end of June, very few of the men who had completed the march were fit for work. But that meant nothing to the engineers, who came into the camps, specified a number of workers and, to make up a quota, regularly dragged men out of the hospital hut to be carried to the workplace.

The camp doctors and orderlies worked tirelessly. Medical inspections and treatments were carried out by firelight. Ulcers were scraped out using sharpened spoons and when the ulcer became too big and a man screamed in pain, the limb was amputated without anaesthetic. Volunteers would hold a man down while the doctor cut through flesh and sawed through bone – his only tools a sharpened knife and sterilized work saw. If the patient was lucky, shock would render him unconscious and he might even survive, his wound stitched with jungle fibres and covered with banana leaves. But if he died, at least he would be free from the pain that a stinking, suppurating, flesh-eating ulcer inflicts on a man.

Beriberi patients walked ponderously around, their legs swollen and their bodies grotesque and, when they were so bloated with fluid that movement was no longer possible, they lay quietly on the sleeping platform, waiting to die.

Stanley Wood-Higgs describes attending to a beriberi patient: 'We go down to where he lies. Grossly bloated under his blankets, swollen with water that comes from a lack of vitamin B1, he has lain still and uncomplaining, quietly drowning in his own serum. Now he is gasping. His breath is laboured. I can feel no pulse in spite of digging my fingers into his inflated wrist. ... There are no drugs to pull this man back from the grave. There are none. There are no injections to alleviate his symptoms. ... What he needs is massive doses of the vitamin. The nearest is thousands of miles and a jungle away. I sit and look at this massive mountain that was once a virile man. ... Steadily his breathing becomes worse. Quietly he dies. He is taken outside.

'There was noise at the far end [of the hut]. Another still form was being carried outside. That must be one of the advanced dysentery cases.

'My relief comes. ... As I walk back to my 6 feet of hut space higher up the hill I pass the long line, it is ten this morning, of those who have found peace in the night. Stretched naked and unashamed, only their faces covered, they lie, mute testimony to the cruelty of man to man.'

In an attempt to make the service road negotiable, work parties were organized to 'corduroy' the surface by cutting down trees to lay across it. But, in spite of the men's best efforts and the whips and sticks freely applied by the guards, the corduroyed road was a spectacular failure. No matter how much material was placed on it, vehicles regularly sank up to their axles in mud, and the prisoners had to haul them out again, driven on like galley slaves of old, under the lash of their tormentors.

Work began on the 'Big Bridge' at Songkurai using the timbers that the POWs had spent weeks felling and preparing. A number of smaller bridges had already been constructed, with the inevitable loss of life, but this new bridge was to have a catastrophic effect on the health of the men who worked on it.

The river was diverted using sandbags and then 'hammer and tap' work made the holes for the explosive charges that blasted out the 'beds' into which the piles for the base of the bridge were sunk. Manpower guided the timbers into place and a primitive style of pile-driver operated by the prisoners drove the piles home. Each day, for weeks on end, emaciated men worked up to their chests in water, shivering violently as they struggled to obey the commands of the guards, flinching when hit by one of the many stones thrown down at them. Bronchitis, pleurisy and pneumonia struck them down but, with no physical evidence of illness to show the guards, sick men were driven out to work. The bridge became commonly known as 'The Bridge of Six Hundred' as it was estimated that 600 men died as a result of working on it, either from injury or through damage caused to their health.

Idris James Barwick said: 'Our men toiled, shivered and groaned as the Nip gave his shrill whistles, one to pull and two to let go. They worked like the slaves of old, no stop for rest, often no stop for food. Frequently men who were dying worked and slaved in that awful river until they died.

'When men didn't move quickly enough they were kicked and beaten, often being kicked or struck on ulcers. One man, sick and weak with dysentery, was unable to get to the privacy of the trees and messed in the road. The Nip beat him until he fell, face down and unconscious, in the mud. Then the Nip promptly placed his foot on the unfortunate man's head and pressed it further into the mud.'

Many accidents were sustained by prisoners working on the bridge. Backs and necks were broken when weakened men fell while carrying the heavy piles. Some slipped on bamboo made greasy by the rain or were beaten off the construction by an irate guard. And after work, arms that had hauled on the ropes of the pile-driver all day were often unable to lift food to the mouths of their owners.

The monsoon that year was the worst on record. The F Force camps were virtually cut off and food deliveries were infrequent. The prisoners ate anything – frogs, snakes, fungus growing on trees, lizards – whatever it was, if they got the chance, they ate it.

Said George Aspinall: 'By the time it [the carcass of a yak] reached us, it was virtually jumping out of the box with maggots. The cooks used to dump the lot into big cauldrons of boiling water, maggots and all. The maggots were skimmed off the top and, after a day of stewing, the meat was fit to eat. Not that there was much of it, just a small piece to mix in with the rice.'

During June and July, the POW medical officers impatiently awaited permission for the evacuation of the sick to the new hospital camp. However, the devastation caused by the monsoon to the service road meant that no movement was possible until the end of July. Then the Japanese informed the medical officers that only 1,700 sick, plus staff, would be moved to Thanbaya. Doctors agonized over the list of men to be transferred and eventually excluded the sickest, fearing that the journey would, in itself, amount to a death sentence. Once again faced with 'playing God', they decided that those with a chance of survival should receive the chance offered by the facilities at the new camp.

Finally, at the end of July, the advance party set off for Thanbaya, followed by two more groups in the following days. No sooner had the Thanbaya parties moved off, than the Japanese announced the closure of three of the F Force camps. In a move designed to provide a workforce of 800 fit men from each camp, all prisoners were to be congregated at Kami Songkurai and Songkurai. As a result, many of the men whom the doctors had considered too sick to move to Thanbaya had to move anyway. The move, on foot, hastened the deaths of many. Prisoners from the British camp at Changaraya were moved to the Australian camp, Kami Songkurai, which initially had held only 396 men.

The provision of 800 fit men each day was an impossible demand owing to the increasing sickness and debility of the men and the rising death rate. So depleted were the workforces that, towards the end of August, the Japanese announced that native workers would take over from the prisoners unless the numbers available for work each day doubled. Should it be necessary to use native workers, all of the prisoners, including the sick, would be ejected from the camps to fend for themselves in the jungle. With Major Wild acting as interpreter, the British and Australian commanders tried to reason with the commander of the 5th Railway Regiment. He eventually conceded that the prisoners could retain two-thirds of the camp accommodation and the remaining third would be used by native workers. As the days wore on, the rising death rate would in itself have provided sufficient space in the camp for the incoming workforce.

Until the beginning of August, when the British prisoners arrived at Kami Songkurai, the health of the Australians there had been fairly good, with the loss of only twenty-three men – fourteen of them to cholera. Having been on the earlier trains from Singapore, the Australians had completed the march through Thailand before the monsoon proper broke and were thus spared the strength-sapping trudge through the mud that the British had had to endure.

However, the influx of men from Changaraya, many of them seriously ill, had a catastrophic effect on the health of everyone at Kami Songkurai. At the same time, the engineers – under pressure to have the railway completed on time – drove the prisoners to efforts beyond their endurance. Punishments increased, hours of work increased – often only a few minutes were allowed to eat the midday rations – and sick men were forced out to work. Between August and November, when the camp was closed, 490 men died.

At Songkurai the men received the same brutal treatment with the result that, during August, an average of ten men died each day, with dysentery and related illnesses accounting for more than half of this number.

Gunner George Gordon died at Songkurai on 21 August 1943 from diarrhoea.

George was from Dornoch, in the north of Scotland.

Gunner Thomas Little died at Kami Songkurai on 12 November 1943 from beriberi.

Thomas had been one of the men at Changaraya whom doctors considered too ill to be moved to Thanbaya – and a few days later was forced to walk to Kami Songkurai.

Gunner Edward Edhouse died at Kami Songkurai on 25 November 1943 from cerebral malaria.

Edward, a married man from Clapham, London, was twenty-five years of age.

125

The journey to Thanbaya proved the ordeal that the doctors had feared. In spite of the 'fittest' of the sick having been chosen for the move, forty-three men died during the journey.

However, conditions at Thanbaya hospital camp were an improvement on the F Force camps. Food was more readily available, although rations were still insufficient to restore sick men to health. Doctors had access to some medical supplies and the operating theatre – though still primitive – gave ulcer patients a better chance of survival by the amputation of limbs in more favourable conditions. Amputees learned to walk on bamboo crutches while waiting for an artificial limb fashioned from bamboo to become available.

Despite the successes, during the six months that the camp was occupied, 748 men died. The ravages of the work camps had taken their toll.

Gunner George Lovage died at Thanbaya hospital on 20 October 1943 from tropical ulcers.

George, from Kent, was twenty-three years of age.

Of the 1,600 men who arrived at Songkurai, only 400 would survive their time on the railway; 600 died at the camp and a further 600 when evacuated to Thanbaya or Kanburi.

The construction of the Burma Thailand railroad was completed on 17 October 1943. During November, the survivors of F Force were moved, in metal, windowless railway wagons, back down to Kanburi, now designated a hospital camp for F and H Forces. More than 200 men, too ill and frail to undertake the return journey of 200 miles, were left behind at Thanbaya to recover sufficiently for a future attempt at the journey or, simply, to wait while their lives ebbed away. A group of carers stayed behind to attend to them and to keep them as comfortable as possible. One of them, Padre Noel Duckworth, who had encouraged the men during the march and sustained them in the camps, now comforted them at the end of their days.

Lance Corporal Bill Smith's last diary entry was made at Thanbaya in December. Although desperately ill, he was still convinced that he would get back home. He wrote:

8 December 1943: Don't worry Ida darling. I'm coming back to you one day.

Sadly, Bill died aged twenty-eight at Thanbaya, just nine days later, on 17 December 1943.

Of the men who made the journey down the line to Kanburi, forty-six died during the journey and a further 186 during the first three weeks there.

Gunner Ian Scott died at Kanburi F & H Forces hospital on 10 December 1943 from pneumonia.

Ian was twenty-three years of age.

Ian, from the small Lanarkshire town of Biggar, had been close friends with Gunner John Mackay Kelly, also from Biggar, who was killed in the ambush at Nee Soon.

In April 1944, the F Force survivors returned to Singapore but in considerably worse condition than when they had left. Their appearance profoundly shocked the men who had remained at Changi. Those who had been considered too sick to go 'upcountry' with F or H Force now looked to be in much better health than their 'fitter' friends of just twelve months before.

Of the 7,000 British and Australians who formed F Force, approximately 44 per cent – 3,096 men – failed to return.

Chapter 10

H Force – The Bridge at Hintock

In spite of the extra manpower provided by F Force and the introduction of native workers, the railway was not progressing as fast as
the engineers demanded. Once again there was the possibility that the
completion date would have to be put back. This was a prospect not
to be contemplated as the high rate of Japanese shipping losses made
supplying their forces in Burma difficult and unreliable. Accordingly,
the completion of the railway on schedule was essential.

The slow rate of progress could have been blamed on any one of
a number of factors but, in reality, it was a combination of them all:
the inhospitable disease-ridden jungle; the difficulties presented by the
terrain over which the railway passed; the treatment meted out to
the unwilling labour force; insufficient food; a lack of medical care; and
long, onerous working hours – in reality, it was a wonder that any of
the men survived at all.

After F Force had left Changi in April 1943 on their ill-fated journey
to the promised 'holiday camp' in Thailand, there were few fit POWs
left in Singapore. However, this did not stop the Japanese from demanding more prisoners for work parties in a 'new place'.

So the 3,270 POWs of H Force were mustered and, under the command of Lieutenant Colonel Humphries (British) and Lieutenant Colonel
Oakes (Australian) they were taken from Changi to Thailand to face the
same horrors as those thousands who had gone there before them.

But ignorance is bliss and, just as F Force had done, they believed the
Japanese promises of a rest camp in a hilly area and gathered together
everything that would help keep them occupied in this wonderful
new place. Books, musical instruments and stage equipment were all
packed up ready for the great move. The Japanese made no objections
when these items were packed onto the lorries waiting at Changi
before the men themselves climbed aboard. And after an exhilarating
ride on open-sided lorries through the streets of Singapore Island, the

POWs were in high spirits when they reached the railway station. There, they were amused to see some Indian officers wheeling a coop of cackling hens along the platform and the sight of some Australians manhandling a piano almost had them doubled up with glee. The high spirits were not shared by the Japanese guards, however, and they ran around yelling and pushing the prisoners into line and onto the station platform.

A moment later, the high spirits of the POWs evaporated.

Major Basil Peacock, 137th Field Regiment RA, explained the reason why: 'Our transport, a long train of steel trucks, was waiting at the platform ... we were met by a scruffy Japanese sergeant major and about a dozen scruffier soldiers armed with our Lee Enfield rifles. For the first time we heard the word "*Speedo!*" and the guards drove us pell-mell into the trucks.'

Seventeen men from the 155th were included in H Force. One of them, Lieutenant Peter Coope, left on 17 May as a member of the 260-strong Officers Party. This officers' party was unusual because this was the only time when officers on the railway were compelled to do the same type of manual work as the ordinary soldier. Many of the officers were older men who had served in the First World War and most of them were unfit. The story is told of one elderly officer who, suffering from dysentery, made a dash for the wagon door to relieve himself. His 'business' finished, he made his way back to his place only to find that his bowels were again in a turmoil and before he could make for the open door once more, he fouled himself and the man standing beside him. Unabashed he announced, 'Sorry, Old Boy! Thought I had finished but there was still one up the spout.'

By the time the five-day journey was over, many other men had suffered the same indignity of bowels erupting forth with their contents and most wagons were awash with the results.

Said Gunner Russell Braddon, 2/15th Field Regiment: 'Perhaps once a day men were allowed out of the trucks to stretch their legs and attend to the various demands of nature. Nature, unfortunately, did not understand this arrangement and made her demands much more frequently, which, in crowded trucks on a jolting train, required all our patience and tolerance of one another.

'Water was the main difficulty. One could overlook the absence of food, but in that intense heat, thirst became an obsession.'

Some poor souls who, back in Singapore had placed their trust entirely in the Japanese, had opted to travel without mess tins or water bottles, thinking that they would be fed at eating places and would not need their messing equipment. These trusting individuals now found

129

themselves in a serious predicament. Having to eat all of the rice provided at the food stop immediately was one thing; having to survive on what water they could manage to drink from the feed pipe for the engine while competing with 600 other thirsty men trying to fill their water bottles at the same time was much harder.

When they finally detrained for the last time, they were almost unable to stand, so stiff were their legs from the enforced immobility of the last five days and nights. However, a screaming guard holding a rifle is an effective antidote for many things and the stiff legs quickly found their strength again. After lining up and being counted several times, they marched to Ban Pong, the exercise and fresh air reinforcing the tonic initially provided by the screaming guards, and they started to feel human again.

The piano that the Australian troops had loaded onto the train at Singapore was nowhere to be seen – it had been abandoned on the station platform at Ban Pong. The hen coop full of chickens had been sold to some Thai traders who appeared as soon as the train stopped, and many of the other 'leisure items' that had been brought along had been bartered for food.

From Ban Pong the men began to march by night, as had F Force the previous month. They started the first stage of the march in good spirits but very soon began to struggle and, during the brief rest periods, fell to the ground exhausted. Feet became blistered and some men removed their boots and marched in stockinged feet. As dawn broke, they could see that they were walking along a plain and making for a range of high mountains. By now they had spoken to prisoners who had been in Thailand for months and had been told about the railway, and they had seen it for themselves as they were marching along. Even the most optimistic of them now accepted that they had been brought here to work and not to rest. They had been tricked, and they had fallen for it hook, line and sinker.

Exhausted, they arrived at their first staging camp just after dawn and collapsed on the ground, falling asleep almost before they had lain down. Later that day some rice was provided and, as darkness approached, they pushed back their shoulders and set out once more. One night, a group of POWs discovered just how unpredictable the guards could be. Stragglers who had fallen behind were kicked, bludgeoned and jabbed with bayonets to make them move on faster. They were forced along, punched and slapped every time they faltered. Then along came a local bus, which the guards quickly commandeered. The stragglers were ordered on board and, once settled on the bus, these same guards who had punched them until they were almost unconscious, offered them cigarettes!

The last night of the march saw them struggling up a steep track on a rain-sodden mountain.

Said Captain Reginald Burton, the Norfolk Regiment: 'It was a long march in the darkness. The man in front of me had a white bowl strapped on his back. It served as a marking disc. I was almost hypnotized by that disc as it bobbed up and down and swayed a little from side to side. Sometimes I could see nothing else and I followed it mechanically.'

Some of the H Force groups walked all the way to their new camps, between Tonchan and Hintock, Tonchan being approximately 139 kilometres from Ban Pong and Hintock almost 155 kilometres away. But in spite of the exhaustion of the march, the beatings of the guards, the sickness of the men and the hunger and the thirst, one thing, above all others, brought home to the marchers of H Force what was in store for them. It was the sight, just south of Kanyu, of a small group of men working on a Japanese truck.

Russell Braddon described the scene: 'It was in the watery light of that next dawn that all laughter was killed for good in Thailand. A handful of grey men working on a Japanese truck ... turned out to be members of F Force. They were emaciated, seemed indifferent to everything and their faces were stamped with a misery that was too awful to look at. Their eyes, inches deep in their sockets, looked mad. ... We walked another 5 or 6 miles in a despairing silence, heightened by drenching rain. These were the first fruits we had seen of Nippon's promises of convalescent camps – skeletons with purplish skins, teeth that looked huge in shrunken faces and haunted eyes. Within three weeks we were all to be reduced to the same travesties of men.'

More fortunate groups were transported some – or even all – of the way. Lieutenant Colonel Newey, one of the group commanders, was stopped by the guards after a march of five nights and told, 'This is your camp.' But there was no camp – only jungle. After being told to clear the area and build a camp, he was issued with tents for the men to sleep in and provided with saws, axes and *chunkels* to do the necessary work. This camp would be known as Tonchan South and was close to Tonchan Central and also to an Asian workers' camp.

The Japanese engineer in charge, Captain Kuwabara, told Lieutenant Colonel Newey that each day he intended to take 60 per cent of the men to work on the railway, leaving the remainder to attend to camp duties. Newey considered this fair; there were enough tents to provide shelter for all of the men and those left in camp would be able to ensure that

131

a hot meal would be waiting for the men working on the railway when they returned in the evening. However, this orderly existence was thrown completely into disarray when the officers' party arrived a few days later, having been transported by train the entire way. No additional tents were provided and many of the ordinary soldiers had to give up their places and sleep in the open.

Before leaving Changi, the officers' party had been told that their duties would be camp administration and supervision. When they discovered that they had been brought to Tonchan South to labour on the railway, many of them were horrified, protesting that officers did not do manual labour. Everyone knew that! But the Japanese either did not know, or did not care. The officers would work and the officers *did* work – at least some of them did – clearing the jungle, felling trees and carting logs just as the Other Ranks did. And they were 'encouraged' to greater effort in the same way – by rifle butts, punches and bamboo staves. However, some of the officers were physically unfit or too old to undertake heavy work and therefore, to meet the daily quota of workers, Lieutenant Colonel Newey had to send out some of the men he had already designated for camp duties, some of whom were themselves sick.

When H Force arrived at Tonchan they worked alongside other POWs already there. It was estimated that the track-laying teams would arrive there in about four weeks and a lot of work still needed to be done to have the trace ready for them. A rough trail already cut through the virgin jungle needed to be widened, a cutting had to be excavated and several small bridges had to be built. Failure to complete the work would mean the track-laying falling behind schedule, a disaster that would have a knock-on effect all along the line.

Huge teak trees were cleared from the track and taken to the saw-mill to provide the timber for bridge-building. After the trees had been cut down and the branches trimmed, the men carried the trunk on their shoulders to the sawmill three-quarters of a mile away. Struggling under the immense weight, they staggered along the slippery downhill path – a dangerous and exhausting job at the best of times but, in the monsoon conditions, almost impossible. The effort of trudging through the thick, slippery mud in the rain while balancing the rough wood on their shoulders caused men to fall, injuring themselves and others. The trunk, meanwhile, would go careering down the path until it eventually crashed against something that was bigger and stronger than it was.

But few things could have been bigger – or stronger – than the tempers of the guards when one of those great tree trunks went crashing down the slope, followed by scrawny men tumbling like ninepins after it.

Shrieking with rage, the guards rushed after the men, slashing with bamboo sticks, kicking out with booted feet, punching faces grey with weariness. Then the great trunk would be lifted again and the men would stagger on.

Everyone was hungry; no food was provided for the sick, so the rations for the camp were reduced, with everyone receiving less to eat, and more men became sick.

The Japanese camp commander, Sergeant Major Aitaru Hiramatsu, nicknamed 'The Tiger', had never been considerate towards the workers but, as the demands of the *Speedo* increased and the numbers of workers decreased, he became maniacal in his demands for work to be completed. Punishments were given out – men standing at attention for hours without food or drink until they collapsed, only to be kicked back to their feet again. Officers, trying to act as intermediaries on behalf of their men were, in turn, beaten up by the guards.

The gravediggers, hospital orderlies, water carriers and cooks were sent out to work. One morning, Hiramatsu attacked the sick in the hospital with the flat of his sword, ordering them out to work also.

Second Lieutenant John Durnford, who had been at the camp at Tonchan since October 1942, described the horror that he felt: 'We took out stretchers with each working party, rice sacks strung between bamboo poles, in order to carry back those who collapsed at work. The men who acted as stretcher-bearers were often themselves scarcely able to bear the weight as the poles cut into their bare shoulders.

'Worst of all were those we carried out to work on stretchers, or those who hobbled there with sticks, without boots, without any kind of clothing save rags, and the hopeless stare of damned souls in their eyes. I shall not forget the day one died at the very side of that monument to human cruelty and folly.'

Life was hard at Tonchan but, at the Hellfire Pass camps – Kanyu, Hintock and Konkuita – life was, if anything, even worse. In the Hintock area, 266 British prisoners from H Force joined the POWs already at Kanyu No. 2 on 16 June and within nine days, seventy-two of them had died from cholera. By the end of June, only 120 men were fit to work; Hellfire Pass was taking its toll on H Force, as it had done with all of the other men sent there.

Each day followed the same pattern. The men were summoned from their sleeping platforms before dawn. They dipped their mess tins into boiling water as a precaution against cholera and queued up for their rice porridge. Then they either lined up for work or for sick parade. The Japanese engineer would come into camp and state how many workers he needed. The medical officer would tell him that there was not that

133

number of fit men in the camp. The engineer would beat up the medical officer. The medical officer would stick to his guns. The engineer would beat up the medical officer again and, if some sort of compromise could not be reached, the engineer would turn some of the sick out to work. The POWs then walked around 4 miles to their work site – the cutting, the embankment or the bridges. When work was over they made their way wearily back to camp, collected their rice ration and, having eaten it, crawled onto their 18-inch space on the sleeping platform to escape the horrors of their existence in sleep.

This area was liberally criss-crossed with gullies and ravines, requiring the construction of several bridges. The bridges were built with whatever wood the jungle had to offer, just as long as the log was the right length. Many of the trees that had to be felled had rooted in the rock and most of them were entangled in the treetop canopy. For men working in bare feet on jagged rocks using only saws and axes in varying stages of rust and bluntness, the tree felling was beset with difficulties. Having cut through the base of a tree, they had to figure out how to make it fall. Sometimes this could only be done by sawing through another tree in which it was entangled, in the hope that the combined weight of the two trees would persuade them to fall together. It was difficult enough for untrained men to try to predict how one tree might fall. It was entirely a different matter when two were coming down at the same time and, just as in the cuttings when explosions were taking place, the men would scatter in all directions.

Once the trees had come to earth, they were trimmed of branches and the bottoms shaped to a point by axes, described by one POW as 'having been left out in the rain more than once.' The trunks were then stacked into piles by another gang of men. Elephants could have moved this timber very easily but why use elephants when you can work men to death?

Bridge building over ravines usually followed the same routine. Firstly, the framework of the bridge would be built from bamboo fastened with wooden wedges or ropes made from cane or rattan. Then the men would be split into teams – some at the top of the ravine, others at the bottom. The men at the top lowered tree trunks to the bottom of the ravine and men at the bottom then manhandled the timber to a place where it would provide a secure base to prop up the bamboo framework. Trying to do this underwater while standing in bare feet on jagged rocks was not easy and took time. But the engineers considered that taking care was equal to wasting time and took the opportunity to beat the men up. So, to safeguard themselves, the men abandoned their attempts to properly secure the timbers and placed them wherever the engineers pointed.

South of Hintock was the Three Tier Bridge – so called because the ravine was so deep that the bridge had to be built in three tiers. Built round a curve, it was a giant of a structure, about 25 metres high and 250 metres long.

The POWs were very wary of the senior engineer on this project and nicknamed him 'Billy the Bastard' as, for his amusement, he would throw rocks down at the prisoners. His aim was good and many a man went back to camp with injuries he had caused. Every day, Billy would point out men whom he wanted to receive a beating and the guards were only too happy to oblige. Weary, emaciated POWs would find themselves being lashed by bamboo sticks or bludgeoned with rifle butts. Raising their arms to defend themselves just encouraged the guards to hit harder and men were often beaten unconscious, tumbling into the water at the foot of the ravine, cracking open heads and breaking limbs as they fell. Friends had to watch silently, knowing that if they intervened, the same 'medicine' would be dished out to them. Later, when the guards were looking elsewhere, they would help their friend – if he could be helped – and, at the end of the working day, carry him gently back to camp.

The 400-yard-long, 80-foot-high Pack of Cards Bridge, located just north of Hintock Station, is one of the most famous bridges in the Hintock area even though there is no known photograph of it. During its construction, the strong current of monsoon water flowing along the ravine dislodged its footings, and it fell down three times, hence its name. It was a temporary bridge and was abandoned in September 1943 when the high earth and rock embankment adjacent to it was completed. By the end of the war, the bridge structure had completely collapsed and disappeared under jungle growth. Built entirely by hand by POWs and native workers, thirty-one men were killed during its construction and twenty-nine beaten to death.

After six weeks at Hintock, some of the men from the 155th were part of a group moved on to speed up the work at Konkuita, the designated joining point for the railway.

The monsoon continued to wreak havoc. The service road was thigh-deep in mud and, under the enormous pressure of the monsoon rains, a road bridge was washed away, with the resulting debris causing the collapse of a railway bridge. Generators were brought in to enable night-time working and a twenty-four-hour shift pattern was put in place. The repairs to the bridge took ten days and the prisoners sighed with relief when it was finished. However, the following day, the raging water caused the bridge to collapse once more and the nightmare of construction began again.

The new target date of October for completion of the railway was drawing closer but the relentless rain and the level of sickness in the POWs still threatened to disrupt the engineers' plans. Every day became a battle of wills between medical staff and the engineers, who refused to accept that so many men were sick. As the completion date drew nearer, desperately sick prisoners were carried to the workplace. In total, 27 per cent of the POWs of H Force died.

On 17 October 1943, the line from Burma joined with the Thailand line at Konkuita. During the week leading up to this, the track-laying parties laid the rails at a frenzied pace, at one stage working continuously for thirty-three hours. A project that the British had once estimated would take six years was completed in twelve months. The track wound along 415 kilometres, spanning rivers and snaking through mountainous terrain. Japanese engineers estimated that the railway involved constructing 4 million cubic metres of earthworks (the embankments), shifting 3 million cubic metres of rock (the cuttings), and constructing 14 kilometres of bridges.

On 25 October 1943, the Japanese chose a group of the healthiest-looking POWs, issued them with new shorts, shirts and footwear, and filmed them celebrating with the Japanese while a senior Japanese officer attempted to hammer in the last spike on the line, which had been specially manufactured from gold in commemoration of this wonderful event. However, legend has it that the spike that was hammered in was not, in fact, the golden spike, but a brass one. It is said that some Australian POWs managed to get a hold of the gold spike and replace it with a brass copy and that the gold spike was sold for a considerable sum of money, which was used to buy food.

When the 'spiking-in' ceremony was over, the new clothes were collected from the POWs and they returned to camp in their jap-happies.

In a report on general conditions in H Force camps, Lieutenant Colonel Humphries wrote:

> The Japanese, while acknowledging the necessity for hospital facilities, did nothing to assist in the provision of the same, and the conditions under which these soldiers suffered, and under which many of them unfortunately died, are indescribable in a report of this nature. They can best be described as filthy charnel houses and, but for the untiring efforts of the medical officers and orderlies, the death toll, heavy as it was, must have doubled or even trebled.

136

Japanese guards were heard to say that they hoped the sick would die and thus save Japanese rice. Medical stores were practically nil, palm leaves having to be used as bandages.

No lighting was ever provided; even surgical operations were performed in the open by moonlight or the light of a camp fire. The hours of work continued long – so much so that the majority of men never saw their camp by daylight.

Lieutenant Peter Coope, Bombardier John Evans and Gunner Edward Padgett [Williams] of the 155th, who had been with H Force, were brought back down the line to the F and H Forces hospital at Kanburi before the completion of the railway as they were seriously ill.

Bombardier John Evans died in Kanburi hospital camp on 7 October 1943 from dysentery.
John, from London, was twenty-three years of age.

———

Gunner Edward Padgett (Williams) died in Kanburi hospital camp on 23 October 1943 from tropical ulcers.
Edward, from Doncaster, was twenty-four years of age.

Lieutenant Peter Coope was eventually well enough to be taken back to Changi, where he continued to keep a record of the men of the 155th.

The survivors of H Force were brought downriver to Kanburi and then taken back to Sime Road camp in Singapore, where those prisoners who had never left Singapore were stunned and horrified at their condition.

By the time the railway was completed in October 1943, it had caused the deaths of 12,400 Allied POWs and almost 100,000 Asian workers.

Gunner David Paton, of the 155th, a member of the track-laying gang, later said: 'Everyone acknowledges the POWs who died working on the Death Railway but no one ever speaks of the poor Asian workers who died there. It's as if they never existed and it has troubled me all my life that these people have been forgotten.'

Chapter 11

'Dark and Gloomy Taiwan'

The Japanese hell ship bucked and pitched as it corkscrewed its way through the South China Sea. Below decks was a detachment of Japanese troops. Much further down, in the very bowels of the ship, 1,000 Allied POWs were distributed throughout the four holds – 239 of them from the 155th (Lanarkshire Yeomanry) Field Regiment RA. The ship, if such it could be called, was the *England Maru*, a rust bucket that the POWs had, only a few weeks previously, emptied of its cargo on the docks at Singapore. Lined up at those same docks on 25 October 1942, they were appalled to discover that they were to be its next load. The memory of being driven down into the holds at the point of a bayonet until every inch of floor space was occupied was something none of them would ever forget. Shared with the rats and cockroaches that scuttled every-where, it was to be their 'Black Hole of Calcutta' for almost three weeks. Lieutenant Colonel Fasson protested furiously to the Japanese and was knocked all over the deck for his impertinence.

Two dim light bulbs relieved the darkness, allowing glimpses of ghostly figures queuing for food, queuing for water, queuing for the bucket that served as a urinal, queuing upwards on the ladders that reached to the deck to use the flimsy toilet platforms slung over the side of the vessel. During the night, diarrhoea sufferers heading desperately for the latrine buckets were often caught short and 'deposits' were left on unwilling recipients, to be discovered on wakening, when shouts of 'What the bloody hell is this?' resounded around the hold. More often than not, a man would return from a toilet trip to find his space on the floor gone and would have to watch for someone else heading for the bucket so that he could, in turn, claim that place.

As the days dragged on and the waves crashed over the decks and poured into the holds, many of them anxiously voiced concerns that the ship would not stay afloat. But the Scots among them reassured everyone, 'Don't worry! She's Clyde-built – she can stand up to these seas.' This assertion was made as a result of the plate – clearly visible on the ship – that proclaimed, 'John Brown's Shipyard, Clydebank'. Fortunately, the Gunners were unaware that the John Brown plate was attached to a piece of another ship that had since been used to make a repair to the *England Maru*.

Twice a day they were fed with rice and watery vegetable stew. Water was in short supply and was supplemented by the rainwater that gathered in puddles on the deck. Conversation regularly turned to food and even the thought of the 'Changi Pie' that the cooks had served up at Singapore made their mouths water. The recipe was recorded in the secret notebook, which Bombardier John Mather kept throughout his captivity: stewed seaweed, boiled potato and boiled rice mixed together, coloured with curry powder and flavoured with pepper and salt – it was a veritable feast.

Occasionally they were allowed on deck for a short period, a welcome respite that served to make their time below seem even more desperate. But this precious time on deck sometimes allowed an opportunity to barter with the Japanese troops on board. This was the case when Gunner Arthur Smith was approached by a young Japanese soldier who offered to exchange a packet of Player's cigarettes for a pair of woollen socks. Agreeing to the trade, the next time he was on deck Arthur handed over the socks and received the promised cigarettes. Safely back in the hold, he gleefully related how he had got one over on the Jap as the socks had holes in the heels. However, the joke was on him when he discovered – not John Player's cigarettes – but a John Player's packet containing the rough native version of smokes. His amused mates, with nothing else to laugh about, considered it a 0-0 draw.

In the close confinement, it was not long before diarrhoea and dysentery broke out. Captain Peter Seed, the medical officer attached to the 155th, moved between the holds, treating the sick with the small amount of medicine he had managed to bring from Singapore. Supported by Lieutenant Colonel Fasson he argued vehemently with the Japanese until they reluctantly agreed to allow the dysentery sufferers to remain on deck. Shortly after this concession was granted some prisoners, including Lieutenant Ronaldson, who had displayed such courage at Slim River, began to show symptoms of diphtheria but with the Japanese refusing to dispense medicines, little could be done to help them. By the time the *England Maru* reached its final destination, Formosa – now known as Taiwan – three men had died and were buried at sea, with only a hurried service being allowed.

On 13 November 1942, the *England Maru* docked at Keelung and the men in the stinking, airless holds did not need to be told twice to disembark. Clad in their well-worn tropical uniform, they shivered in the cold and the rain that was typical of this location in the north of the island. Having spent the last year in the heat of the tropics, the cold cut deeply into them. After being sprayed all over with disinfectant, they were lined up, counted and separated into two groups. Under the gaze of the local population, one group, comprising 523 filthy, bearded, exhausted men from the 155th and the 80th Anti-Tank regiments, were marched to the railway station and hustled onto a waiting train where they collapsed gratefully onto the hard wooden seats of the carriages. After about an hour and a half it stopped at the station at Zeiho and the weary prisoners, having left the train, were allowed a short *yasume* to eat a small bun – the first food they had received that day. During their short break, they were humiliated to see the local people holding their noses as they passed.

At a shout of '*Kioski!*' (Attention!) the prisoners were lined up to 'march to new campu' and set off along a rough road that led upwards into the hills ahead. On and on they went, jostled and pushed constantly by the guards. No rest was allowed, no pity shown to the exhausted captives. Sharp stones pierced through worn boots, wet socks raised blisters, diarrhoea and dysentery sufferers doubled up with pain – but still the guards forced them on. Those who collapsed were beaten and kicked back to their feet. Men with dysentery who stopped at the side of the track to relieve themselves were knocked off their feet, forced to continue the march, fouling themselves as they struggled on. Packs with their precious possessions were thrown off and abandoned, the extra weight proving an impossible burden.

This was the pattern of a march of more than 6 miles, at the end of which, confined in the playground of a Chinese school, they stood shivering in the rain and waited. No one was allowed to sit on the ground or even lean against a wall. Anyone who did received a savage beating from the Japanese and Formosan guards who stood around eager to spot any misdemeanour. They were punched and kicked and beaten into line, the sick kicked back to their feet. A lengthy speech by the commandant of Kinkaseki camp, Yoshio Wakiyama, followed, translated for their benefit by a fat little interpreter. 'You men all disgrace to country. You surrender in battle. Nippon soldier not surrender. All time England say Nippon coolie. Now you coolie and will work like coolie. You will be punish hard like coolie.'

When he eventually finished, the men marched on to what would be home to many of them for the next two and a half years.

This was Kinkaseki – a name that would be etched into their brains for the rest of their lives.

That first night the men were introduced to the requirement of a night guard, or 'Fu Shimbun'. Camp regulations demanded that in each hut two prisoners were to be on duty during the night in case of fire or theft. A tally of men going to and returning from the latrines had to be kept as a precaution against escape attempts. If anyone should be foolish enough to attempt to escape, the Fu Shimbun would be regarded as accomplices and dealt with accordingly – summary execution.

Personal possessions were given up and clothing and boots were replaced by worn Japanese uniforms and wooden clogs known as *gaitas* – a wooden sole with a strap made from a strip of canvas. In the almost constant rain of Kinkaseki the clogs were treacherous and wet feet slipped on the wooden sole, which, in turn, slipped on the mud underfoot and caused many a twisted ankle.

By the time the formalities were over – searches, counting, questioning – it was 0200 hours before the men were allowed into the waiting huts to lie on the wooden boards of the sleeping platforms, which served as beds. In rows against the wall were piles containing two blankets, a small pillow and a shirt for each of them. Space on the sleeping platforms amounted to approximately 30 inches per man. Other than the bun provided at the railway station the previous day, they received no food or water until 1000 hours that morning. During the searches Red Cross milk was confiscated, never to be seen again.

At 0600 hours, after just a few hours' sleep, the prisoners were terrified out of their wits by screaming guards bursting into the huts, attacking them with rifle butts until everyone was on his feet. Bewildered men struggled up from the depths of exhaustion, trying to make sense of the screams and the thuds and the slaps. During their time in the camp, this was to be their 'wake-up call'. Never again would any of them sleep deeply, alert even in repose for the sound of the bugle that signalled the attack of the guards. For the remainder of their lives, the majority of the Kinkaseki men would have trouble sleeping.

Within days of arriving at the camp, men began to die from the privations endured on the *England Maru* and the savagery of the forced march to the camp. The cold, rainy weather, the shortage of nourishing food and the lack of medicines made recovery almost impossible in spite of the devotion of Captain Seed and the hard-working medical orderlies who included Lance Bombardiers Joseph Black and Joseph Wallace from the 155th. Lieutenant Hinton, also from the regiment, volunteered to help as an orderly and this was recorded after the war when he was Mentioned in Recognition of Distinguished Service while a POW.

Lieutenant Colonel James Fasson later reported: 'By far the most disgraceful thing in the camp was the hospital, run by Sergeant Tashiro [nicknamed Sanitary Sid] and two Japanese corporals – Ueno and Kurabayashi. There was accommodation for forty, Japanese standard 30 inches per man on a hard wooden bench, with only blankets being provided. On occasions, blankets were taken away for several days for washing. There was also a small room with accommodation for seven, into which the worst cases were placed and there left to die. From November to April, all drugs, including those brought by the medical officer, were locked up and issued erratically in minute quantities. The only food provided for the hospital was thin rice gruel, not even sufficient water being provided for the dysentery cases. On several occasions food was cut for everyone in hospital as a punishment for unknown offences.'

Lance Bombardier Gordon Ellerby died at Kinkaseki on 18 December 1942 from dysentery.

Gordon, from Bury, Lancashire, was twenty-six years of age.

———

Gunner Alexander Gunn died at Kinkaseki on 18 December 1942 from dysentery.

Alexander, a married man from Springburn, Glasgow, was twenty-seven years of age.

———

Gunner Hugh Warnock died at Kinkaseki on 19 December 1942 from dysentery.

Hugh, a married man from Shettleston, Glasgow, was thirty-three years of age.

Sentries and guards had to be saluted by bowing at all times. With only 523 POWs in the camp and six sentry posts, this meant a lot of bowing. Failure to spot a sentry – and they often hid to surprise unsuspecting POWs – was sufficient excuse for a beating to be administered, as was any infringement of camp rules, real or imagined.

Said Bombardier Benny Gough of the 155th: 'Kinkaseki was a hell of a place. I saw guards beating men every chance they got. We had to learn to number off in Japanese and if you put a foot wrong they were into you with a rifle butt. They kept us standing in the parade square in the rain for hours one day and a Hamilton chap commented to his pal that his feet were freezing. One of the guards saw him talking and asked him what he had said. When he told him all the guards set about the poor lad and battered his feet black and blue.'

In the camp, meals were eaten in the huts. Each POW squad leader collected the food from the cookhouse and 'dished it up' to the men in his hut, making sure that there was enough to go round. Occasionally there was a little left over and this extra, or 'leggi' rice, as it was known, was distributed in turn to the men in the hut. Camp rules stated that meals had to be eaten with the POWs squatting cross-legged at small wooden tables. Guards regularly interrupted and anyone not squatting properly was beaten. Anyone not standing at attention quickly enough was beaten. Anyone not bowing low enough was beaten. Anyone with the courage to look defiant was beaten. Meanwhile, the food – a small cupful of rice and another of watery vegetable stew – was left to go cold.

During the night, guards often rushed into the huts – one from each end – and assaulted any prisoner who did not rise quickly enough to bow to them. A favourite trick was for guards to stand one on each side of a man who, unable to bow both ways at once, could not escape a beating. Singing and games, even cards, were forbidden except on holidays given by the Japanese.

In his Official Report on the camp after the war, Major J.F. Crossley, 80th Anti-Tank Regiment, commented:

> The general policy of beating and ruthlessness was very quickly apparent. ... During the first three weeks the beatings were too numerous to give in detail; and we doubt if there was a single prisoner who escaped; the officers coming in for particular attention.

On 12 December, all prisoners were ordered to learn Japanese at the rate of six words per day. No official instruction was provided but, by now, all prisoners had realized that it was to their benefit to learn fast. Some expressions they were already familiar with were:

Tenko!	Roll call!
Atsumarei!	Line up!
Bango!	Number off!
Kioski!	Attention!
Yasume!	Stand at ease!
Bagerro!	Stupid!
Hakko! Hakko!	Hurry up!
Koora!	Hey you there!

Lieutenant Mike Brown of the 155th was a fluent Japanese speaker and acted as interpreter within the camp until February 1945, when he was part of a large contingent of POWs sent from Taiwan to Japan.

143

Unfortunately for Lieutenant Brown, just translating the dialogue meant that he was often on the receiving end of a beating.

On 22 December 1942, the prisoners had their suspicions confirmed about the type of work they were to do when an advance party went down the Kinkaseki Copper Mine. The British officers were then informed that, beginning the following week, most of the POWs would be required to work underground each day. A formal protest was submitted to the camp commandant, pointing out that many men were not fit to work in the mine. Before leaving Singapore in October, they had been told that weak men could be included in the party as they were only required for light work. The protest was ignored!

The next day Sergeant Major Brookes of the 155th, in charge of the cookhouse, decided to ignore the Japanese directive that sick men receive half rations and drew half a bag of rice too much from the stores. For his crime he was sentenced to five days' imprisonment. Known to the Japanese as the 'eiso' and to the POWs as 'the ice box', the punishment cell was a small, cramped room with a hole in the corner for a toilet. For their amusement, guards would demand that the prisoner sit squatting back on his heels and forbid him to move. In this position, legs very soon became numb but any attempt to ease his discomfort would incur a savage beating. Mealtimes brought only one small rice ball and a cup of water.

Christmas Day came, the first of their captivity, and everyone's thoughts turned to home and their families. The special day brought no respite from the cruelty of the camp and the Christmas dinner of rice and salted turnip brought no consolation to anyone.

On 29 December 1942, the parade ground at Kinkaseki took on a different aspect. In the cold, misty dawn, hundreds of POWs, destined to be underground slaves, lined up for the first time in their mine apparel of green shirt and shorts, green canvas cloven-toed boots and black compressed cardboard mining hats. To the order 'Bango!' they expertly numbered off 'Ichi; ni; san; see . . .' and so on until the last number was called. They had become quick learners under their Japanese masters, having learned the hard way that the sadistic Formosan and Japanese guards relished any opportunity to beat them up.

The green-clad men, their bento (lunch) boxes tied at their waists, followed the guard out of the camp gates and up the 200 rough steps that led to the top of the hill. From there the ocean stretched before them, with freedom somewhere beyond. Dragging their eyes from the water and their minds from dreams of happier times, they focussed on the mine head far below with its tin sheds and railway lines on which sat the bogeys (trolleys), which would become the bane of their lives.

It was not an easy path; this tortuous trail of steps cut into the hillside over which they had climbed and crawled some weeks before. But, noticing a cable railway leading to the top of the hill, they consoled themselves with the hope that they would be allowed to use it to get back to camp. Slipping and slithering they completed the descent and, after counting them, the camp guards handed them over to the mine *hanchos*.

These new supervisors with stripes painted on their black hats were no more pleasant-looking than the camp guards had been. The more stripes a *hancho* had (from one to four), the more senior he was but they were all more than happy to beat the prisoners. Following a demonstration of how to light the carbide lamps with which they had been issued, the novice miners were led to a small Shinto shrine beside the mine entrance. Hats were removed and all bowed low as the *hancho* chanted a prayer asking for safety during the day. That first morning the bemused prisoners watched and listened. Thereafter, they surreptitiously joined in with their own chant. Some, encouraged by Regimental Sergeant Major Peter Scullion, muttered 'Up the Celts!' or 'Up the Gers!' Others mouthed their favourite swear words but, as the days went on, more and more men prayed for their own safety and for those at home.

Prayers over, and having been organized into squads, the POWs entered the dark, yawning chasm of the mine entrance, keeping one eye on the *hancho* in front and the other on the precarious loose boards on which they were walking. Just one moment's carelessness could mean slipping into the stagnant water below. On into the blackness they walked, realizing now why such importance had been placed on taking care of their lamps. Eventually, the *hancho* led them into a tunnel on the left – a different kind of tunnel, un-timbered and very hot. It led downwards to the many different levels of the mine and seemed to become hotter with every step. Some of the prisoners were destined for the lowest levels, which had been closed for some time as civilian employees refused to work there.

Sergeant Jack Edwards, Royal Corps of Signals attached to the 155th, described the experience: 'Down we went, getting hotter and hotter. After another four flights, we found another tunnel with two sets of trolley lines. ... Instead of stopping, as we hoped, down we were taken again, the steps becoming rougher and the ceiling lower until we were bent double. There were cries all around as others, like me, caught backs or arms on the jagged walls and low ceiling. I will never forget that first morning. I thought we were descending into hell. The sweat was pouring from us; our knees were shaking.'

145

Having reached the level where they were to work, each squad of panic-stricken miners was directed to its work hole. Gasping for breath and streaming with sweat, the men climbed the ladder into the blackness of their own particular abyss.

Gunner John McEwan of the 155th later told of the horror: 'What a mess we were in as we climbed up that shambles of a ladder within the claustrophobic tunnel, with the acid water dripping from above and stinging our eyes and making the rungs slippery. ... We finally found ourselves at the top – in a wide, low-roofed cavern where the heat was so ferocious that it left us gasping for air that was not there. I began to wonder if I had been killed in battle and this was Hell. But this was no nightmare in a dream world. ... This was our world now. ... I had a vision of Hell as I stood in the searing heat, watching our grotesque shadows writhe on the walls of this awesome hole in the bowels of the earth.'

In some of the work holes it was so hot that the men could only work for a minute or two before collapsing unconscious. Containers of water were reluctantly provided by the mine authorities to allow the men to cool down, although this water itself often reached a very high temperature. In other holes there was an incessant flow of acid water from the roof, which stung and burned the skin and caused eye injuries. Gunner Andy Coogan of the 155th was temporarily blinded by this acid water and was only able to find his way around the mine by placing his hand on the shoulder of his mate, Gunner Hugh Carroll.

Chunkels were used to scrape copper ore into flat, two-handled bamboo baskets, which were then tipped into a chute in the floor of the cavern to fall into a bogey below. It took fifty baskets of ore to fill a bogey. It was then pushed along to the assembly point, where it was checked by a civilian worker and credited to the appropriately numbered work hole. About noon, a shout of *'Yasume!'* signalled a break and the workers were taken to the hole where they had left their meal boxes that morning. As they entered, they were aware of the scuttling of rats and noticed that many of the *bento* boxes had been nibbled by the same rodents. Then yells of dismay echoed all around when the boxes were opened to reveal cockroaches availing themselves of the contents. But the men had eaten nothing since 0630 hours and, in spite of the unwelcome dining companions, the rice was eaten.

In later years, Johnny Kane of the 155th would tell his family: 'We were that hungry we'd have eaten the cockroaches as well if we could have caught them.'

During the *bento* break, civilian workers carried out blasting in the work holes to provide more copper ore for collecting by the POWs. This

146

blasting was the cause of many injuries caused by roof falls or by falling over rocks in the dark, smoke-filled interiors of the holes. Just one of the men injured as a result of the blasting was Gunner William Barrie from Lanarkshire. Complications from a leg injury he suffered in the mine resulted in the limb being amputated after the war.

The blasting also caused major concern for Gunner William Holt's team when they went back to their work hole to find one of the *chunkels* trapped under a pile of large rocks. Losing or breaking a tool was always punished by a severe beating by the *hanchos*. Frantically the men scrabbled at the debris but it was useless. No matter how hard they heaved at the rocks they were unable to move them. One of them appealed to a team of civil workers and, within minutes, the problem was solved. A small trench was scooped out under the rocks; the *chunkel* fell into it and was retrieved by the relieved POWs.

After the *bento* break, work resumed until it was time to go back to camp. What had been a wearisome march down the hill and down into the depths of the mine at the start of the day now became a test of strength and willpower as tired men climbed out of the work holes and up the steps out of the mine. There was no easy ride back to camp on the cable railway. After being counted, the camp guards harassed them all the way up the 800 steps of the hill back to camp. More than 2,000 steps were climbed from the work holes to the top of the hill.

Gunner Arthur Smith, the regimental trumpeter, was an accomplished musician and amateur poet and used both of these skills to the benefit of the Kinkaseki POWs. He composed the 'anthem' of Kinkaseki, *Doon the Mine*, which the prisoners used to sing in defiance of the guards who stared, incredulous, at the gaunt, emaciated miners who sang as they struggled to and from work. Arthur also composed the poem *Dark and Gloomy Taiwan* in memory of the men who lay buried there, worn out and killed by Kinkaseki.

> *O frowning hill I'll see thee still though I be far away.*
> *When shadows fall I'll oft recall each dark and gloomy day.*
> *When we began the ascent steep, bereaved and sore distressed,*
> *To see a soldier set to sleep within thy stony breast.*

An Intelligence Report on POW camps and conditions in Formosa compiled in October 1945 commented:

Although mining conditions universally are severe, it is emphasized that few can equal the hazards of this tunnel. There was no lighting (POWs used carbide lamps), no props, rock falls were a daily occurrence and down the steps there ran a stream of sulphurous acid

147

water. Passage through the tunnel, made twice daily by the POWs, constituted a severe mental strain and a physical risk. In their under-fed condition, often too ill to work in the opinion of the Senior Medical Officer of the POWs, the trials of this tunnel alone brought extreme suffering to the men.

There was no ventilating system whatsoever in the mine. Heat and humidity was intense throughout. ... Conditions were so extreme that many men collapsed ... and were succoured by their colleagues. Many men experienced a delayed asphyxiation owing to lack of oxygen in the non-ventilated tunnels. In the very worst of the chutes, of the comparatively fit men, none could work for more than five or six minutes without collapse.

Lieutenant Colonel James Fasson recorded in his diary that during the winter months the men were without warm clothing of any description, many of them having to walk to the mine barefoot. He also noted that from November to March, torrential rain fell unceasingly, but no waterproofs were provided. The average temperature was 45 degrees F (approximately 7 degrees Centigrade) and usually each day there were high winds.

Gunner John Topping died at Kinkaseki on 8 January 1943 from dysentery.

John, a married man from Manchester, was twenty-three years of age.

Lieutenant Patrick H.D. Ronaldson died at Kinkaseki on 9 January 1943 from dysentery and diphtheria.

Patrick, a married man from Edinburgh, had never recovered from the horror of the **England Maru** *and the forced march to Kinkaseki.*

Japanese officers appeared at his funeral and presented flowers.

Gunner Hope-Scott Ramsay died at Kinkaseki on 21 January 1943 from dysentery and anaemia.

Scott, a married man from Forfar, Angus, was twenty-three years of age.

Work down the mine became progressively harder. For the first few weeks, the quota of bogeys to be filled was achievable – one or two per man – but then the quotas were increased to five and six and, later on, to impossible amounts. Towards the end of January 1943, the names of some of the workers were called out after they returned to camp. A

148

hancho had reported that they had not worked well in the mine that day and, as a punishment, they were made to run up and down a hill and were beaten as they ran.

Later that same day, the parade ground was the setting for a punishment that would long remain in the memories of all of the POWs. Confined to their huts, they saw through the windows fifteen men stripped to the waist ordered onto the parade ground to do strenuous exercise. For a full hour they watched, horrified, as many of these, their comrades, collapsed, only to be kicked back to their feet again by the guards. Then, led by 'Rubberneck', a Japanese sergeant, and Sanitary Sid, the beatings started, blow after blow from bamboo sticks and rifle butts raining down on the helpless men, many of whom had been ordered from the camp hospital to be victims of this savagery. The courageous Doctor Seed tried to intervene, but was pushed aside and also beaten. What crime had these men committed? They had all been in hospital when the others had been photographed for camp records – and their photographs had not been taken.

Sergeant Jim Watson of the 155th commented: 'The only good point about this bleak prison camp was the weekly bath that we were allowed to take. There was a communal wash house consisting of a small pool heated by a vertical steam boiler made by Cochrane's of Annan, a small town near my home in Scotland. The drill was to take a little water out of the pool using a small wooden tub, wash yourself, if you had a piece of soap so much the better, and then soak in the main pool until one was ordered out to have a cold shower.'

The officers were not allowed to take a bath until all of the men had bathed, and there was only one lot of water provided for all of the camp. Often, by the time the men had had their bath, the water resembled a muddy soup. Other petty rules were introduced, which affected everyone. No one was allowed to lie down on the sleeping platforms before 'lights out' and during 'sleeping time' no one was allowed to pull the blankets over their head. Regular checks by the guards would see any offender punished by having his head beaten by the butt of a rifle, then being forced to stand to attention at the foot of his sleeping space.

Tashiro conducted a reign of terror, ably assisted by Corporals Ueno and Kurabayashi. Each of them regularly beat hospital patients who they maintained were only pretending to be ill. On 28 January 1943, Tashiro arrived unexpectedly in the hospital hut and found seven dysentery patients playing cards. He sentenced them to be handcuffed in pairs for three days (two pairs, one three). For a dysentery sufferer who might need to visit the latrines twenty or more times a day, being handcuffed to another man similarly afflicted meant double the trips required for each of them. Bad enough during the day but during the night it was almost intolerable. Gunner Gordon W. Vacher of the 155th was another victim of assault while suffering from dysentery. He was knocked down and kicked by the camp commandant for sitting outside the hospital.

Towards the end of January 1943, three men reported to Major Crossley that a two-bar *hancho* in the mine had beaten them with the shaft of his hammer. The men were black and blue all over. When the Japanese officer in charge of mine work was told of the incident, he found it very amusing. This signalled the start of beatings in the mine for men who had not filled their quota of bogeys. Sergeant Jim Watson was on the receiving end of one of these beatings. Blow after blow rained down on his back, one of them being so severe that he lost consciousness and had to be carried back to camp. On later asking Captain Seed for something to ease the pain, the anguished doctor had nothing to give him except the advice to try to work a little harder the next day to avoid another beating.

These beatings heralded a reign of terror by the *hanchos* down the mine. 'Frying Pan', 'Goldie', 'Pan Face', 'Blackie', 'The Eagle', 'The Ghost' and others relished any opportunity to beat the prisoners mercilessly. Usually the prisoners were aware of the approach of a *hancho* by the light from his lamp, which shone stronger than their own. However, the two-bar *hancho* Nagi Takegoro, nicknamed 'The Ghost', was familiar with the layout of the mine and regularly extinguished his lamp so that he could sneak up on the prisoners and catch out anyone not working hard enough. Gunner Willie Williamson, a spirited Dumfries man, sometimes defiantly downed tools and announced to his workmates, 'I'm not doing their work for them!' before redoubling his efforts so that the quota of bogeys could be filled. However, The Ghost caught him out and beat him savagely on the head with his hammer. Williamson was knocked senseless and thereafter suffered from severe headaches. In later years, during tests to find out the cause of the pains in his head, it was discovered that Williamson had a fractured skull – the legacy of the beating by The Ghost.

Lieutenant Cross of the 80th Anti-Tank Regiment noted in a report on camp conditions after the war:

From this time onwards, the savage and brutal conduct of the mine *hanchos* would have to be seen to be believed and, instead of using the shafts of their hammers, they used the metal end, i.e. the hammer itself on the heads and bodies of the men.

Every evening when the men finished work, they were lined up by the *hanchos* in the tunnels of the mine and those who, in their

150

opinion, had not done enough work, were beaten with hammers until they were unconscious and had to be carried back to camp by their comrades. It can be imagined the effect of this on all the men, the mine had become a veritable 'Hellspot' and the men dreaded the coming of each dawn when they would have to go to the mine again. It was learned later that the threat of being sent to the copper mines was used constantly in the other POW camps as intimidation.

On 1 February 1943, the first death occurred in the mine when Gunner Harry Millership of the 80th Anti-Tank Regiment fell down a chute and was killed. The Japanese staged an elaborate funeral but refused to erect protective barriers and claimed that no fault could be attributed to them. During the following two years these unguarded chutes were responsible for many serious injuries to men who fell down them in the dark.

The graves in the camp cemetery were dug out in terraces on a hill about 3 miles from the camp. The naked bodies of the dead were encased in flimsy wooden coffins and carried by POWs to the makeshift cemetery, which later became known to them as 'Boot Hill'.

Lance Bombardier William Calland died at Kinkaseki on
5 February 1943 from dysentery.
William, a married man from Lancaster, was thirty-two years
of age.

The first week in February saw some of the officers beaten savagely. On one occasion, a Taiwanese guard nicknamed the 'Nasty Carpenter' went into the officers' billet and knocked many of them out. A few days later, eight Taiwanese guards beat up Captain Andrew Sewell of the 155th for an hour. The beating finished with one of them hitting Captain Sewell on the head with his rifle butt and bayonet, knocking him unconscious – savage and cowardly treatment for the man who had won the Military Cross for gallantry at the Pelandok Defile.

Gunner James Cowan died at Kinkaseki on 8 February 1943
from dysentery.
James, from Eastriggs, Dumfriesshire, was twenty-three years
of age.

A week later, eleven men who, through no fault of their own had no mining lamps, were kept standing to attention for four hours and beaten

151

if they moved. They were then forced to dig all day with no food or rest. That same week, the officer of the guard went around, beating up everyone he met. At the end of February, 'bad mine workers' were again severely beaten and made to run up and down the hill.

In an attempt to curb the brutal behaviour of the guards, Major Crossley, the personnel administrator, complained to the camp commandant that:

On the morning of 18 February, Lieutenant Colonels Napier and Fasson were knocked off a bench when the commander of the guard knocked them both to the ground with the butt of his rifle. Shortly afterwards, Gunner Roy Buchanan was sick in his billet when some Japanese guards came in and searched the kits of men who were working in the mine. On finding a pair of green mining trousers they beat Gunner Buchanan until he was unconscious. For twenty-four hours afterwards he lost all power of speech.

Later, all of the Taiwan guards appeared with sticks and beat up all the sick men in camp. A Japanese soldier entered the hospital and beat up a man who was lying seriously ill with dysentery.

Then, in the afternoon, a work party was going out of the gates when Gunner Bilham stopped to tie his shoelace. By the time he had done this, the gates were closed. Ten minutes later, the party returned and the Japanese officer sent for Gunner Bilham. He was beaten and knocked senseless by the Taiwanese guards.

He continued:

The present state of the men in this camp is one of nervous tension, for no one knows at what moment he will be knocked off his feet, or for what. I submit that if it is the intention of the Nippon Army to continue this treatment then all prisoners will become mentally unbalanced within the next few months.

Another typical example has just occurred whilst I am typing this letter. The commander of the guard walked into the office and with the butt of his rifle knocked me straight off the typewriter and almost through the window of the office. I now request that you investigate the above instances and ensure that we may be treated at least as human beings.

At the end of February, after the officers had spent a day working at the mine head, a letter of protest was written to the camp commandant stating that this type of work was aiding the Japanese war effort contrary to the Geneva Convention and that the officers were not prepared to do this. As a result, they were imprisoned for nineteen days, with an extra five and three days for Lieutenant Colonels Napier and Fasson. During this time the officers received only one rice ball per meal and had to clean out the dysentery latrines. While serving out the sentence, Captain Hope-Johnston of the 155th was admitted to hospital with dysentery.

In spite of the number of deaths that were occurring, the Japanese refused to issue medicines in adequate quantities. The officers contributed money for the purchase of drugs but these also were issued erratically and effective treatments for the many ailments in the camp were almost non-existent. In the absence of traditional medicines, Doctor Seed improvised, administering charcoal powder and rice water to dysentery patients. Although many of them realized that the powder might only be a placebo, they accepted it gratefully as there was still a possibility that it might work.

Gunner Harold Barker died at Kinkaseki on 3 March 1943
from dysentery.
Harold, from Bulwell, Nottinghamshire, was twenty-five years
of age.

Malnutrition as well as vitamin deficiency diseases began to take their toll. Myriad complaints affected the men: malnutritional oedema, better known as beriberi, pellagra, worms, bedbugs, wounds from the mine or from beatings by the camp guards, bronchitis from the perpetual cold and wet. If ever a doctor's heart came close to breaking it must have been Doctor Seed's. But still he carried on, tirelessly, courageously. Even while suffering from dysentery himself, he continued to treat the sick.

Lance Bombardier Joseph Black died at Kinkaseki on 11 March
1943 from malnutritional oedema.
Joseph, from Sanquhar, Dumfries, had been a regimental orderly
with the 155th and was one of the men who was beaten on the
parade square for not having his identification photograph taken
while in hospital.

The men were expected to work and maintain their health on three bowls of rice and two watery vegetable stews per day, the midday meal being cold. Meat was non-existent and, on the rare occasions when it did appear, it was eaten by the Japanese.

153

Gunner Ernest Andrews died at Kinkaseki on 23 March 1943 from malnutritional oedema.

Ernest, from Leatherhead, Surrey, was twenty-five years of age.

On March 25, Sergeant Jack Cresswell of the 155th recorded in his diary:

> Rock falls on me from mine roof. Injured back, head, hands. In camp hospital two weeks then discharged to make room for other men.

Also injured in the mine at this time was Lance Sergeant John Farmer. A falling rock caused a deep gash in his leg but the wound was not considered sufficiently serious to allow him time out of the mine. As the days passed, the acid water dripping onto his leg from the roof caused the wound to become poisoned. Within days the injury had become so bad that a red line visible on John's leg indicated that the poison was travelling towards his heart. The wound had to be lanced by the only tool available to Captain Seed – a sharpened pair of broken scissors.

During 1943, the Japanese began to issue extra food to men whom they considered had worked well in the mine. They manipulated a situation where everyone was always hungry, the daily ration of 400 grams of rice and a little vegetable stew per man being insufficient to maintain health when so much energy was required in the mine. The promise of extra food encouraged some men to work beyond their strength and actually helped increase the sickness levels within the camp. This was compounded by the fact that the Japanese did not increase the amount of food provided. The 'extra food' for good workers was taken from the total rations for the camp and penalized everyone else, including the sick. The practice was eventually stopped when the Japanese realized that prisoners who received extra food were sharing it with others.

Gunner George Brown died at Kinkaseki on 6 April 1943 from malnutritional oedema and dysentery.

George, from Carluke, Lanarkshire, was twenty-three years of age.

The daily medical inspections were held by Tashiro and usually began with him severely beating up Captain Seed and his orderlies. POWs who reported sick were regularly beaten to the ground with the *kendo* stick, which he carried everywhere, and for this reason, some prisoners who were really sick did not attend sick parade. Captain Seed, at the

154

risk of a harsh beating, visited seriously ill men in their huts and argued furiously with Tashiro to get them into hospital.

Lieutenant Colonel Fasson reported: 'Total collapse was generally speaking the only form of sickness that excused a man from work. Men with dysentery and other such diseases were frequently carried down to the mine head, left lying there during the day and carried back by their comrades at night, on many occasions being beaten up for their inability to walk.'

Eventually, a system was devised whereby men who were sick enough were admitted to hospital; men considered seriously ill and who should be in bed were given a red card and allowed to lie down in their billets. Men considered sick and still not fit to work in the mine were given a white card but had to work at other duties in the camp. In all cases the distribution of cards was decided by Tashiro and, said Lieutenant Cross, 'if the doctor tried to intervene on behalf of any man, he finished up on the floor.'

Even in hospital the men were not safe as Tashiro regularly visited just to beat up some of the patients.

In April 1943, the death rate started to decline but so also did the health of the prisoners. Captain Seed was of the opinion that 50 per cent of the men were not fit enough to walk to the mine, never mind work there. At the end of each day, many men had to be supported or carried back to camp by their friends. On one occasion, the camp commandant ordered that Lance Bombardier Harold Askew, who was very sick, be picked up and carried down the mine. It was only after much argument that the fortunate Askew was taken instead to hospital.

As the health of the men declined and the quota of bogeys crept up, desperate measures were taken by the POWs to try to meet their quota. As a bogey was pushed past the civilian at the checking point, the POW shouted out the work hole number and the checker marked it up for that hole. But if the checker could be distracted it was occasionally possible for a lurking POW to mark up extra bogeys for difficult holes and save their mates from a beating, but with savage repercussions for anyone who was caught. Another ruse was to pack pieces of old timber into the bottom of the bogey so that less copper ore was required to make it look full. But, as William Holt recorded in his secret diary:

The top-heavy bogey jumped the points and the strewn timber shouted, 'See this! See me!'

The *hancho* who came rushing over beat William on the head with his hammer for putting the wood into the bogey and for letting the bogey jump the rails.

From the Intelligence Report on POW camps and conditions in Formosa October 1945:

Bearing in mind the frequent despatch to work of men so ill they had to be helped to the mine, and their inevitable collapse in the lower depths, and their journey up the almost perpendicular shaft to the mine's main tunnel to the camp, the ordeal was an ultimate in brutality.

Throughout the course of the POWs' use in the mine, no medical attention was permitted in the mine. Ranging from light injuries, collapses of the sick, to the maimed or killed in the mine, all were without medical relief until the camp was reached at 1800 hours. Early departure from the mine was forbidden, no matter what the reason.

By August 1943, even the Japanese were forced to accept that many men were no longer fit to work underground and, to bolster the work force, an influx of prisoners from Taihoku 6 camp arrived that month. Included in the party was Major Ben Wheeler, a Canadian doctor. He was a godsend in the midst of so much sickness and injury in the mine.

Said Andy Coogan of the 155th: 'I used to say my prayers every time I went down the mine. The roof fell down in front of me one time and I was trapped there in the dark. I kept hammering on the compressed air pipe to let them know I was still alive. When they got me out and I got back to camp there was no food left for me. This Formosan was shouting his head off and he dragged me out and thumped me.'

All of the men were afraid of going down the mine but Dominic 'Doc' Sweeney often voiced his concerns to his friends that he would be killed there.

Gunner Dominic 'Doc' Sweeney died in the Kinkaseki mine on 18 August 1943 when the roof fell on him.
Dominic, a married man from Kinning Park, Glasgow, was thirty-four years of age.

On 20 August, twenty-three officers left for the officers' camp at Shirakawa. More than 100 prisoners also left the camp on this first 'thin man party'. These groups were made up of POWs considered unfit for work in the mine. Every man was desperate to be included on the list. On this occasion, of the 'thin men' from the 155th, twenty-three were sent to Shirakawa and forty-seven to Taihoku 6. One of those sent to

Taihoku 6 was Lance Bombardier David Hiddleston, who had been beaten on the head with a sword by Rubberneck.

Lieutenant Mike Brown, referring to the conditions in the camp said: 'To appreciate fully the peculiar difficulties of maintaining health, nothing but a month spent in Kinkaseki and several visits down the mine would really be satisfactory. Kinkaseki had one of the heaviest rainfalls in the world. Four completely dry summer months were more than made up for by the winter, when spells of ten days of incessant downpour were quite usual. This meant that when a sick man was left in camp for rest, improvement in his health was made practically impossible by the necessity of staying inside the billet [in itself damp enough], while just to visit the latrines meant returning covered in mud and soaked through. Consequently, once a man became sick, he was virtually broken with no hope of recovery unless he was lucky enough to be transferred to another camp.'

Gunner Hugh Smith died at Kinkaseki on 23 August 1943 from malnutrition, dysentery and chronic gastroenteritis.
Hugh, a married man from Coalburn, Lanarkshire, was thirty-seven years of age.

In the secret diary that he kept, Major Ben Wheeler commented on the death of Hugh Smith:

Another death, Smith – beriberi, starvation, mental depression or what-have-you. Just gave up, and who can blame him? Only thirty-seven but he was wasted away and his hair had gone white, he looked at least sixty-seven.

During August and September an influx of more than 300 prisoners arrived at Kinkaseki and, with a lesser number leaving on thin man parties, the strength of the camp was brought up to 678. On 12 August, John Mather noted in his secret diary:

100 new POWs arrived in camp. Look very fit.

That same month the mine authorities started some of the POWs working with pneumatic drills in the mine to make the holes for the blasting materials. Shortly after that, it was decided that the drill operators should also be responsible for laying and detonating charges. If the men thought that the introduction of 'modern' equipment would make things easier for them, they were soon to be disabused. In his diary, John Mather recorded on 13 September 1943 that he was made to stand

157

for an hour with his arms in the air for not working hard enough. On 30 September, he began work on a new level and his diary entry includes the comment:

It is very warm indeed.

Rather than helping the POWs, the 'modern' equipment contributed to injuries suffered in the mine.

Said Ken Pett, 80th Anti-Tank Regiment: 'I was placing the explosive one day and it detonated prematurely. It injured my hand and my chest. Doctor Seed treated the wounds and told me that I must keep them clean. He said that if my hand became poisoned it might have to be amputated. I was so desperate to get out of the mine that I used to rub dirt into the wound because if my hand was amputated I would be allowed to stay in camp. But it got better after all and I ended up back down the mine again.'

In the first week of November 1943, more men left on a thin man party and were sent to Taihoku 6. One of them was Arthur Smith, the 'Bard of Kinkaseki'. On his arrival at his new camp he was met by Frank Kelso, his friend of many years who had been moved from Kinkaseki on the first thin man party. The men who had moved out of the mining camp were replaced by prisoners from Heito in the south of the island, where the climate was very different to that at Kinkaseki. The thin men of Kinkaseki, racked with bronchitis and with their skin stained yellow from the acid water that dripped on them daily in the mine, marvelled at the healthy tans of the newcomers. They, in turn, looked with horror at the men of Kinkaseki and wondered what was in store for them.

In the middle of November 1943, a further twenty-one desperate men from the 155th were moved to Heito on a thin man party. One of them was Les Puckering, who said: 'We had been told that some of the sick were going to be moved out of Kinkaseki. We were lined up and this Jap was going along the line picking men out. He didn't pick me and I was so desperate to get away that I slipped along to the end of the line and stood there. This time I was picked out and we were sent to Heito. I don't think I would have survived if I hadn't got away from Kinkaseki.'

Gunner James Powell died at Kinkaseki on 25 November 1943 from malnutritional oedema with gastroenteritis.
James, from Willesden, Middlesex, was twenty-seven years of age.

In December, Yoshio Wakiyama, the camp commandant, was replaced by Captain Immamura, who initially seemed to herald a new age for the camp. On meeting with the officers, he agreed that beatings in the mine and in the camp should stop. But they were empty words because the guards were still beating the prisoners just as much and just as hard two years later. When the War Crimes Trials were held, *hanchos*, who were themselves accused of war crimes, said that Immamura had told them to extract maximum work from each prisoner.

At the War Crimes Trials in Hong Kong, one of the guards gave evidence against some others: 'Cho Kon Toku (Frying Pan), a squad supervisor, beat prisoners of war so often his beatings were an almost everyday occurrence. He beat them with mine hammers, the head, not the handles, and with his fists and open hands. His blows came on the head, the body, the legs, the arms of the prisoners.'

John Marshall, the 'Quiet Man' of Kinkaseki, provided perhaps the only piece of beauty for the POWs in this grim place of confinement and terror. After lights out he would quietly play his harmonica for the men in his hut and, in the silence of the night, the sound drifted over the whole camp. The beauty of the music carried the prisoners out of captivity into the freedom and memories of the past. For some it would be the last sounds they heard as death carried them away from Kinkaseki. It was always the same tune, *Brahms' Lullaby*. No one wanted anything else.

> *Slumber sweetly my dear, for angels are near,*
> *To watch over you, the silent night through,*
> *And to bear you above, to the dreamland of love,*
> *And to bear you above, to the dreamland of love.*

John played the lullaby every night until Kinkaseki took its toll on his lungs and he was no longer able to play the instrument.

Tashiro, 'Sanitary Sid' – the so-called medical sergeant who had made life terrifying for everyone in the camp, left in January 1944 to resume his civilian occupation as a foreman in the Sugar Company at Heito. His position was taken by Corporal Ueno, whose malice and cunning were almost as bad as Tashiro's brutality.

Gunner James Douglas died at Kinkaseki on 25 January 1944 from dysentery and malnutritional oedema with ascites.
James, a married man from Guardbridge, Fife, was thirty-four years of age.

There was never enough food for the prisoners at Kinkaseki and Lieutenant Brown, in a report submitted after the war ended, said:

159

Another malevolent enemy was Suzuki 'Chui', who assumed the duty of quartermaster in Spring 1944. If anything could be withheld from us in the matter of rations or canteen, Suzuki more than did himself justice, and Moriyama 'Gunso' and Mishima 'Gunso' loyally helped him. The food gifts of the mine company, who seemed to be required by regulations to furnish us with meat, flour etc., were regularly withheld by this trio and sold outside the camp. We managed to obtain the commandant's attention to this matter, after which we were required to sign receipts (often for more than we were given). Even to the end, if the commandant left camp for a day, Suzuki would have a pig killed and sold down the town.

The canteen never at any time started to function and when I left in February 1945, £15,000 was in the camp unspent, despite the fact that no money had been issued by the Japanese for four months.

A nominal sum for each working man was paid to a fund held by the officers, which the prisoners could spend in the canteen. Benny Gough of the 155th concurred with Lieutenant Brown's report and said, 'There was a canteen at Kinkaseki but there was never anything in it. There was nothing to buy. There was no way that we could get anything extra to eat.'

In March 1944, Major Ben Wheeler recorded in his secret diary:

All the men have been issued with British anti-gas capes – what a tremendous thing – only we who have lived here and seen the men out in rain day after day, always wet, always cold, can realize. They still only have rags for their feet and that is the next greatest necessity. How their feet stand up, even as well as they do, I can't imagine.

In June, the officers were told that a Red Cross representative was on the island but would not visit No. 1 Camp, although a list of articles that were needed could be submitted. Only one item on the list was ever received – 'Bug Powder'. Kinkaseki was never at any time visited by the Red Cross. Conditions in the camp and in the mine were never inspected or investigated during the time the POWs were there.

Said John Marshall: 'For a while I wasn't fit to push the bogeys and, because I had learned a fair bit of Japanese, the *hanchos* used me as a messenger in the mine. One day in June 1944, the men in hole 179 told me that it was dangerous – dust was trickling down from the roof. I told one of the *hanchos* and he said to tell them to go to hole 180. After they moved, they were arguing about who was going to push the bogey. Eventually one of them took it and when he came back he discovered the other two men had been killed – the roof had fallen on them. I tapped on the pipe to get the Jap overseer to come. When he came he was smiling and poking at the bodies. You were a hero to them if you died in the mine.'

On this occasion, the unfortunate victims were not from the 155th.

In 1944, the workload at Kinkaseki caught up with Captain Seed and he became very ill with gastric ulcers caused by overwork and anxiety. Major Wheeler was left to care for the sick on his own – just as Captain Seed had done during the first year in the camp. Repeated requests were made for another doctor to be sent to Kinkaseki but the response was that there was not another doctor on the island. It was later discovered that more than thirty doctors were working in the gardens at Shirakawa.

The health of Captain Fraser Stewart also suffered a breakdown in 1944. To his great misfortune, the Japanese had taken a particular dislike to him and made his life particularly difficult. Repeated requests that he and Captain Seed be moved to another camp before winter were foiled each time by Corporal Ueno.

On 20 March 1944, John Mather wrote in his diary:

More mail arrived in camp. No luck so far. Propaganda photos taken today. Prayed for peace? Bullshite! One pig killed. Miserable little pasty. Have had diahorea [sic] for about three weeks now.

Gunner Richard Docherty, who had earlier cheated death when he was caught up in a bomb blast just before the fall of Singapore, now had the misfortune to fall down a chute in the mine. He was brought back to camp, his back broken and paralysed from the waist down. Following Major Wheeler's instructions, Freddie Thomas of the 80th Anti-Tank, a former carpenter, made a wooden cradle with a sand 'mattress' in which Docherty was placed and a rota of prisoners was organized to massage his legs. After a while, he managed to move a toe and a type of exercise cycle was made by the carpenter with a weighted plank of wood instead of pedals. Gunner Docherty spent hours each day pushing his feet on each end of the plank and eventually, although with difficulty, he walked again. Richard was moved to Shirakawa in October 1944 and survived his time in captivity.

In November 1944, it seemed that life for the men at Kinkaseki was to become a little easier with the blasting of a tunnel down through the mountain into the main tunnel of the mine. The POWs began to think that, at last, things were looking up for them until the implications of the two heavy iron doors, which enclosed a section of the tunnel, dawned on them. It could not be a coincidence that the tunnel and the doors had appeared after the Americans started bombing Formosa. The more astute among them figured out that, if the island were to be invaded, the Japanese were going to shut them in the tunnel and bring the mountain down on them. They were never going to get home again!

But the Japanese had not reckoned on the determination and the spirit that still burned in many of the POWs. A small group, including Ken Pett, organized itself. They planned to steal explosives from the mine when they got the chance. Then, if they were ordered into the tunnel, they would use the explosives to blow the doors off and hide in the mine until they were rescued. Stealing the explosives would be risky but possible as, at the end of the day, the mine *hanchos* only checked lamps that had gone out. Stolen explosives could be hidden under the carbide in lamps still burning and later concealed, ready for use if the situation demanded.

In December, it was clear that the poor food, overwork and extreme cold were having a devastating effect on the health of the men and Major Wheeler sent a strong letter to the camp commandant pointing this out. As a result, from the beginning of January 1945, it was agreed that all men should receive a minimum of six days' holiday per month and that weak men should be used for sweeping and cleaning only. In addition, reveille was changed from 0600 to 0630 hours. But the concessions came too late for some of the men of Kinkaseki.

Sergeant William G. Anderson died at Kinkaseki on 13 January 1945 from acute encephalitis, complicating malnutritional oedema with ascites and diarrhoea.

William, a married man from Kirkfieldbank, near Lanark, was thirty-four years of age. His wife never got over the shock of her husband's death and their children were taken into care.

Major Ben Wheeler was of the opinion that the combination of working in the mine and the cold, wet climate simply did not allow for recuperation. 'A man might have a day's fever or stomach trouble and be sent down the mine. That day in a hot place [and temperatures of up to 184 degrees F. were recorded] and he would return with cheeks hollow, 5 kilograms lighter, never to work again, steadily sinking. Generally beriberi [malnutritional oedema] was the form the decline took.'

162

Gunner Samuel Pickles died at Kinkaseki on 24 January 1945 from
malnutritional oedema with ascites and terminal diarrhoea.
Samuel, from Burnley, Lancashire, was thirty-three years of age.

Lance Bombardier William B. Blair died at Kinkaseki on
6 February 1945 from malnutritional oedema with ascites and
terminal acute diarrhoea.
William, from Dunbar, East Lothian, was twenty-nine years
of age.

Gunner Henry Burns died at Kinkaseki on 8 February 1945 from
malnutritional oedema with ascites, acute gastroenteritis and
terminal pneumonia.
Henry, a married man from Edinburgh, was thirty-six years of age.

On 21 February 1945, Lieutenant Brown of the 155th was one of three officers and 257 Other Ranks who left Kinkaseki to join with a large party from other camps in Formosa who were leaving for Japan. Captain Fraser Stewart, in spite of being seriously ill, had been listed for departure by Corporal Ueno. However, his poor state of health made such a journey a virtual death sentence and, after strenuous representations to the camp commandant, he was allowed to remain at Kinkaseki.

Men were still going down the mine every day but less work was demanded of them. Then, on 9 March 1945, the weary men of Kinkaseki heard the wonderful news that the mine had closed.

Said Lance Bombardier John Douglas: 'You couldn't find the words to tell someone how bad Kinkaseki was and, even if you could find the words, they wouldn't believe you. It gave us all a lift when the mine closed.'

John was one of a party of sick men who left Kinkaseki for Shirakawa on 22 March. Both doctors went with them and Doctor Seed was one of fifteen men carried on stretchers. From 22 March till 31 May, the men who remained at Kinkaseki were without doctors or drugs.

After the closure of the mine and the departure of personnel to Japan and Shirakawa, there were around 350 men left at Kinkaseki. Of that number, eighty-nine remained from the original group of 523 that had arrived in November 1942, the others having either died or been moved to other camps. The men remaining were impatient to move on, away from the twin threats of the mine and the tunnel in the mountain.

They were kept busy during the next few weeks moving stores and equipment from Kinkaseki to a small mineral railway line about 3 miles from the camp. Then, in the middle of May, a group of around 100 men left Kinkaseki, with Sergeant Jim Bingham of the 155th in charge. Their destination was Kukutsu – the jungle camp.

Unaware that they were probably walking away from one planned place of execution to another, the men retraced the tortuous path of two and a half years earlier with light hearts. Their feet hurt in the rigid leather of the boots that had been returned to them, but that was a small price to pay for leaving Kinkaseki behind. 'Napoleon', one of the guards, told them that they were moving to 'a Red-Crossu campo, very rovery' in the mountains and they were happy to believe him.

At Zeiho they were packed onto the train, where they welcomed the rest offered by its wooden benches. But at Shinten Station, when they were confronted with the piles of stores that they had carried to the mineral railway line a few weeks previously, their optimism began to waver. The guards made it clear that they were to carry the items to the new camp. Sacks of rice, rice boilers, bags of sand and of cement, blankets, office supplies for the Japanese – the prisoners carried all of it and, in many cases, a load weighed more than the man carrying it.

Having left the village, the men sweated, staggered and were beaten up a rough track for roughly 6 miles into the mountains. Some hours later, they arrived at a clearing in the jungle where they were met by Immamura, of Kinkaseki fame, whom they had hoped never to see again. There was no food for them and no shelter; the two bamboo and *attap* huts already built were for the use of Immamura and the guards. His words of welcome included the statement, 'You orru die here!'

During the next few weeks, constantly beaten by the guards, the men cleared away jungle and collected materials to build the huts for the camp. Over the following weeks, two more groups from Kinkaseki arrived.

Every day, work parties went out to clear ground in preparation for the planting of sweet potatoes and peanuts. Previously the site of a tea plantation, the old tea plants had to be stripped out before the ground could be cultivated. Daily quotas for clearing and planting were set and failure to meet a quota meant a beating. The bamboo sticks carried by the guards were constantly in use, delivering savage blows to anyone who even straightened his back. Napoleon regularly taunted the prisoners: 'You no good soljas! Good soljas die – they no surrender.'

The guards had orders that 16,000 sweet potato plants had to be planted every day from 2 June. It was an impossibility, and they knew

164

it, but they beat and tortured the prisoners in a vain attempt to make it happen.

There were two new guards at Kukutsu; one of them, Lieutenant Tamaki, had been commandant at Heito before the camp was closed. The prisoners there had feared him. So now did the men at Kukutsu, and they named him 'The Madman'. The other new guard was a thin-faced Japanese corporal with a small moustache. John Marshall of the 155th later said: 'We called him "Tashi" because of his moustache. He was evil – he beat us all the time.'

A favourite punishment at Kukutsu was to make a man kneel with a bamboo rod behind his knees. Ordered to sit back on his heels, it did not take long before the lower legs lost all feeling. After a time, the man would be ordered to stand at attention and when his knees buckled under him and he fell, he was kicked to his feet until he stood sufficiently straight to satisfy the guards.

In the middle of June, Lance Bombardier Joe Bentley of the 80th Anti-Tank Regiment became ill and the doctors diagnosed pneumonia. In spite of repeated requests, the Japanese refused to provide drugs. Instead they gave the following remedy for pneumonia: 'Dig up ten worms, wash them, cut in half, boil and administer the soup to the patient.'

In spite of the best efforts of the doctors, which included ignoring the Japanese remedy, Lance Bombardier Bentley died on 24 June.

Groups regularly made the 6-mile trek to Shinten to collect supplies. One *yasume* in each direction was all that was allowed. On one of these 'town parties' John Marshall and John McEwan were amongst those staggering back up the mountain, carrying bags of rice on their backs. At the resting place everyone collapsed to the ground. The prowling Tashi saw some grains of rice lying beside the two friends and accused them of trying to steal the Emperor's food. The rice was probably from a previous stop but, although both men protested their innocence, Tashi beat them severely on the head with his rifle butt. Both men later said that they saw stars and John McEwan carried a scar on his forehead for the rest of his life.

With only 250gms of rice allowed per day for each man, the prisoners were reduced to eating grass, snails and insects. One day, Gunner Pat Dobbie of the 155th heard a rustling, which, on investigation, turned out to be a snake. He killed it and wrapped it around his waist under his jap-happy so that it would not be claimed by the guards. The camp cooks agreed to cook the snake for him in return for a share of it. What was left was shared with his friends.

Said Ken Pett: 'When we were planting peanuts we used to leave a trail of stones from the planting area back to the huts. Then, when it was dark we would follow the stones and root about in the ground for the nuts. We washed them in the stream that ran past the edge of the camp because the ground was fertilized with human manure. When we got back to the hut we often discovered that what we thought was twenty peanuts might be three peanuts and the rest just stones.'

Gunner Robert Daly of the 155th and an American soldier were accused by the guards of stealing sugar. Arbitrary justice saw Gunner Daly end up with a broken jaw, which the doctor fastened together with wire. The American soldier was tied up outside the guardroom for days with little water and no shelter from the sun. This was just one of the many incidents investigated by the War Crimes Commission after the war.

But in spite of the cruelty, the beatings and the starvation, the POWs were unanimous that, although Kukutsu was brutal, it wasn't as bad as Kinkaseki – at least they were in the fresh air and the mine couldn't fall on them.

Elsewhere on Taiwan, men of the 155th were struggling.

The camp at Taihoku 6, also in the north of the island, opened on 14 November 1942 and received half of the POWs from the *England Maru*. As well as farming labour, the men built a memorial park and excavated a man-made lake. The camp also acted as a feeder for Kinkaseki, transferring POWs to replace men no longer fit to work in the mine. On 20 August and 8 November 1943, desperately sick thin man parties, including men from the 155th, were sent to Taihoku 6 from Kinkaseki.

In later years, Gunner Arthur Smith of the 155th recorded in his memoirs:

> The gentler work of Taihoku allowed the hammer marks of Kinkaseki to heal as we toiled where the sky was a safer roof and the sun a brighter lamp.

But for many, the damage that had been caused at Kinkaseki was irreparable.

Lance Bombardier David M. Hiddleston died at Taihoku 6 on 20 September 1943 from cardiac failure.
David, from Dumfriesshire, was twenty-three years of age.
He had been transferred from Kinkaseki on a thin man party one month earlier.

———

Lance Bombardier Robert Thomson died at Taihoku 6 on 16 December 1943 from malnutritional oedema.

*Robert, from Port Clarence, near Middlesbrough, was twenty-nine
years of age.*

———————

*Bombardier Harold Speed died at Taihoku 6 on 11 May 1944 from
malnutritional oedema.*

Harold, from Nottingham, was twenty-five years of age.

———————

*Gunner Alonza Medlock died at Taihoku 6 on 30 July 1945 from
acute melancholia.*

*Alonza, a married man from Liversedge, Yorkshire, was
twenty-six years of age.*

On 1 August 1944, POW camp commanders were issued with a copy of
the 'Final Disposition' – the organized killing of all POWs in the event
of the invasion of Japanese territories or the possible rescue of the
POWs by Allied forces.

In preparation for the Final Disposition, 150 men were sent from
Taihoku 6 in July 1945 to build a new camp in the hills north of the city.
It was intended that all of the POWs from Taihoku 6 would be moved
there and killed in the event of the Allies invading Taiwan. Conditions
at Oka, the new camp, were bad. Food was scarce, the treatment brutal
and more men died.

*Gunner Robert Glendinning died at Oka on 1 August 1945 from
malnutritional oedema and pellagra.*

Robert was a married man from Lanark.

At Heito the prisoners were involved with the production of sugar.
Work included clearing rocks and stones from a dried-up riverbed
in preparation for planting sugar cane or labouring in a nearby sugar
processing factory – a much sought-after job! On 13 November 1943,
twenty-one men from the 155th who were no longer fit to work in the
Kinkaseki mine were sent to Heito. One of them, Lance Sergeant John
Farmer, later recounted an incident when a large amount of sugar was
spilled on the factory floor and, by the next morning, every grain had
been carried off by the huge army of ants. It was a change from the
POWs carrying off spilled sugar.

*Gunner Frank Collins died at Heito on 16 December 1943 from
malnutritional oedema and malaria.*

Frank, from Glasgow, was twenty-three years of age.
He had been transferred from Kinkaseki less than five weeks before
he died.

Gunner Roy Buchanan died at Heito on 1 January 1944 from
malnutritional oedema.

Roy, from Biggar, Lanarkshire, was twenty-three years of age.

It was Roy who had lost the power of speech after guards beat
him unconscious because they found a pair of mine trousers in
his billet while he was lying there sick.

Gunner Michael Lowther died at Heito on 8 December 1944 from
malaria and neurasthenia.

Michael, from Beattock, Dumfriesshire, was twenty-eight years
of age.

On 7 February 1945, an American bombing raid damaged a large part of the camp, killing more than twenty prisoners and injuring more than eighty. The injured received no medical assistance, as a result of which more men died. The camp was closed after the bombing and the prisoners distributed between Shirakawa, Toroku and Taihoku 6.

Gunner Donald McCallum died at Heito on 7 February 1945 from
bomb splinters to the temple.

Donald, from Glasgow, was twenty-nine years of age.

Gunner Archibald McLean died at Heito on 11 February 1945 from
malnutrition and malaria.

Archibald, a married man from Airdrie, Lanarkshire, was forty
years of age.

The camp at Taichu was situated on the west of the island where POWs laboured in excavating a flood diversion channel to prevent main rail and road bridges from being washed away by flooding caused by the seasonal typhoons and monsoon rains. Several men from the 155th who had previously slaved in Kinkaseki were moved to Taichu from Taihoku 6. For many of them, their situation was hopeless and, inevitably, the effects of Kinkaseki caught up with them.

Gunner Albert Spurrier died at Taichu on 14 June 1944 from dysentery and pellagra.

Albert, from Aston, Birmingham, was twenty-seven years of age.

In late spring 1944, a tropical storm raged across Taiwan for several days. The torrential rain flooded the river and, in spite of the diversion channel, Taichu's rail and road bridges were washed away.

Gunner Sydney D. Stone died at Taichu on 17 June 1944 from pellagra.

Sydney, from Avon, near Bristol, was twenty-four years of age.

Part of the camp was flooded and it closed in June 1944. The men who were still fit to work were distributed to other camps on the island. Sick prisoners were sent to the newly established camp, Inrin, which was situated about 20 miles from Taichu.

Lance Bombardier George Perman died at Inrin on 25 September 1944 from tuberculosis and malnutritional oedema.

George, from London, was twenty-four years of age.

In spring 1945, many of the prisoners at Inrin were moved to the camp at Toroku.

Gunner Edwin B. Rose died at Toroku on 16 March 1945 from malnutritional oedema and malaria.

Edwin, from London, was thirty-five years of age.

He was the only man from the 155th who died on Formosa but had not previously slaved at Kinkaseki.

Located to the south-east of Formosa, the camp at Shirakawa was initially used mainly for officers but gradually developed into a hospital camp. Men from the 155th were transferred to Shirakawa from Kinkaseki on 20 August 1943, 25 October 1944, and 22 March 1945. Sergeant Jack Cresswell, who was transferred with the first group, recorded in a hidden diary for 16 October 1943:

Have suffered from beriberi and a poisoned leg at this camp, but still better by 200% since coming here. Able to purchase coffee, tea, strawberry syrup, pepper and curry at canteen.

But, although conditions were better at Shirakawa, some men who had slaved at Kinkaseki were beyond recovery.

169

*Lance Sergeant Samuel Henderson died at Shirakawa on
27 December 1944 from tuberculosis.*

*Samuel, from Motherwell, Lanarkshire, was twenty-four years
of age.*

―――――――――

*Gunner Stuart H. Tuck died at Shirakawa on 26 January 1945
from malnutritional oedema.*

Stuart, from Middlesbrough, was thirty years of age.

―――――――――

*Gunner Andrew Vere died at Shirakawa on 14 April 1945 from
malutritional oedema and enteritis.*

*Andrew, from Canonbie, Dumfriesshire, was thirty-three years
of age.*

―――――――――

*Lance Bombardier Frederick S. Lindley died at Shirakawa on
16 May 1945 from malnutritional oedema and enteritis.*

Frederick was twenty-four years of age.

―――――――――

*Captain J.H. Fraser Stewart died at Shirakawa on 9 June 1945
from malnutrition and dysentery.*

*Fraser, from Ravenstruther, near Lanark, was thirty-one years
of age.*

Chapter 12

Spread Across the Far East

On 31 March 1943, six men from the 155th, Bombardier Tom Tadman, Gunner Charles Shun, Staff Sergeant John Parker, Gunner Frederick Wain, Gunner Rodger Campbell and Gunner David Laing, left Changi as part of E Force, a group of 500 British and 500 Australians sent to Borneo to work at building and extending airfields. The airfields were necessary to allow Japanese aircraft flying from Singapore to the Philippines to refuel.

Borneo was of prime importance to the Japanese for its oil fields – Tarakan, Sangasanga and Balikpapan on the east coast and Seria (now Brunei) and Miri on the west coast. The oil was vital for the supplying of the Philippines and the whole of the Japanese-occupied Asia/Pacific territories.

The men of E Force were transported on the *De Klerk*, a captured Dutch freighter that had seen better days. After five days they were unloaded at Kuching and worked there on the docks for about a week. The Australians were then moved to Jesselton for a short time before moving on to Sandakan, where a large camp of British and Australians was already established.

The British POWs remained at the camp at Kuching, also known as Batu Lintang. This was also the location of an internment camp, although the internees and POWs were kept strictly apart. The officers' camp was fairly comfortable, set in a roomy compound with a plot of land for growing vegetables. The Other Ranks were kept in grossly overcrowded barracks with inadequate cooking, lighting, water and sanitary services. The arrival of E Force swelled the camp numbers to around 2,000.

As well as working on the docks, the prisoners were tasked with extending an existing airstrip where large planes had difficulty landing owing to the proximity of a nearby hill. To enable the airstrip to function effectively, the prisoners had to remove the hill. Using *chunkels* and baskets the earth was excavated and carried away. To make the work even harder for the steadily weakening POWs, one of the guards amused himself by stamping on the earth in the baskets so that more soil needed to be added to fill them to his satisfaction. This piece of malevolence earned him the nickname the 'Kuching Stamper'.

Another hated guard was named the 'Big Pig' because he used to line the prisoners up in such a way that, on striking the first man a vicious blow to the head, the rest of the line would fall like dominoes.

Keat Gin Ooi, one of the internees at Batu Lintang, was witness to the brutality and later said: 'The trying conditions of life under internment at Batu Lintang camp tested to the limits the human struggle for survival. Food shortages, disease and sickness, death, forced labour and harsh treatment were daily occurrences in camp. We, the civilian internees, were treated less harshly than the POWs. Of those POWs, the Other Ranks were subjected to far worse treatment than the officers.'

The mortality rate among the British POWs was extremely high, with men dying from malaria, beriberi, dysentery, dengue fever, diphtheria and tropical ulcers. Scabies, skin infections, septic bites and sores were commonplace. No medicines were provided for the sick and a man's weight could drop from 10 stones to 4 or 5 stones as a result of starvation, dysentery or a combination of both. The many dead were buried in makeshift shrouds fashioned from rice sacks and carried to the cemetery in a wooden coffin with a hinged bottom so as to allow re-use.

In August 1944, Tom Tadman, Charles Shun, John Parker and Frederick Wain were among a group of 300 sent to Labuan to construct an airfield intended for the defence of a fleet anchorage planned for Brunei Bay. At first, life was not too bad for the POWs but when the Allies began bombing airfields in the region in October, rations were reduced for the prisoners and deaths began to mount significantly.

Gunner Charles Shun died at Labuan on 5 November 1944 from malaria and beriberi.

Charles, from London, was twenty-five years of age.

Staff Sergeant John Parker died at Labuan on 29 December 1944 from beriberi.

John, a married man from Urmston, Lancashire, was thirty-three years of age.

Gunner Frederick Wain died at Labuan on 20 February 1945.

Frederick, from Rugeley, Staffordshire, was twenty-five years of age.

By March 1945, 188 of the prisoners taken to Labuan had died. Due to the proximity of Allied shipping, the remainder began the move back to Kuching. They completed the first stage – to Brunei – on 8 March and remained there until the beginning of May. By this time, only eighty-two men remained of the initial 300.

Lance Bombardier Thomas Tadman died at Brunei on 3 April 1945.
Thomas, from London, was twenty-five years of age.

The remaining eighty-two men were taken to Kuala Belait and on to Miri on 28 May. Then, on 8 June, the POWs, now numbering just forty-six, were ordered to make their way into the jungle along a rough track where they rested for two days. There the Japanese officer in charge, Sergeant Major Sugino, received news that the Australian 9th Division had landed at Brunei Bay, only 125 miles away. As a precaution against the prisoners being rescued, Sugino decided to put into operation the Final Disposition – the murder of all POWs.

The prisoners were shot out of hand and their bodies buried hurriedly by the guards in a nearby swamp.

Of the 300 POWs who had left for Labuan the previous year, not one was left alive.

Conditions in the camp at Kuching were deteriorating rapidly and the POWs dying in increasing numbers.

Gunner Rodger Campbell died at Kuching on 15 February 1945.
Rodger, from Annan, Dumfriesshire, was twenty-four years of age.

Gunner David Laing died at Kuching on 3 August 1945.
David was twenty-eight years of age.

At the end of the war, the bodies of Rodger Campbell and David Laing were recovered at Kuching and removed to the War Graves Cemetery at Labuan.

The bodies of the four men who died as part of the Labuan group were never recovered. They are commemorated on the memorial at Kranji Cemetery in Singapore.

On 16 May 1943, four men from the 155th, Gunners William Barnes, Francis Divers, Stephen McElligott and Peter Rhodes, together with Signalman Herbert Horrocks, were the first to be sent from the regiment to Japan, as part of J Force. They were transported on the *Wales Maru*, and, although some of its unwilling passengers renamed it the '*Mukki Maru*', Peter Rhodes felt compelled to comment: 'Although the *Wales Maru* was certainly a "hell ship", it did not smell anything like as badly as did the SS *Ekma*, which had carried the 155th from Bombay to Port Swettenham.'

The journey of twenty-two days ended at Moji in Japan. Some of the men from the 155th were sent to work in the heavy industries at Fukuoka. The others were sent to Hakodate on Hokkaido Island. During the summer at Hakodate the POWs worked in the fishing industry and in the winter they slaved in a coal mine. Conditions in the camp were harsh. Food was in short supply and in the cold winters the huts were not well heated.

During the winter of 1944–45, when the snow was deep on the ground, Herbert Horrocks was caught taking a shortcut between two huts by one of the guards. As a punishment he was forced to stand in the snow all night with his arms above his head. Next morning he was suffering from hypothermia but was revived by his friends wrapping him up in blankets.

Elsewhere in Japan, another of the 155th was receiving special attention. In November 1943, Lance Bombardier Donald Bruce was taken from Kinkaseki to the Bunka camp in Tokyo, where he was one of twenty-seven POWs forced on pain of death to write scripts for the Japanese radio propaganda programme, *The Zero Hour*. The scripts written by the POWs were read by a young American/Japanese typist, who was herself forced to take part in the programmes. She referred to herself as 'Orphan Anne' but was infamously known by American servicemen who heard the broadcasts as 'Tokyo Rose'.

Orphan Anne befriended Donald Bruce and the others and, at great risk to herself, helped keep them alive by taking food, medicines and clothing to them in the cells where they were held.

In 1945, the men were moved to the Omori camp on a man-made island in Tokyo Bay that had been constructed to isolate the POWs. Donald Bruce was evacuated from the Omori camp on 23 August 1945. After the war, he worked as a journalist for the *Glasgow Daily Record*.

In June 1944, following the completion of the Death Railway, a large number of POWs were moved back from Thailand to River Valley Road camp in Singapore. From there, they were taken to Japan to provide slave labour for the camp at Funatsu/Nagoya, where they worked at mining or refining lead and zinc. Included in the group were thirty-seven of the 155th, including George Mair, the bombardier who at Slim River had joined with Captain Gordon Brown in fighting off the Japanese with rifles.

Conditions in the camp were severe. Harsh punishments were given out for very little reason and sick men were often forced out to work. Beatings were administered with leather belts, sticks and steel rods.

There were around 300 men in the camp and most were in poor health suffering from malnutrition, dysentery, beriberi and other complaints. No medical help was given to the medical officers by the Japanese.

During the winter it was very cold and heavy snowfalls were common. A small fire in each hut was permitted only for two hours in the evening. Many prisoners suffered the loss of toes due to frostbite.

Some of the guards were later to be the subject of investigation at the War Crimes Trials. The charges brought included an incident where an American prisoner had attempted to escape and was beaten on the head with a stool after he was recaptured. He was then tied up outside and beaten with sticks till he was unconscious. Over the next fifteen days he was systematically beaten to death with steel rods, the other POWs being aware of his agonized screaming during much of this time.

Another atrocity occurred early in 1945, when an American POW was discovered to have stolen some cigarettes from the store room. The entire camp was paraded and the American POWs present ordered to lash the back of the culprit with a leather belt. After the Americans had done as they were ordered, the British POWs were ordered to do the same. The Allied officer in charge, Lieutenant Orrock, formerly of the Death Railway, refused the instruction and also refused to allow the British POWs to comply with the order. Lieutenant Orrock received a severe beating for his bravery.

Around the same time, six British prisoners were caught with pieces of coke in their pockets, which they had taken to add to the small fire in their hut. After being beaten, they had to stand to attention outside in 6 feet of snow for almost two hours.

After the war, Norman Churchill, a war crimes investigator reported: 'The prisoners' quarters were filthy and infested with lice, fleas and rats. There were no beds and the men had to sleep on mats on the floor. The camp was in the mountains and the weather was often very cold, with the temperature usually well below zero. On the night that I slept at this camp, I had eight blankets and was still cold and uncomfortable. The POWs had two or three blankets. The men were in very poor physical condition, many of them suffering from frostbite.'

Another group of POWs, known as 'Japan Party 3', was sent to Japan on 4 September 1944. Made up of prisoners who had been returned to River Valley Road camp in Singapore from Tamuang in Thailand, the group, 1,548-strong, included four men from the 155th: Bombardier George Flint, and Gunners Bernard Goodchild, John Kay and Thomas Menzies. At the docks in Singapore they were among those herded onto the *Kachidoki Maru* – the former *President Harrison*, a captured American ship, which sailed on 6 September.

On the night of 12 September 1944, the *Kachidoki Maru* was attacked by the submarine US *Pampanito*, which had been shadowing the convoy. With only one narrow staircase and two vertical ladders allowing exit from the holds, many of the prisoners drowned, unable to escape from the sinking ship. Survivors of the sinking who had managed to struggle onto life rafts were, in many cases, beaten off them by Japanese soldiers.

Bombardier George Flint died in the carnage that night,
12 September 1944.
George, from London, was twenty-five years of age.

The other three men from the 155th survived the sinking and after some time were picked up by a Japanese ship. They eventually arrived at Japan and were taken to the Shinkai POW camp, where they were destined to slave in a carbide manufacturing factory. At first the rations in the camp were adequate but deteriorated as time went on. Punishments by the guards were severe, with men being sentenced to time in the cells for minor or perceived infringements. On one occasion, the entire camp was made to kneel for a lengthy period of time on the parade square because a tap had been broken.

The Allied officer in charge, Captain Wylkie, requested that the Japanese allow him to deal with infringements of camp rules and this was eventually agreed. Camp rules were tightened up and offenders sentenced to punishments such as withholding rations or cigarettes for a period imposed by Captain Wylkie. Being punished by their own officer might have saved everyone from harsher punishments by the camp guards but it led to ill feeling and resentment among the men. The camaraderie, respect and support for each other that was evident while the men worked on the railway in Thailand were sadly missing in this camp.

The sinking of POW transport vessels by Allied shipping is often blamed on the fact that the Japanese did not mark POW ships as such. In fact, the Americans were often aware that the ships that they were attacking contained POWs, as the Allies had broken the Japanese shipping codes. According to Greg Michno in *Death on the Hellships*, they opted to attack POW transports because to leave them untouched while sinking other Japanese shipping would have indicated to the Japanese that their codes had been compromised.

Most of the POWs were eventually moved from Changi to slave in other locations until the only men left in the camp were the badly injured and the very sick. Conditions were not as savage at Changi as in most other Japanese POW camps, but food and medicines were still in short supply.

Gunner Robert Logan died at Roberts Hospital, Changi, on
5 October 1944 from hemiplegia.
Robert, from Alloa, Clackmannanshire, was twenty-eight years
of age.

On 21 February 1945, 700 POWs from camps on Formosa were herded into the holds of the *Melbourne Maru* for transportation to Japan. Included in the party were Lieutenant Mike Brown from Kinkaseki and the other officers of the 155th who had been moved to Shirakawa in August 1943. Arthur Smith later said: 'We were hurried and helped down into the hold by blows from bamboo poles and, when we were battened down, 700 of us were stowed into a space that would have made half that number uncomfortable.'

After a few hours sailing, the ship ran aground and limped back to Keelung.

The POWs were eventually transferred to the *Taiko Maru*, formerly the captured *Winchester Maru*, and finally docked at Moji, in Japan, on 10 March. On arrival, the prisoners were, for the most part, divided into groups according to their last camp on Formosa and were distributed between four camps in Japan.

The Kinkaseki men were sent to Fukuoka 5B (Kawasaki), which supplied labour for the Omine Coal Mine at Kyushu. The treatment and conditions in this camp were harsh. The document 'Provisions for the handling of POWs at the Omine Coal Mine' clearly stated that supervisors could use weapons such as bamboo lances and clubs to 'control' prisoners.

Bill Nottley of the 155th noted that the POWs were forced to work a twelve-hour day on very little food. On one occasion, in an attempt to force the guards to give them a rest, he deliberately broke a piece of machinery. It did little good for, although the guards did not suspect sabotage, the prisoners had to repair the damage and were not allowed out of the mine until they had filled their quota for the day. On another occasion, convinced that the roof would fall in and kill him, Bill deliberately dropped a large piece of coal on his foot in an attempt to crush it and save him from further work in the mine. Despite being seriously injured, he was allowed only a few days off work.

Another of the 155th labouring at Omine was Jim Fergusson who, in the uncensored letter sent to his wife following the battle at Slim River, had spoken of his 'many and varied experiences' during the Malayan Campaign. Little had he known then that these experiences would include the hell of Kinkaseki and then the alternative dark depths of the Omine Mine.

The POWs from Taihoku 5 and 6 were sent to Hakodate 2 on Hokkaido Island, a trip that entailed a three-day train journey followed by a ferry boat sailing. At their new camp they worked at a large dockside railway terminus shovelling coal or fish from railway trucks into horse-drawn carts. Occasionally it was possible to steal a piece of fish to add to their rations but it was in such small quantities that the poor diet and lack of medical attention soon became the cause of deaths among the workforce.

Gunner Ernest Barnes died at Hakodate 2 on 16 April 1945 from beriberi and pneumonia.
Ernest, from Rossendale, Lancashire, was twenty-six years of age.

Shortly after the POWs at Hakodate 2 received the news that Germany had surrendered, they were moved to a new camp, Sorachi, for a short time before being moved again to work in a coal mine owned by the Sumimoto Mining Company.

Prisoners who had been held at Shirakawa or Taichu were sent to Fukuoka 9, where they also laboured as coal miners. As the Allies stepped up pressure on the Japanese mainland, the prisoners were aware of the heavy air raids in the district and Jack Cresswell described how, at this time, some of the prisoners were forced to dig a deep ditch in the camp. Ostensibly, this was an air raid precaution but may, perhaps, have been part of the preparations for the Final Disposition.

The officers who had accompanied the group on the *Taiko Maru* were sent to Fukuoka 12 (Miyata). Then, in April 1945, some of them were removed to Hotten camp, Mukden, in Manchuria. But one was missing. It was the popular D Troop commander, 'Wee Andy' Anderson, about whom 'his men' used to fondly sing, *'Wee Andy, gie's yer candy'*, and who had proved so effective during the fighting at Batu Pahat.

Captain Michael L. Anderson died at Number 12 camp, Miyata, on 23 April 1945.
Michael, from New Malden, Surrey, was twenty-five years of age.

The group from Heito was sent to Fukuoka 24B, where they worked in the Senryu Coal Mine owned by the Sumimoto Coal Mining Company.

After several days' training by experienced miners they began work underground. Sadly, the time spent in the holds of the *Melbourne Maru* and the *Taiko Maru* had had a devastating effect on the health of some of them and a week after arriving at the camp, the 155th lost another of its men.

Lance Bombardier John Farmer died at Fukuoka 24B on 17 March 1945 from acute enteritis.

John, from Essex, was twenty-six years of age.

The overseers in the mine were more considerate about the welfare of the prisoners than in other POW camps, and beatings were rare. But the long hours underground in confined spaces and the poor diet took their toll on the men.

Bombardier Thomas Donnelly died at Fukuoka 24B on 10 April 1945 from acute enteritis.

Thomas, a married man from Hamilton, Lanarkshire, was forty-three years of age.

It was Thomas who had had his feet battered black and blue at Kinkaseki when a guard heard him whisper to a friend that they were cold.

Lance Bombardier Harold Askew died at Fukuoka 24B on 11 May 1945 from acute enteritis.

Harold, from Crook, County Durham, was twenty-nine years of age.

On 2 February 1945, more than 2,000 POWs were packed into the holds of the *Haruyasa Maru* at the Singapore docks. They had been moved back from Thailand to River Valley Road camp in Singapore the previous September and the contingent from the 155th comprised forty of the track-laying gang and four from the drivers' party. Three of them were Tom Hannah, Pat McCready and Geordie Shannon, the three buddies who had supported each other throughout the dangers and hardships on the railway. Left behind at River Valley Road were Bombardier Len Woodcock, Lance Bombardier Sammy Cuthbertson and Gunners George Ashness, Tom Douglas, William Moffat and Edgar Rook, who were considered unfit for the journey. Sadly, Sammy Cuthbertson's health continued to deteriorate and he died in May 1945.

Lance Bombardier Samuel Cuthbertson died at Roberts Hospital,
Changi, on 7 May 1945 from dysentery and malaria.
Samuel, a married man from Motherwell, was thirty-nine years of
age. He left behind a wife and five children and was the uncle
of Gunner Jim Johnston, who had died in India in 1941.

The POWs on the *Haruyasa Maru* were very aware of the presence of Allied shipping. Each night they held their breath as they listened to the explosions coming from other ships in the convoy and wondered when it would be their turn, while keeping their fingers crossed that they would survive unscathed.

Five days after leaving Singapore, the ship docked and the men, hardly able to walk after their confinement in the packed holds, staggered onto dry land. Having expected to arrive in Japan, they were somewhat surprised to find themselves in Saigon, in French Indochina, where the Vichy French went about their business in freedom. Signs of bomb damage were evident in the number of half-sunken ships lying in the harbour and the many damaged buildings nearby.

The rations were better in Saigon than they had been in Thailand but the behaviour of the guards was no different – there was still brutality and cruelty. But, just as they had experienced on the railway, the guards could be very unpredictable. At times they would blow up for no apparent reason and at other times would laugh when a beating might be expected. This kept the prisoners on edge all the time, never able to trust, never able to relax.

For a time, the POWs worked on the docks. One morning one of the guards, a former taxi driver in the United States, lined them up to give them a lecture about stealing. He was a bit of a show-off and, during his talk placed his 'visual aid' – a tin of pineapples – on the ground and indicated to the prisoners that the fruit could not be touched. Turning his back for a second or two, he turned back round again and, to his consternation, the tin of pineapples had gone. He immediately started to shout, demanding to know who had stolen his fruit but, needless to say, no one owned up. The prisoners remained standing until reinforcement guards arrived and, although they were repeatedly searched, no fruit was forthcoming. Eventually, they were ordered to remove all of their clothing and yet another search was carried out. Still no fruit! Enraged, the guard ordered the men to get dressed and as he began to walk away in a fury, an Australian voice shouted, 'Here's your bloody fruit back,' and the tin landed at the feet of the dumbstruck former taxi driver.

The culprit was never discovered but the incident provided many a good laugh afterwards. The fruit had been under an Australian bush hat all the time. Although the men had been searched many times, none of the guards had thought to check under the hats, which had been placed on the ground.

Said Tom Hannah: 'It just goes to show how good the Aussies were at lifting stuff.'

During the next few months, the POWs worked at a few locations near Saigon, building airfields before returning to Saigon to see the war out, working once again at the docks.

Back in Thailand, the POWs were still labouring. Near the end of February 1945, Andrew McKay from the 155th was amongst a group taken from the base camps in Thailand to Ubon in the north-east of the country near the Chinese border to build an airstrip. There was no camp when they arrived, so the first objective was to build huts for themselves and the guards.

Once work on the airstrip began, some of the POWs cleared the ground while others worked in a quarry digging out stones for the runway. The project was almost completed when the guards ordered the POWs to dig trenches roughly 2 yards deep and 5 yards wide across the surface that they had worked so hard to make smooth and level. For the POWs, the destruction of the airstrip suggested that the Allies – and the end of the war – might not be too far away.

In May 1945, a group of men from the 155th were in a group of around 300 men without officers sent to Pratchai, 125 kilometres north of Bangkok on the River Daun Naung. The camp was close to the original Thai State Railway. After building the camp huts, some of the POWs were set to work tunnelling into the hillside to make petrol and ammunition dumps for the Japanese. At the same time, others were cutting down trees and sawing them into logs to provide wood for the engines using the railway line.

The camp was extremely isolated but the prisoners received a welcome boost one morning when they found leaflets, which had been dropped by Allied planes, announcing that the war in Europe was nearly over. But the mood of the camp guards was becoming ever darker and the treatment more brutal so the men had to hide their elation at finding the leaflets. And the sight of the bund (deep ditch) that had been dug around the camp, with a machine-gun pit at each corner, reminded them of just how precarious their situation was. The men kept their fingers crossed for their survival – even in the event of an Allied victory.

In July 1945, a group of POWs, including Lieutenant David Ffolkes and others from the 155th, was moved from Thailand to a camp at

Nakon Nyok, 180 kilometres north-east of Bangkok. The camp was in the middle of a Japanese defensive position from which 30,000 troops were actively preparing to resist any further Allied advance. The tension in the POW camp was intense and the Japanese became steadily more moody. So afraid were the prisoners of an organized massacre that the officers prepared and concealed sharpened bamboo staves with which the prisoners could attempt to defend themselves.

Over on the west of Thailand, Gunners Tom McKie and Edgar Webster drew a desperate short straw when they were sent to the Mergui Road.

In early 1945, with the Death Railway being regularly bombed by the Allies, the Japanese urgently needed a new route to supply its army in Burma. The sea lanes of the Andaman Sea were also denied them by the increasing presence of Allied warships. Using native labour, a road between Pratchup Kirrikan and Mergui was under construction but, by the early months of 1945, many of the natives had died and the others had drifted away. A new labour force was required and it was found in Nakon Pathon camp.

One thousand of the men who had previously laboured on the railway were conscripted. Some were tempted by the promise of a new camp where 'good food would be provided for light work', while others, from previous experience, were more sceptical. The group left Nakon Pathon in April 1945 by train for Pratchup Kirrikan, and from there they walked to where they were to work on the Mergui Road. And, once again, they found the reality of empty promises.

There was very little food and often no shelter other than the undergrowth for this unfortunate workforce. The monsoon rain fell steadily as they cleared away the jungle, cut down trees and hacked out roots from the earth. All the while they suffered the vicious bites from red ants, endured the tenaciously-fastened leeches and fended off centipedes that fastened their jaws on any part of a man that they could reach. And no matter how hard they tried to work, it was never good enough for the guards and they were beaten mercilessly.

Under the gloomy, dripping canopy of the jungle, men suffered and died. They died from malaria, beriberi, dysentery, typhus fever, starvation and hopelessness. Too weary to listen to the urging of their friends to 'hang on a bit longer', they gave up and accepted the peace that death gave. Those who were determined to live ate snakes, frogs, leaves, grass – anything that appeared edible – but they died also. They had often been hungry on the railway but this was worse – they had nothing. And then the road was finished and the skeletons who had survived waited to go back to Thailand.

Said Tom McKie: 'We were relieved when the road was finished and thought that we would be going back to Thailand. But the guards told us we weren't going back. The monsoon had turned the road into a right mess and we had to cut down trees and lay them on top of it to make a surface so that the lorries could carry the troops and supplies to Burma. Laying the tree trunks on the road didn't work. The lorries sank up to their axles in mud and we had to pull them out! One day a lorry full of wounded Jap soldiers came down from Burma and got stuck. The men had to get out so that we could pull the truck clear. They were in a terrible state – they tumbled onto the ground and lay there. They were filthy and covered in blood. One of our guys went over to one of them to give him a drink of water. The Jap who had been driving the lorry beat them both almost to death. That made us think that there was no hope for us. We were hanging on from day to day.'

One thousand men, including Tom McKie and Edgar Webster from the 155th, went to work on the Mergui Road. Only half of them survived. Tom was one of them.

Gunner Edgar Webster died on the Mergui Road on 15 June 1945. Edgar, from Leeds, was thirty-three years of age.

Epilogue

The morning sun glinted on the fuselage of the *Enola Gay*, a B29 Super-fortress bomber, as it droned its way steadily over the ocean to the island of Honshu, Japan. From the cockpit nothing was visible save the sky and the sea but the twelve crewmen on board knew that throughout the Japanese Empire, towards which they were flying, their fellow comrades were scattered far and wide in prisoner of war camps, camps that would, sooner rather than later, bring death to them all.

For the prisoners of the Japanese, 6 August 1945 was a day like any other. As usual, they would be starved, beaten and forced to work. Thousands of them had already died and others would die until there were none left. They did not know it but the clock was ticking fast. In twelve days, 18 August 1945, the extermination of the prisoners, the Final Disposition, would begin. The instructions to camp commanders began:

> At such time as the situation became urgent and it be extremely important, the POWs will be concentrated and confined in their present location and, under heavy guard, the preparation for the Final Disposition will be made.

Already, not a single POW in North Borneo was left alive. Whether they had been sent to Sandakan or to Labuan, all had either died or been killed. The forty-six survivors of the Labuan group of 300 realized what was about to happen to them and were shot as they tried to run away. The sick, frantically trying to crawl into the undergrowth to safety, were shot or beaten to death but several of the POWs were still alive when they were buried. (Eyewitness report at War Crimes Trials.)

The order for the Final Disposition continued:

The Methods

(a) Whether they are destroyed individually or in groups, or how-
    ever it is done, with mass bombing, poisonous smoke, poison,

184

drowning, decapitation or whatever, dispose of them as the situation dictates.

(b) In any case, it is the aim not to allow the escape of a single one, to annihilate them all, and not to leave any traces.

The extermination camp at Kukutsu was steadily starving its occupants to death. After the mass extermination it would be easy to leave no trace of the prisoners, so remote was the location. The extermination camp at Oka, to be used for the disposal of the Taihoku prisoners, was well under construction. Just building the camp caused the deaths of seventeen of the 100 men who worked there.

Bunds had been dug at Chungkai, Nakon Pathon and other railway camps in Thailand. Machine-gun nests graced the four corners of each. Ditches had been dug at some of the camps in Japan, ostensibly as air raid precautions, and in the mining camps there were the mine tunnels and the explosives that would bring the roofs down on the helpless captives.

The *Enola Gay* approached the island of Honshu and its crew readied itself for action. Hiroshima was ahead of them ... under them. At 0815 hours the bomb doors opened and a single missile plummeted to earth. Immediately, the plane veered away, banking high, away from its target, towards the ocean and home.

Suddenly, a flash 'brighter than a thousand suns' flared over the entire countryside. An enormous roar and a deafening explosion announced Death. Even at its tremendous height the *Enola Gay* was buffeted so that its occupants – all veterans of many bombing raids – shouted out, 'Oh my God!' and the pilot, Colonel Paul Tibbets, called on every ounce of his skill to keep the plane on track.

This was the first delivery of the 'prompt and utter destruction' promised by the Allies on 26 July 1945 if Japan did not agree to surrender. The Japanese decided to call the Allies' bluff and the use of 'Little Boy', the first atomic bomb, was the result. The Japanese Government chose not to heed the warning and decided to fight on.

Three days passed and the POWs were three days closer to the Final Disposition.

On 9 August 1945, Major Charles Sweeney piloted the *Bockscar*, a B29 Superfortress, towards Kyushu Island, Japan. His target had initially been Kokura but the city was obscured by clouds and smoke so he was redirected to Nagasaki, the secondary target. At 1102 hours, 'Fat Man', the second atomic bomb, was released and exploded over the city. The Japanese were no longer in any doubt that the Allies could deliver the 'prompt and utter destruction' promised at the end of July.

But still the government prevaricated. The civilian representatives pushed for surrender, the military refused to countenance it. It took the intervention of Emperor Hirohito to settle the matter and, on 15 August 1945, a recorded address by him was broadcast to his people announcing the surrender of Japan.

The prisoners, who had for some time been aware of heavy bombing raids by the Allies, noticed the silence and the emptiness in the skies above them and knew that something had happened. Bit by bit the news filtered through to them.

At the coal mine in Japan where Peter Rhodes of the 155th had slaved, the rumour was passed around, 'The Japs have surrendered!' When the guards tried to force the prisoners out to work with the words, '*Shigoto! Shigoto!*' (Work! Work!), the prisoners replied '*Shigoto Nai! Senso wa owari!*' (No work. War finished!), and the guards retreated in tears.

At Nakon Nyok, in Thailand, some of the Korean guards decided that their chances of survival were greater if they threw in their lot with the Allies and approached the officers, offering to release weapons to them should the Japanese guards turn nasty.

In many camps the POWs noticed a change in the guards, a sudden friendliness where before there had been antagonism and cruelty. Some of the worst overseers tried to make friends with POWs, who, just hours before, they had been beating ruthlessly.

At Kukutsu, some natives approached a working party and whispered, '*Senso sunda! Taxan bomb. Boom! Boom!*' (The war is over! Big bomb. Boom! Boom!) The word was relayed back to camp and the prisoners held their breath.

Said John Marshall: 'When we heard that the war was over, Suzuki – one of the worst guards – came up to me and asked if I would say that he had been kind to us while we were POWs. I told him where to go! He was later convicted of war crimes.'

Napoleon, who had previously taunted the POWs, 'You no good soljas. Good soljas no surrender,' found himself taunted by Willie Williamson: 'When are you going to kill yourself? You said we were no good because we surrendered. Now you've surrendered. When are you going to kill yourself?'

Napoleon did not kill himself. He surrendered meekly, as did most of the Japanese Army.

The survivors at Kukutsu had to make their own way down the mountain, carrying the sick on stretchers. The Japanese did not help, but merely supervised. Most of the camp's inmates were mere skeletons, weighing between 5 and 6 stones. In later years, John McEwan would say, 'You could have hung your jacket on our hip bones.'

The war had finished but the deaths had not.

Gunner Thomas Gordon died at Oka on 20 August 1945 from cerebral malaria.
Thomas, from Auchenheath, Lanarkshire, was twenty-five years of age.

In later years, Tom Hannah described how he and other prisoners on Saigon discovered that they were free men. 'We saw this GI walking up to the camp. He was like a walking arsenal with machine guns strapped across him and grenades hanging from his belt. As he passed the guardhouse, one of the Japs bowed to him. Without breaking stride the American punched the Jap right off his feet.'

On the Mergui Road, the guards disappeared overnight and the survivors guessed that the war was over. Tom McKie was one of the emaciated wrecks who tottered back to Kirikan, there being no transport. Anyone not able to make the effort to save himself perished.

Said Tom McKie: 'It took us days to stagger back along the road. On the way we came across lots of lads who had died and we buried them where they lay. In one of the camps there wasn't a single man left who could even stand. They were all just lying on the ground, staring into space.'

On Formosa, John Douglas, who had been moved to Shirakawa when the mine at Kinkaseki was closed, was seriously ill with pellagra. He was not able to be evacuated when the majority of the camp moved out and was flown to Manila later. Some others from the 155th lacked the strength to recover.

Gunner Richard Vanstone died at Shirakawa on 22 September 1945.
Richard, from Bodmin, Cornwall, was twenty-five years of age.

Gunner Ronald Callan died at Shirakawa on 30 September 1945.
Ronald, from Prestwick, Ayrshire, was thirty years of age.

The American Navy came to Keelung to pick up the survivors of Formosa. The Kinkaseki/Kukutsu men were first to go, on 5 September. Skeletal figures were carried on board ship by marines who wept openly at the state of the men they cradled in their arms. The former POWs also wept, unable to comprehend kindness after three and a half years of systematic brutality.

Some of the men from Formosa went home via Australia. Others travelled via Manila and San Francisco, Canada and New York, where they embarked on the *Queen Mary* – the luxury liner turned troopship. Up until then they had been treated with kindness, had gifts pressed on them, were offered tea, coffee, doughnuts, cigarettes. Then, on the *Queen Mary*, some of the 'paying passengers' on board objected to the soldiers having access to all of the ship and asked the captain to restrict them to certain areas only. The captain's response was, 'After what these men have been through, as long as they leave the funnels in place, they can do what they like.' It was the last piece of respect that the men were to have for quite some time.

As the *Queen Mary* approached Southampton on 19 November 1945, the troops lined the railings along the decks, eager for their first glimpse of 'home'. There was no welcoming party, no band to strike up a tune, and when they had disembarked and were shown into a shed for a meal of roast beef, they discovered that it was cold. It had been served two hours earlier, the time the ship had been expected.

Next day they were given a train ticket home. They stood – or sat – in the corridors, the seats occupied by passengers who had paid for their own tickets. John Douglas arrived at Carlisle and discovered that he had missed his last train home. He went into an empty carriage in a siding and settled down for the night. A station employee discovered him there and turned him out. John spent the rest of the night shivering on the platform.

Tom McKie, who had endured the railway and the Mergui Road, was flown to Rangoon with other Mergui survivors. After a time in hospital they began the sea journey home on the *Empire Pride*. They were well looked after and nothing was too much trouble for those looking after them. That is, until the ship arrived at Liverpool! There was a dockers' strike in progress and the captain was told that the ship would have to lie at anchor until things were settled. Arguments went to and fro until the dockers finally agreed that, in the circumstances, they would permit the returning troops to land. Their first night back in Britain was spent on camp beds under the stands at Everton football ground.

Tom Hannah remembers being flown to Rangoon from Saigon and after that his mind is a blank. Having endured the horrors of Japanese captivity, his brain had finally 'shut down' and needed time to adjust to freedom. His next memory is of arriving at Carstairs Junction, in the wilds of Lanarkshire, in the middle of the night. A considerate railway employee phoned the local police and Tom arrived home in a police car. He had gone to war with the help of the police and returned home in the same way.

On his evacuation from Thailand, John Durnford wrote to his girl-friend with a proposal of marriage. On the ship back home he received a letter from her turning down his proposal as she had married some-one else.

Robert Brentnall, a former Formosa prisoner of war, arrived at Motherwell Railway Station. His family had not been informed that he was due to come home that day and there was no one there to meet him. Robert was so weak after his years of captivity and the strain of the journey home that he was unable to find his way to a bus stop. Some kindly ladies became aware of his distress and bought him a cup of tea in a nearby tea room before calling a taxi to take him home to Craigneuk, in Wishaw.

Jimmy Tominey's family had had no word from him for a long time and, at the end of the war, did not know whether he had survived. As each of the local men returned from the Far East, Jimmy's father went to their homes, frantically seeking news of his son, but receiving none. Then, one day, there was a knock at the door. Jimmy had come home.

John MacKay Kelly's parents waited and waited for him to come home. They had had no word from him since before the surrender in February 1942. In April 1946, he was presumed dead. John had been killed on February 14, 1942, at the ambush at Nee Soon, and his parents had never been informed.

None of the 155th who were sent to Borneo survived and four of them have no known grave. The Tadman family have spent a lifetime and made several visits to Borneo to try to find out what happened to their brother Tom.

John McEwan married Nan, whose memory had sustained him in his times of despair. Les Puckering married Jean, the girl he had met at a dance in Haddington in 1941. Bobby Findlater married Peg, the young girl from Thornhill who had liked the look of him and used to wave shyly to him before he went off to the war with the fireside soldiers. Pat Campbell realized his dream and qualified as a solicitor. He married Margaret, worked in London and later retired to his home town of Dumfries. Roy Russell, the former regimental police sergeant, was turned down for both the police and the fire service. His health had been irretrievably damaged during his years in Thailand but he later used his knowledge of horses to open a riding school, which he called Tao Ha – the name of one of the POW camps in Saigon!

Dick Gwillim, the 'Gunner with nine lives', married his sweetheart Betty but throughout his life was haunted by the fact that the wound to his hand and arm had kept him at Changi, while his mates had suffered and died elsewhere. He felt this despite the fact that conditions for the prisoners at Changi had never been pleasant. For the rest of his life, he and Betty were stalwarts of the Far East POW Association, which looked after the interests of the former prisoners and their families.

Tom McKie, the first of the Thornhill contingent to come home, was constantly asked by others in the village about their own family members. Tom, still trying to come to terms with the trauma of his own experiences, found himself unable to communicate with the worried relatives. When the Army sent him to Birmingham for a medical, he found a job as a prison officer and stayed there, exchanging one form of imprisonment for another!

But all the Far East prisoners of war returned to a world that did not understand them and one that they, in turn, did not understand. In the camps they had supported each other, helped each other, confided in each other. Now they were cast adrift, without the support of their mates, living with the nightmares and the memories.

And although relieved to be back with their families, sorrow was never far away. Sorrow for the mates who had not come home, sorrow for their lost youth, sorrow and bemusement for the times they were called cowards for a surrender they had not wanted but could not avoid.

They had expected some justice for what they had suffered but instead they were ordered not to speak about what had happened to them; told that it would cause hurt to families who had lost someone. And in that silence they were lost.

Said John Durnford: 'Only because the Western world saw the survivors of Belsen and Buchenwald do men imagine that the horrors of concentration camps are synonymous with the names of Nazism and, in our day, communism. It is not so. The callous neglect of human suffering shown by Oriental minds, the working and starving of human souls and bodies to a pitch of exhaustion over years, was a more deliberate and refined piece of cruelty.'

Nominal Roll of the 155th (Lanarkshire Yeomanry) Field Regiment, RA

The following is a list of Men of B and C Batteries of the 155th (Lanarkshire Yeomanry) Field Regiment, RA, who fought during the Malayan Campaign and were killed or taken prisoner of war. The list includes Army number, surname and first names, rank and details of their experience and movement as prisoners, including the POW group to which they were attached. Where the individual was killed in action or died as a POW, this is indicated, along with his place of burial or commemoration.

Owing to the large number of camps on the Death Railway, it has not been possible to list them all against each individual. However, the POW group to which they were attached is listed against their name and the camps used by these groups are outlined in the chapters that tell of their involvement on the railway.

For ease of reference, the following abbreviations are used:

Ranks

Lt. Col.	Lieutenant Colonel
A/Lt. Col.	Acting Lieutenant Colonel
Maj.	Major
Capt.	Captain
Lt. Qm.	Lieutenant Quartermaster
Lt.	Lieutenant
2/Lt.	Second Lieutenant
R.S.M.	Regimental Sergeant Major
B.S.M.	Battery Sergeant Major
R.Q.M.S.	Regimental Quartermaster Sergeant

B.Q.M.S.	Battery Quartermaster Sergeant
Sgt.	Sergeant
S/Sgt.	Staff Sergeant
L/Sgt.	Lance Sergeant
Bdr.	Bombardier
L/Bdr.	Lance Bombardier
Gnr.	Gunner

POW Camps

Singapore
Ch.	Changi

Formosa
Kin.	Kinkaseki
T6	Taihoku 6
T5	Taihoku 5
Tc.	Taichu
Ht.	Heito
Kuk.	Kukutsu
Sh.	Shirakawa
In.	Inrin
To.	Toroku
Ka.	Karenko

Japan
Fuk. 9	Fukuoka 9
Sen.	Senryu
Funa.	Funatsu
Miy.	Miyata
Hak. 2	Hakodate 2
Hokk.	Hokkaido

Borneo
Kuch.	Kuching (Batu Lintang)
Lab.	Labuan

* * *

Movement of POW groups from the 155th

Singapore to Thailand
2/Lt. Durnford, Lt. Ffolkes, Drivers' Party	October 1942
Track-Laying Gang (Rw. Track)	November 1942
D Force	March 1943

F Force	April 1943
H Force	May 1943
Singapore to Formosa	October 1942
Singapore to Borneo	March 1943
Singapore to Japan	May 1943
Singapore to Japan (ex Thailand)	June 1944
	September 1944
Singapore to Saigon (ex Thailand)	February 1945
Formosa to Japan	February 1945
Japan to Manchuria (ex Formosa)	April 1945

* * *

Place of Burial/Commemoration

B/W	Brookwood Memorial, London
Lanark	Lanark Cemetery, Scotland
Kirkee	Kirkee War Cemetery, India
Kranji	Kranji War Cemetery, Singapore
Kranji Mem.	Kranji Memorial, Singapore
Sing. Hos. Mem.	Singapore Civil Hospital Memorial, Kranji, Singapore
Sai Wan	Sai Wan War Cemetery, Hong Kong
Taiping	Taiping Cemetery, Malaya
Chungkai	Chungkai War Cemetery, Thailand
Kanburi	Kanchanaburi War Cemetery, Thailand
Thanbyuzayat	Thanbyuzayat War Cemetery, Burma (Myanmar)
Yokohama	Yokohama War Cemetery, Japan

ASN	Surname	First Name	Rank	POW Camps	Place of burial/Commemoration
977214	Allan	Harold S.M.	Gnr.	Ch.; Rw. Track; Japan Funa.	Yokohama NB 10
129328	Anderson	Michael L.	Capt.	Ch.; Kin.; Sh.; Japan Miy. (died)	
310000	Anderson	J. Thomas	Sgt.	Ch.; Rw. Track; Japan Funa.	
309928	Anderson	William G.	Sgt.	Ch.; Kin. (died)	Sai Wan V11 F25
959350	Andrews	Ernest G.	Gnr.	Ch.; Kin. (died)	Sai Wan VF1
942866	Anniss	F.A.	Bdr.	Changi (died)	Kranji 7A 13
325650	Armstrong	James	L/Bdr.	Ch.; Rw. Track; Ubon	
322234	Arnott	William	Gnr.	Ch.; Rw. F Force; Ch.	
950086	Ashness	George A.	Gnr.	Ch.; Rw. Drivers; Changi	
974739	Askew	Harold	L/Bdr.	Ch.; Kin., Ht.; Japan Sen. (died)	Yokohama NA 3
919354	Bailey	Henry A.	Gnr.	Ch.; Rw. Track (died)	Kanburi 8K 11
977215	Baillie	Thomas W.	Gnr.	Ch.; Kin., Sh.	
954916	Baines	Frederick G.	Gnr.	Ch.; Rw. H Force; Ch.	Sai Wan V11 F16
963257	Barker	Harold	Gnr.	Ch.; Kin. (died)	Chungkai 8L 5
954912	Barnes	Edward F.	L/Sgt.	Ch.; Rw. Track (died)	Yokohama AA 10
942756	Barnes	Ernest	Gnr.	Ch.; Kin., T6; Japan Hak. 2 (died)	
970652	Barnes	Hubert E.	Gnr.	Ch.; Rw. H Force; Ch.	
871488	Barnes	William C.J.	Gnr.	Japan Fuk. 3	
322235	Barrie	William	Gnr.	Ch.; Kin.; Japan Omine	
740690	Bartlett	Alfred G.	BQMS	Ch.; Rw. Track (died)	Kranji Mem. Col. 37
942861	Batrick	William C.F.	Gnr.	Ch.; Kin., T6; Japan Hak. 2	
309549	Bell	James W.	BSM	Ch.; Rw. Track; Japan Funa.	
929697	Bennett	George J.E.	Bdr.	Killed in action	Taiping 2H 7-8
317950	Bennett	Robert	BSM	Ch.; Rw. Track; Saigon	
779106	Berry	Robert L.	Gnr.	Ch.; Rw. Track; Saigon	
837976	Bilham	Lawrence	Gnr.	Ch.; Kin., T6; Japan Hak. 2	
1423985	Billings	Francis J.	BSM	Killed in action	Kranji Mem. Col. 37
325661	Bingham	James	Sgt.	Ch.; Kin., Kuk.	
949558	Birch	Thomas F.	Gnr.	Ch.; Rw. F Force; Ch.	
97721	Birrell	Robert M.	L/Bdr.	Ch.; Rw. H Force; Ch.	

194

ASN	Surname	First Name	Rank	POW Camps	Place of burial/Commemoration
968374	Black	Douglas J.	Gnr.	Ch.; Rw. Track; Saigon	Sai Wan V B6
322402	Black	Joseph	L/Bdr.	Ch.; Kin. (died)	
1105152	Blair	David	Gnr.	Ch.; Kin.; Sh.	
982191	Blair	William B.	L/Bdr.	Ch.; Kin. (died)	Sai Wan V1 M6
791186	Bland	George	Bdr.	Ch.; Rw. D Force	
954926	Bliss	Rex	Gnr.	Ch.; Rw. H Force; Ch.	
960004	Bradley	Richard	L/Bdr.	Ch.; Rw. Track	
1105153	Brandon	William J.	Gnr.	Ch.; Kin.; Kuk.	
954915	Brennan	James C.	Bdr.	Ch.; Kin.; Ht.; Japan Sen.	
322887	Brentnall	Robert	Gnr.	Ch.; Kin.; T6	
963511	Brewer	Douglas C.	L/Bdr.	Ch.; Rw. Track; Japan Funa.	
950240	Broadrick	Herbert G.	Gnr.	Ch.; Rw. Track	
129289	Brocklehurst	Michael J.C.	Lt.	Pudu; Rw. 14.10.42	
325658	Brodie	John	Sgt.	Ch.; Kin.; Kuk.	
1065703	Brookes	Wallace S.	BSM	Ch.; Kin.; Ht.; Japan Sen.	
4968245	Broughton	Frederick	Sgt.	Ch.; Rw. Track; Ubon	
89538	Brown	Charles G.	Capt.	Changi	
325663	Brown	George M.	Gnr.	Ch.; Kin. (died)	Sai Wan V A7
324167	Brown	James	L/Sgt.	Ch.; Kin.; Kuk.	
2983588	Brown	R.A. (Ginger)	L/Sgt.	Escaped 14.2.42	
977273	Brown	Robert	Gnr.	Ch.; Rw. F Force; Ch.	
325656	Brown	William	L/Bdr.	Ch.; Rw. Track; Saigon	
164316	Brown	W. Michael G.	Lt.	Ch.; Kin.; Japan Miy.; Manchuria	
977274	Bruce	Donald C.	L/Bdr.	Ch.; Kin.; Japan Omuri; Bunka	
954903	Bruce	Edward	Gnr.	Ch.; Kin.; T6; In.; Sh.; Japan Fuk. 9	
977275	Buchanan	Robert D.	L/Bdr.	Ch.; Rw. H Force; Ch.	
326271	Buchanan	Roy	Gnr.	Ch.; Kin.; Ht. (died)	Sai Wan V11 F27
977276	Buckham	John	Gnr.	Ch.; Kin.; Kuk.	
987279	Buckton	Thomas E.	Gnr.	Ch.; Kin.; Japan Omine	
977277	Burgess	John	Gnr.	Ch.; Kin.; T6; Sh.; Japan Fuk. 9	

ASN	Surname	First Name	Rank	POW Camps	Place of burial/Commemoration
977278	Burke	Thomas S.	Gnr.	Ch.; Rw. F Force; Ch.	
1105156	Burns	Henry	Gnr.	Ch.; Kin. (died)	Sai Wan V M4
977279	Burns	James G.	Gnr.	Ch.; Rw. Track; Saigon	
987280	Burns	William D.	L/Bdr.	Ch.; Rw. Track; Japan Funa.	
949574	Butler	Robert E.	Gnr.	Ch.; Rw. Track; Pratchai	
325657	Byers	William (Jimmy)	Gnr.	Ch.; Rw. D Force (died)	Chungkai 2H 6
977280	Caddell	David	Gnr.	Ch.; Rw. F Force (died)	Kanburi Mem. 9M4
381026	Caldow	James	Gnr.	Ch.; Kin.; Kuk.	
977218	Callan	Ronald R.	Gnr.	Ch.; Kin.; Sh. (died)	Kranji Mem. Col. 38
797981	Calland	William J.	L/Bdr.	Ch.; Kin. (died)	Sai Wan V L3
859716	Cameron	William	Gnr.	Ch.; Kin.; Japan Omine	
977219	Cameron	William J.R.	Gnr.	Ch.; Kin.; Sh.	
977281	Campbell	Alexander	Gnr.	Ch.; Kin.; Kuk.	
977283	Campbell	Gilbert	Gnr.	Ch.; Kin.; Kuk.	
977284	Campbell	John	Gnr.	Ch.; Rw. Track	
977286	Campbell	John	Gnr.	Ch.; Rw. Track; Japan Funa.	
325672	Campbell	Patrick	Bdr.	Ch.; Rw. Track	
3185583	Campbell	Reginald G.	Gnr.	Ch.; Rw. F Force; Ch.	Labuan P B12
977220	Campbell	Rodger	Gnr.	Ch.; Borneo Kuch. (died)	
977288	Campbell	William G.	Gnr.	Ch.; Kin.; Kuk.	
977221	Capitalli	Louis	Gnr.	Ch.; Rw. Track; Nakon Nyok	
309667	Carlyle	Irving	L/Bdr.	Ch.; Kin.; Kuk.	
323100	Carmichael	Andrew	Gnr.	Ch.; Rw. Track; Nakon Nyok	
977289	Carmichael	Archibald	Gnr.	Ch.; Kin.; Japan Omine	
977290	Carmichael	John	Gnr.	Ch.; Rw. Track; Ubon	
977292	Carr	Alexander	L/Bdr.	Ch.; Kin.; Ht.; Japan Sen.	
977293	Carroll	Hugh A.	Gnr.	Ch.; Kin.; Sh.	
318003	Carroll	John J.	Gnr.	Killed in action	Kranji Mem. Col. 38
325925	Carruthers	William	Gnr.	Ch.; Kin.; Kuk.	
977294	Carson	Benjamin	L/Bdr.	Ch.; Kin.; Kuk.	

ASN	Surname	First Name	Rank	POW Camps	Place of burial/Commemoration
977295	Carson	George R.	Gnr.	Ch.; Rw. Track; Saigon	
954920	Carter	Charles F.	Gnr.	Ch.; T6; Kin.; Kuk.	
872653	Cartwright	Donald	Gnr.	Ch.; Kin.; Kuk.	
326263	Cavers	Alex S.L.	Bdr.	Ch.; Rw. F Force (died)	Kanburi Mem. 9M4
949592	Cheeseman	Aubrey C.	Gnr.	Ch.; Rw. Track	
325669	Christie	Alexander H.	Gnr.	Ch.; Rw. D Force (died)	Kanburi 4B3
977299	Clark	William	Bdr.	Ch.; Rw. Track; Pratchai	
977300	Clark	William McK.	Gnr.	Ch.; Rw. Track	
963262	Clarke	George F.	Gnr.	Ch.: Rw. Track; Ubon	
942851	Claydon	Reginald G.	Gnr.	Ch.; Rw. Track; Japan Funa.	
977302	Clifford	William J.	Gnr.	Ch.; Rw. Track; Saigon	
977303	Clinghan	William C.	Gnr.	Ch.; Kin.; T6; Japan Hak. 2	
318179	Clisby	Robert (Bunny)	Gnr.	Ch.; Rw. Drivers	
973106	Clorely	William	L/Bdr.	Ch.; Rw. Track; Saigon	
930715	Coleman	Charles H.	L/Bdr.	Ch.; Rw. Track	
146967	Coles	Guy Roger	Capt.	Ch.; Rw. Track (died)	Kanburi 8A 39
977306	Collins	Frank G.	Gnr.	Ch.; Kin.; Ht. (died)	Sai Wan V11 E32
324668	Collins	Thomas M.	Gnr.	Ch.; Rw. Track; Ubon	
1105157	Constable	George	Gnr.	Ch.; Rw. Track	
977309	Coogan	Andrew	Gnr.	Ch.; Kin.; Ht.; Japan Sen.	
987281	Cooke	Edwin	Gnr.	Ch.; Rw. H Force; Ch.	
160642	Coope	Peter R.	Lt.	Ch.; Rw. H Force; Ch.	
326796	Copeland	Norman H.	Gnr.	Ch.; Rw. Track	
1105158	Corbett	David	Gnr.	Ch.; Rw. Track; Saigon	
325665	Cowan	James	Gnr.	Ch.; Kin. (died)	Sai Wan V1 F4
1105159	Cox	John	Gnr.	Ch.; Kin.; T5; Japan Hak. 2	
318092	Craig	David L.	L/Bdr.	Ch.; Kin.; Ht.	
1105160	Crawford	Thomas	Gnr.	Ch.; Rw. Track (died)	Chungkai 8M6
894512	Cresswell	Jack S.	L/Sgt.	Ch.; Kin.; Sh.; Japan Fuk. 9	
950446	Crowther	Joseph	Gnr.	Ch.; Rw. Track; Pratchai	

ASN	Surname	First Name	Rank	POW Camps	Place of burial/Commemoration
977313	Cunningham	William	Gnr.	Ch.; Rw. Track (died)	Chungkai 9L5
1105161	Currie	James	Gnr.	Ch.; Rw. Track; Saigon	
977314	Currie	Robert H.	Gnr.	Ch.; Rw. H Force; Ch.	
309572	Cuthbertson	Samuel	L/Bdr.	Ch.; Rw. Track; Ch. (died)	Kranji 16 D15
326920	Dalgleish	George	Gnr.	Ch.; Kin.; Sh.	
977316	Daly	Robert W.	Gnr.	Ch.; Kin.; Kuk.	
1105162	Daly	William	Gnr.	Ch.; Rw. D Force (died)	Kanburi 4 G35
977223	Dalziel	William R.	Gnr.	Ch.; Rw. D Force (died)	Kanburi 4 F29
1105163	Davidson	Thomas N.	Gnr.	Ch.; Kin.; Ht.; Japan Sen.	
963562	Davis	Eddie G.	Sgt.	Ch.; Kin.; Japan Omine	
954952	Davis	George	Gnr.	Ch.; Rw. Track	
937128	Dean	Thomas V.	L/Bdr.	Ch.; Rw. Track; Japan Funa.	
954955	Dell	Ronald	L/Bdr.	Ch.; Kin.; T6; Tc.; Sh.; Japan Fuk. 9	
1051696	Dewsnap	David	Sgt.	Ch.; Kin.; Kuk.	
325673	Dick	William	L/Bdr.	Ch.; Rw. Track; Japan Funa.	
324168	Dickie	William	Gnr.	Ch.; Rw. Track	
326795	Dickson	Alexander	Gnr.	Ch.; Kin.; Kuk.	
977317	Dickson	William J.	Gnr.	Ch.; Kin.; T6; Sh.; Japan Hak. 2	
1105164	Divers	Francis A.	Gnr.	Ch.; Japan Hokk.	
318133	Dobbie	Patrick	Gnr.	Ch.; Kin.; Kuk.	
977318	Docherty	Richard	Gnr.	Ch.; Kin.; Sh.	
1195165	Dodds	Thomas	Gnr.	Ch.; Kin.; T6; Japan Hak. 2	
1073225	Donaldson	Leslie A.	Sgt.	Ch.; Kin.; Sh.; Japan Fuk. 9	
9987284	Donnelly	Herbert H.	Gnr.	Ch.; Kin.; T6; Japan Hak. 2	
317907	Donnelly	Thomas F.	Bdr.	Ch.; Kin.; Ht.; Japan Sen. (died)	Yokohama NA 9
1105166	Douglas	James W.	Gnr.	Ch.; Kin. (died)	Sai Wan V1 M3
326282	Douglas	John C.	L/Bdr.	Ch.; Kin.; Sh.	
1105167	Douglas	Thomas T.	Gnr.	Ch.; Rw. Track; Ch.	
954925	Douglas	William H.	L/Bdr.	Ch.; Rw. Track; Japan Funa.	
169531	Douglas-Home	Edward C.	2/Lt.	Ch.; Rw. Track	

ASN	Surname	First Name	Rank	POW Camps	Place of burial/Commemoration
318175	Downie	Alexander	Bdr.	Ch.; Kin.; Kuk.	
325675	Downie	James	L/Bdr.	Ch.; Kin.; Kuk.	
817090	Doyle	Arthur S.	Gnr.	Ch.; Rw. Track	
963019	Drewer	Albert E.	Gnr.	Ch.; Rw. H Force; Ch.	
977320	Drysdale	James	Gnr.	Ch.; Rw. Track; Saigon	
977321	Duncan	Alexander	Gnr.	Ch.; Kin.; T6; Oka	
325674	Dunn	William	Gnr.	Ch.; Rw. Track; Saigon	
977323	Dunsmore	William H.	Gnr.	Ch.; Rw. Track; Japan Funa.	
165459	Durnford	S. John H. (Dinky)	2/Lt.	Ch.; Rw. No. 4 Group	
977324	Eadie	Gerard	Gnr.	Ch.; Rw. Track; Japan Funa.	
951132	Eaton	Thomas W.	Gnr.	Ch.; Rw. Track	
934634	Edel	Bernard	Bdr.	Killed in action	Kranji Mem. Col. 38
977325	Edgar	Peter F.	Gnr.	Ch.; Kin.; Kuk.	
1075337	Edgar	Thomas	Gnr.	Killed in action	Kranji Mem. Col. 38
950217	Edhouse	Edward	Gnr.	Ch.; Rw. F Force (died)	Thanbyuzayat B3 Z2
318021	Edmonds	R.D.	Gnr.	Ch.; Rw. Track	
929378	Ellerby	Gordon	L/Bdr.	Ch.; Kin. (died)	Sai Wan V G11
954900	Ellis	Thomas	Gnr.	Changi	
954813	Emery	Thomas A.	Gnr.	Ch.; Rw. D Force (died)	Chungkai 1E8
118417	Eustace	Maurice J.R.	Capt.	Killed in action	Sing. Hos. Mem. Col. 1
915076	Evans	John H.	Bdr.	Ch.; Rw. H Force (died)	Kanburi 8 B4
929732	Farmer	John A.	L/Sgt.	Ch.; Kin.; Ht.; T6	
950025	Farmer	John C.	L/Bdr.	Ch.; Kin.; T6; Tc.; Ht.; Japan Sen. (died)	Yokohama HC 16
977327	Farrell	John R.	Gnr.	Ch.; Rw. Track; Japan Funa.	
63201	Fasson	James C.	Lt. Col.	Ch.; Kin.; Sh.; Japan Miy.; Manchuria	
961383	Fazackerley	John	Bdr.	Ch.; Rw. Track; Saigon	
977328	Feehily	John J.	Gnr.	Ch.; Rw. D Force	
977329	Fegan	James	Gnr.	Ch.; Rw. Track	
318244	Fergusson	James	Bdr.	Ch.; Kin.; Japan Omine	
149765	Ffolkes	David N.	Lt.	Ch.; Rw. No. 4 Group; Nakon Nyok	

ASN	Surname	First Name	Rank	POW Camps	Place of burial/Commemoration
325679	Findlater	Robert J.	L/Sgt.	Ch.; Rw. Track; Saigon	
951129	Finlay	George	Bdr.	Ch.; Rw. Track; Saigon	
950220	Fitzgerald	James A.	L/Bdr.	Ch.; Kin.; Kuk.	
977325	Fleming	William	Gnr.	Ch.; Kin.; Japan Omine	
963260	Fletcher	Walter	Gnr.	Ch.; Kin.; Sh.; Japan Fuk. 9	
950227	Flint	George V.	Bdr.	Ch.; Rw. D Force; Japan (drowned)	Kranji Mem. Col. 37
963537	Ford	John	L/Sgt.	Ch.; Kin.; Japan Omine	
91544	Forster	Alfred R.	Capt.	Killed in action	Taiping 2H 7-8
172448	France	Brian A.	Lt.	Ch.; Kin.; Sh.; Japan Fuk. 9	
951128	Francis	William I.	Gnr.	Ch.; Rw. Track; Japan Funa.	
1105171	Fraser	Thomas	Gnr.	Ch.; Rw. Track; Japan Funa.	
1075339	Freeman	Walter	Gnr.	Ch.; Kin.; T6; Sh.; Japan Fuk. 9	
318222	Frew	Samuel	Gnr.	Ch.; Kin.; T6; Tc.; Ht.; T6	
929979	Frost	Reginald J.	L/Bdr.	Ch.; Rw. Track	
954943	Gaillard	Robert P.	Bdr.	Killed in action	Kranji 11 C2
963538	Gale	Frederick	Gnr.	Ch.; Kin.; T6	
946149	George	John F.	L/Bdr.	Ch.; Rw. Track	
317992	Gibson	A.T.	Sgt.	Wounded, evacuated 15.1.42	
987288	Gibson	Thomas	Bdr.	Ch.; Rw. Track; Japan Funa.	
977343	Gill	John M.	Gnr.	Ch.; T6; Kin.; Kuk.	
322222	Glencross	William	Bdr.	Ch.; Kin.; Japan Omine	
323802	Glendinning	Robert	A/Lt. Col.	Ch.; Kin.; Ht.; T6; Oka (died)	Sai Wan V1 C11
53618	Gold	Philip R.	Gnr.	Escaped 14.2.42	
1075311	Goodchild	Bernard J.	Gnr.	Ch.; Rw. D Force; Japan Shinkai	
954901	Goodman	Raymond G.	L/Sgt.	Ch.; Kin.; Kuk.	
998847	Gordon	George	Gnr.	Ch.; Rw. F Force (died)	Thanbyuzayat B4 H1
977345	Gordon	Thomas	Gnr.	Ch.; Kin.; T6; Oka (died)	Sai Wan V C7
977347	Gough	Benjamin	Bdr.	Ch.; Kin.; Kuk.	
977348	Graham	George M.	Gnr.	Killed in action	Kranji Mem. Col. 38
318002	Graham	James	Gnr.	Ch.; Kin.; Kuk.	

200

ASN	Surname	First Name	Rank	POW Camps	Place of burial/Commemoration
977349	Graham	John	Gnr.	Ch.; Rw. Drivers; Saigon	Kanburi 2Q 22
977350	Graham	John C.	L/Bdr.	Ch.; Rw. D Force (died)	
177368	Graham	Maurice Y.N.	Lt.	Ch.; Rw. F Force; Ch.	
1105173	Graham	Robert	Gnr.	Ch.; Rw. Track; Nakon Nyok	
1105174	Gray	John	Gnr.	Ch.; Rw. H Force; Ch.	
318265	Gray	John G.	Bdr.	Ch.; Rw. Track; Saigon	
977352	Green	James	Gnr.	Ch.; Rw. Track	
977353	Green	Joseph	Gnr.	Ch.; Kin.; Kuk.	
318028	Greer	Albert T.	Gnr.	Ch.; Rw. Track; Japan Funa.	
977355	Greig	John (Tony)	Gnr.	Ch.; Rw. D Force (died)	Kanburi 8L 33
977356	Grierson	James	Gnr.	Ch.; Rw. Track; Saigon	
322020	Grierson	William J.	Gnr.	Ch.; Rw. Track (died)	Chungkai 8L8
954919	Griffin	Frederick	L/Bdr.	Changi	
977357	Gunn	Alexander	Gnr.	Ch.; Kin. (died)	Sai Wan V11 F5
1105175	Gunn	Andrew P.	Gnr.	Ch.; Rw. Track; Saigon	
1105176	Guthrie	John	Gnr.	Ch.; Kin., T6; Tc.; Sh.	
324670	Gwillim	Richard	Gnr.	Changi	
318264	Halifax	John	L/Sgt.	Changi (died)	Kranji 10 B8
936272	Hall	Maurice (Nobby)	Gnr.	Killed in action	Kranji Mem. Col. 37
963193	Hallsworth	Arthur	Gnr.	Ch.; Rw. Track	
3318105	Hamilton	J.	Gnr.	Escaped 14.2.42	
318289	Hands	Joseph A.	Gnr.	Ch.; Kin.; Ht.; T6	
977359	Hannah	Thomas (Chad)	Gnr.	Ch.; Rw. Drivers; Saigon	
942847	Harbird	James	Gnr.	Ch.; Rw. Track; Saigon	
963543	Hardingham	Victor	L/Bdr.	Ch.; Rw. Track	
861257	Harlow	Richard F.	Gnr.	Ch.; Rw. Track; Japan Funa.	
1056554	Harrison	Thomas	L/Sgt.	Ch.; Kin.; Japan Omine	
317961	Harvey	David A.	Gnr.	Ch.; Kin.; Kuk.	
318178	Hay	William L.	Gnr.	Ch.; Kin.; Kuk.	
4030845	Haynes	George H.	L/Sgt.	Ch.; Kin.; T6; Ht.; Japan Sen.	

ASN	Surname	First Name	Rank	POW Camps	Place of burial/Commemoration
831644	Heaver	Leonard A.	Sgt.	Ch.; Kin.; Japan Omine	
7889335	Henderson	D.J.	Gnr.	Ch.; Rw. Track	Sai Wan V1 F9
325683	Henderson	Samuel	L/Sgt.	Ch.; Kin.; Sh. (died)	Kanburi 2A 26
977232	Hendry	John	Gnr.	Ch.; Rw. Track (died)	
325684	Hendry	John S.	L/Bdr.	Ch.; Rw. Track; Ubon	
789122	Henley	Eric A.	Bdr.	Ch.; Rw. H Force; Ch.	
963773	Hewitt	A.J.	L/Bdr.	Ch.; Rw. Track	
323393	Hiddleston	Andrew	Gnr.	Ch.; Kin.; Sh.	
325690	Hiddleston	David M.	L/Bdr.	Ch.; Kin.; T6 (died)	Sai Wan V1 J1
1074007	Higgins	Richard P.	Gnr.	Ch.; Kin.; T6; Tc.; Sh.; Japan Fuk. 9	
987289	Hill	Arthur	Gnr.	Ch.; Rw. Track; Japan Funa.	
1075313	Hindle	Alfred	Gnr.	Ch.; Rw. Track; Japan Funa.	
149766	Hinton	George N.	Lt.	Ch.; Kin.; Sh.; Japan Fuk. 9	
867098	Holt	William G.	Gnr.	Ch.; Kin.; Kuk.	
44090	Hope-Johnston	Percy W.	Capt.	Ch.; Kin.; Sh.; Japan Miy.; Manchuria	
951138	Hopkins	George L.	Gnr.	Ch.; Kin.; Kuk.	
950242	Hoskins	Frederick	Gnr.	Changi (died)	Kranji 9 B8
1028094	Howell	Harold	Sgt.	Ch.; Rw. Track	
960029	Hudson	Robert	L/Bdr.	Ch.; Rw. Track; Japan Funa.	
960014	Hufton	Ronald	Gnr.	Ch.; Kin.; T6; Kin.; Kuk.	
71677	Hugo	James W.	Lt./Qm.	Ch.; Kin.; Sh.; Japan Fuk. 9	
1105179	Ingram	Harry	Gnr.	Ch.; Kin.; T6; Tc.; Sh.; Japan Fuk. 9	
4910519	Jackson	Leonard	Gnr.	Ch.; Rw. Track; Japan Funa.	
963195	James	John W.	Gnr.	Ch.; Rw. D Force (died)	Kanburi 8 J18
325692	Jess	Samuel H.	Gnr.	Ch.; Kin.; Sh.	
950244	Johnson	Albert G.	Gnr.	Ch.; Rw. Drivers	
961098	Johnson	Edward	Gnr.	Ch.; Rw. D Force (died)	Chungkai 2 G1
324606	Johnston	William J. (Jim)	Gnr.	Died India	Kirkee 13 D7
323102	Johnstone	A.M.	Gnr.	Ch.; Rw. Track	
326812	Johnstone	T.L.	Gnr.	Escaped 14.2.42	

ASN	Surname	First Name	Rank	POW Camps	Place of burial/Commemoration
950057	Joliffe	James M.	Gnr.	Ch.; Rw. D Force	
325694	Kane	John	Gnr.	Ch.; Kin.; Kuk.	
1103120	Kay	John	Gnr.	Ch.; Rw. D Force; Japan Shinkai	
791190	Keen	Oliver J.	L/Sgt.	Killed in action	Kranji Mem. Col. 37
942155	Kelly	John	Gnr.	Ch.; Rw. Track; Saigon	
326276	Kelly	John MacKay	L/Bdr.	Killed in action	Kranji Mem. Col. 38
855776	Kelly	Patrick M.	Gnr.	Ch.; Rw. Track; Japan Funa.	
760115	Kelly	Thomas	Bdr.	Ch.; Rw. F Force; Ch.	
318176	Kelso	Francis D.	Gnr.	Ch.; Kin.; T6	
1075704	Kennedy	Maurice	Gnr.	Ch.; Kin.; T6; Japan Hak. 2	
987280	Kilvington	Norman	Gnr.	Ch.; Kin.; T6; Sh.; Japan Fuk. 9	
1105121	King	Anthony D.	Gnr.	Ch.; Rw. Track; Saigon	
925031	Knotman	Thomas H.	Bdr.	Ch.; Rw. D Force	
322238	Knox	Samuel	Gnr.	Ch.; Rw. Track	
1105122	Laing	David A.K.L.	Gnr.	Ch.; Borneo Kuch. (died)	Labuan NC3
1105123	Larkin	Francis	Gnr.	Ch.; Kin.; Kuk.	
930964	Latham	Douglas H.	Gnr.	Ch.; Rw. Drivers	
317861	Laurie	Joseph	Gnr.	Ch.; Rw. Drivers	
998849	Lawford	A.J.	Gnr.	Wounded, evacuated 15.1.42	
950230	Ledwidge	Victor	Gnr.	Ch.; Kin.; Ht.; T6	
160645	Legard	Peter H.	Lt.	Ch.; Rw. Track	
888360	Leith	Thomas	Gnr.	Ch.; Rw. Track	
963034	Levett	Charles A.	L/Bdr.	Ch.; Kin.; T6; Japan Hak. 2	
963253	Limb	Raymond	Gnr.	Ch.; Kin.; T6; Japan Hak. 2	
326939	Lindley	Frederick	Gnr.	Ch.; Kin.; Sh. (died)	Sai Wan V1 F5
781812	Lindup	D.	Sgt.	Escaped 14.2.42	
317888	Little	Thomas G.	Gnr.	Ch.; Rw. F Force (died)	Thanbyuzayat B3 S10
3186956	Lockhead	Samuel	L/Sgt.	Ch.; Kin.; Kuk.	
977233	Logan	Robert	Gnr.	Changi (died)	Kranji 14 A13
854107	Lovage	George	Gnr.	Ch.; Rw. F Force (died)	Thanbyuzayat B6 Q15

ASN	Surname	First Name	Rank	POW Camps	Place of burial/Commemoration
317966	Lowther	Charles S.	B.S.M.	Ch.; Kin.; Japan Omine	Sai Wan V M12
322016	Lowther	Michael B.	Gnr.	Ch.; Kin.; T6; Tc.; Ht. (died)	
134370	Mackenzie	James	Capt.	Ch.; Kin.; Sh.; Japan Miy.; Manchuria	
977479	Mackie	Robert	Gnr.	Ch.; Kin.; T6; Sh.	
77480	Mair	George	Bdr.	Ch.; Rw. Track; Japan Funa.	
977318	Manning	Joseph G.	Gnr.	Ch.; Rw. Track	
977483	Marshall	John (Ginger)	Gnr.	Ch.; Kin.; Kuk.	
325706	Mather	John	Bdr.	Ch.; Kin.; Sh.	
977484	Matthewson	John	Gnr.	Ch.; Kin.; T6; Ht.; Japan Sen.	
963465	Maw	William T.	Gnr.	Ch.; Rw. Track; Saigon	
309287	McAuslan	James A.	R.Q.M.S.	Ch.; Kin.; Ht.; Japan Sen.	
982204	McCallum	Donald	Gnr.	Ch.; Kin.; Ht. (died)	Sai Wan V D11
1105125	McCallum	James	Gnr.	Ch.; Kin.; T6; Sh.	
324675	McCready	Patrick	Gnr.	Ch.; Rw. Drivers; Saigon	
317940	McCutcheon	John	Gnr.	Ch.; Kin.; Kuk.	
977235	McDonald	James	Gnr.	Killed in action	Kranji Mem. Col. 38
857953	McElligott	Stephen	Gnr.	Ch.; Japan Hokk.	
325724	McEwan	John	Gnr.	Ch.; Kin.; Kuk.	
926776	McGhie	Fergus	Gnr.	Ch.; Kin.; Japan Omine	
977238	McGhie	Robert	Gnr.	Ch.; Kin.; Japan Omine	
322223	McGill	Robert	Gnr.	Ch.; T6; Kin.; Japan Omine	
3236821	McGuinness	John L.	Gnr.	Ch.; Kin.; Japan Omine	
317853	McKay	Andrew	L/Bdr.	Ch.; Rw. Track; Ubon	
325700	McKay	Hector	Gnr.	Ch.; Kin.; T6	
858557	McKee	Cyril H.	Gnr.	Ch.; Rw. Track; Saigon	
322158	McKenna	James	Gnr.	Drowned *Arandora Star*	B/W Panel 4 Col. 1
722616	McKenna	Patrick	Gnr.	Changi	
322403	McKie	Thomas W.	Gnr.	Ch.; Rw. Track; Mergui	
317982	McLachlan	John	Gnr.	Ch.; Rw. Track; Saigon	
325707	McLean	Archibald	Gnr.	Ch.; Kin.; T6; Tc.; Ht. (died)	Sai Wan V1 B9

ASN	Surname	First Name	Rank	POW Camps	Place of burial/Commemoration
164341	McLean	Ian G.	Lt.	Ch.; Kin.; Sh.; Japan Fuk. 9	
325320	McLellan	John	Gnr.	Ch.; Rw. Drivers	
1105128	McLeod	John A.	Gnr.	Ch.; Kin.; Sh.	
1105129	McMaster	Alexander	Gnr.	Ch.; Rw. Track; Saigon	
325720	McNair	John	L/Bdr.	Ch.; Rw. Track	
318220	McPhail	Archibald	Sgt.	Ch.; Kin.; Kuk.	
982207	McWhirter	Robert W.	L/Bdr.	Ch.; Rw. Track; Saigon	
942991	Medlock	Alonza	Gnr.	Ch.; Kin.; T6 (died)	Sai Wan V1 B6
318009	Melrose	Robert G.	Gnr.	Ch.; Kin.; Japan Omine	
325717	Menzies	Thomas	Gnr.	Ch.; Rw. D Force; Japan Shinkai	
954924	Miles	Robert (Tom)	L/Sgt.	Ch.; Kin.; T5; Japan Hak. 2	
3185935	Millar	Thomas E.	Gnr.	Ch.; Rw. Track; Japan Funa.	
977486	Miller	Alexander	Gnr.	Ch.; Rw. F Force; Ch.	
1105132	Milne	John C.	Gnr.	Ch.; Rw. Track; Japan Funa.	
977488	Milne	William	Gnr.	Ch.; Kin.; Kuk.	
950047	Milner	William H.	Gnr.	Ch.; Rw. Track; Japan Funa.	
868159	Mitchell	Charles B.	Sgt.	Ch.; Kin.; Kuk.	
1105133	Mitchell	David M.	Gnr.	Ch.; Rw. Track; Japan Funa.	
324141	Mitchell	George H.	Bdr.	Ch.; Kin.; Sh.	
324685	Mitchell	Robert W.	L/Bdr.	Ch.; Rw. Drivers	
977489	Moffat	William	Gnr.	Ch.; Rw. Track; Ch.	
861579	Mogg	Henry C.	Gnr.	Ch.; Rw. Track	
963468	Moon	John L.	L/Bdr.	Ch.; Rw. Track	
317969	Moore	Thomas D.	Gnr.	Drowned *Arandora Star*	B/W Panel 4 Col. 1
317954	Mottley	Ronald A.H.	L/Bdr.	Ch.; Kin.; Sh.	
891680	Moule	Frank	Gnr.	Ch.; Rw. Track	
25586	Murdoch	Alan A. (Jiggy)	Lt. Col.	Killed in action	Kranji Mem. Col. 37
818101	Murgatroyd	Joshua	Sgt.	Ch.; Kin.; Kuk.	
1105134	Murphy	Daniel	Gnr.	Ch.; Rw. Track; Saigon	
954778	Nash	Robert S. (Joe)	Gnr.	Ch.; Kin.; Japan Omine	

ASN	Surname	First Name	Rank	POW Camps	Place of burial/Commemoration
930810	Nightingale	J.F.	Gnr.	Ch.; Rw. Track	
1105135	Nolan	James (Gerry)	Gnr.	Ch.; Rw. Track	
835896	Norbury	Frederick	Bdr.	Ch.; Kin.; Kuk.	
963472	Notley	William R.	Gnr.	Ch.; Kin.; Japan Omine	
3245565	O'Brien	Patrick	Gnr.	Ch.; Rw. Track; Japan Funa.	
309721	O'Connor	Joseph	Bdr.	Ch.; Rw. H Force; Ch.	
929370	Ogden	John A.	Gnr.	Ch.; Kin.; Kuk.	
950234	Ostler	James A.	Gnr.	Ch.; Kin.; Kuk.	
950097	Padgett	Ed (Williams)	Gnr.	Ch.; Rw. H Force (died)	Kanburi 2B 9
952044	Pannell	William G.	Gnr.	Ch.; Kin.; T6	
1069558	Parker	John J.	S/Sgt.	Ch.; Borneo Kuch.; Lab. (died)	Kranji Mem. Col. 37
325727	Paterson	James	Gnr.	Ch.; Kin.; Kuk.	
1105136	Paterson	John McE.	Gnr.	Ch.; Rw. Track (died)	Chungkai 9M7
3184627	Paterson	William J.	Bdr.	Ch.; Kin.; Kuk.	
998877	Paton	David McK.	Gnr.	Ch.; Rw. Track; Saigon	
317955	Paton	William	Gnr.	Ch.; Rw. Drivers	Kranji 32 A13
802800	Pennington	Robert C.	Bdr.	Killed in action	Sai Wan V1 D11
963477	Perman	George	L/Bdr.	Ch.; Kin.; T6; Tc. (died)	
1105137	Petrie	John	Gnr.	Ch.; Rw. Track; Saigon	
317980	Picken	William	Gnr.	Ch.; Rw. Track	Sai Wan V K13
1085246	Pickles	Samuel	Gnr.	Ch.; Kin. (died)	
961692	Plumridge	Laurence	Gnr.	Ch.; Kin.; Japan Omine	
950043	Poland	Raymond	Gnr.	Ch.; Rw. Track; Saigon	
953336	Polley	Norman D.	L/Bdr.	Ch.; Rw. Track; Saigon	
1749348	Poole	James W.	B.S.M.	Ch.; Rw. Track; Japan Funa.	
946274	Popple	Charles	L/Bdr.	Ch.; Kin.; Kuk.	
3236772	Porteous	Hugh	L/Bdr.	Ch.; Rw. Track; Saigon	
929813	Powell	James	Gnr.	Ch.; Kin. (died)	Sai Wan V G6
581666	Pratt	Frederick	Gnr.	Ch.; Rw. Track; Japan Funa.	
963479	Price	Ernest G.	Gnr.	Ch.; Rw. Track	

ASN	Surname	First Name	Rank	POW Camps	Place of burial/Commemoration
950221	Puckering	Leslie V.	Bdr.	Ch.; Kin.; Ht.; Sh.	Kranji Mem. Col. 38
930602	Quertier	Albert G.	Gnr.	Killed in action	Sai Wan V1 F7
998859	Ramsay	Hope-Scott	Gnr.	Ch.; Kin. (died)	
954898	Read	George W.A.	Gnr.	Ch.; Kin.; T6; Oka	
840973	Reek	Bernard	Bdr.	Ch.; Rw. D Force; Pratchai	
318646	Renfrew	Roderick	Gnr.	Ch.; Rw. F Force; Ch.	
959103	Rhodes	Peter S.	Gnr.	Ch.; Japan Fukuoka	
2691562	Road-night	Charles	Sgt.	Escaped 14.2.42	
325731	Robertson	Wm. (Big Bill)	Sgt.	Ch.; Rw. D Force	
929998	Robinson	Dennis H. (Tiger)	Gnr.	Ch.; Rw. H Force; Ch.	
1068987	Robson	Norman	Sgt.	Ch.; Rw. Track	
309811	Rogerson	Nesmith	Sgt.	Ch.; Rw. Track	
165395	Ronaldson	Patrick H.D.	Lt.	Ch.; Kin. (died)	Sai Wan V M9
950107	Rook	Edgar T.	Gnr.	Ch.; Rw. Drivers; Ch.	
930700	Rose	Edwin B.	Gnr.	Ch.; T6; Tc.; In.; To. (died)	Sai Wan V H10
840697	Ross	David	Bdr.	Ch.; Rw. H Force; Ch.	
318066	Russell	Robert	Sgt.	Ch.; Rw. Track; Saigon	
1105139	Russell	Thomas	Gnr.	Ch.; Rw. Track; Japan Funa.	
985263	Sams	Reginald J.	Gnr.	Ch.; Kin.; T6; Tc.; Sh.	
35588	Sanderson	Gerald B.	Major	Ch.; Kin.; Sh.; Japan Miy.; Manchuria	
952048	Sanderson	Walter	Gnr.	Ch.; Kin.; T6	
325732	Sandilands	John	L/Bdr.	Changi	
1105140	Scott	George	Gnr.	Ch.; Kin.; T6; Japan Hak. 2	
326279	Scott	Ian	Gnr.	Ch.; Rw. F Force (died)	Kanburi 2 D3
323294	Scott	James	L/Bdr.	Ch.; Kin.; Sh.	
322881	Scott	John	Gnr.	Died from illness	Lanark West Plot 37
325737	Scott	John	Gnr.	Ch.; Rw. Drivers	
326813	Scott	Joseph	Gnr.	Ch.; Kin.; Sh.	
325734	Scott	William	Gnr.	Ch.; Kin.; Kuk.	
317984	Scott	William	Bdr.	Ch.; Rw. Track; Japan Funa.	

ASN	Surname	First Name	Rank	POW Camps	Place of burial/Commemoration
460443	Scullion	Peter	R.S.M.	Ch.; Kin.; Ht.; T6	
937466	Sephton	Reginald	Sgt.	Ch.; Kin.; Sh.; Japan Fuk. 9	
118443	Sewell	E.R. Andrew	Capt.	Ch.; Kin.; Sh.; Japan Miy.; Manchuria	
318005	Shannon	George	Gnr.	Ch.; Rw. Drivers; Saigon	
1096286	Shaw	Thomas	Gnr.	Ch.; Rw. Track; Japan Funa.	
853176	Shelley	Patrick	Gnr.	Ch.; T6	
1018809	Shelvey	Dennis A.	B.S.M.	Ch.; Kin.; Japan Omine	
325531	Shields	William	Gnr.	Ch.; Kin.; Japan Omine	
963486	Shipcott	Charles	Gnr.	Changi	
810223	Shone	M.M. Joseph	Bdr.	Ch.; Rw. D Force	
963487	Shun	Charles W.	Gnr.	Ch.; Borneo Kuch.; Lab. (died)	Kranji Mem. Col. 38
963688	Sibley	Neville A.H.	Bdr.	Ch.; Kin.; Ht.; Japan Sen.	
3248921	Sim	John D.	Gnr.	Ch.; Kin.; T6; Tc.; Sh.; Japan Fuk. 9	
977210	Sinclair	Thomas A.S.	Bdr.	Changi (died)	Kranji 9 B12
961444	Siviter	Albert	Gnr.	Ch.; Rw. Track	
324677	Skilling	Joseph	Gnr.	Ch.; Rw. Drivers	
317922	Smith	Arthur (Tpr.)	Gnr.	Ch.; Kin.; T6; Japan Hak. 2	
950371	Smith	Charles	Gnr.	Ch.; Rw. D Force	
323103	Smith	George (Butcher)	Gnr.	Ch.; Rw. D Force	
1105141	Smith	George	Gnr.	Ch.; Rw. Track; Saigon	
318093	Smith	Hugh C.	Gnr.	Ch.; Kin. (died)	Sai Wan V B10
1105142	Smith	John M.M.	Gnr.	Ch.; Kin.; Kuk.	
941551	Smith	Leslie T.A.	L/Sgt.	Ch.; Rw. Track; Japan Funa.	
322587	Smith	Robert G.	L/Bdr.	Changi	
998863	Smith	William	Gnr.	Ch.; Rw. Track; Saigon	
26814	Smith	W.J.	Bdr.	Escaped 14.2.42	
942845	Smithies	Frederick	Gnr.	Ch.; Rw. Track	
948472	Snowdon	William A.	Gnr.	Ch.; Rw. Track	
1096284	Southerton	Harold	Gnr.	Ch.; Kin.; Kuk.	
948483	Speed	Harold	Bdr.	Ch.; Kin.; T6 (died)	Sai Wan V N6

ASN	Surname	First Name	Rank	POW Camps	Place of burial/Commemoration
963016	Spooner	Reginald	Gnr.	Ch.; Kin.; Ht; T6; Oka	Sai Wan V1 E5
961129	Spurrier	Albert W.	Gnr.	Ch.; Kin.; T6; Tc. (died)	
1089478	Stanhope	Thomas E.	Gnr.	Ch.; Kin.; Sh.; Japan Fuk. 9	
1105143	Stevenson	James D.	Bdr.	Ch.; Kin.; Kuk.	
953819	Steward	Ernest	Gnr.	Ch.; Rw. Track (died)	Chungkai 8 L8
125568	Stewart	J.H. Fraser	Capt.	Ch.; Kin.; Sh. (died)	Sai Wan V11 E22
325739	Stitt	J.M. (Tom)	Gnr.	Ch.; Rw. Track; Japan Funa.	
950239	Stockford	Richard R.	Gnr.	Ch.; Kin.; T6; Japan Hak. 2	
813660	Stokes	George A.	Gnr.	Ch.; Rw. Track; Saigon	
1096282	Stokes	Harry	Gnr.	Ch.; Rw. Track	
919276	Stone	Sidney D.J.	Gnr.	Ch.; Kin.; T6; Tc. (died)	Sai Wan V F4
1089480	Straw	Arthur	Gnr.	Ch.; Rw. Track	
880103	Street	Alfred C.	Gnr.	Changi (died)	Kranji 7 E16
996515	Sullivan	Francis J.	Gnr.	Ch.; Rw. Track	
1099481	Swan	George E.	Gnr.	Ch.; Kin.; Sh.	
309362	Swan	Walter	Gnr.	Ch.; Kin.; Ht.	
1105145	Sweeney	Dominic (Doc)	Gnr.	Ch.; Kin. (died)	Sai Wan V A10
963490	Tadman	Thomas	L/Bdr.	Ch.; Borneo Kuch.; Lab. (died)	Kranji Mem. Col. 38
1105146	Taylor	Alex McG.	Gnr.	Ch.; Rw. Track	
963491	Taylor	Alfred J.	Gnr.	Ch.; Rw. Track; Saigon	
942188	Taylor	George	Gnr.	Killed in action	Kranji Mem. Col. 38
1105147	Telford	James	Gnr.	Ch.; T6; Kin.; Japan Omine	
999629	Terry	Ernest	Gnr.	Ch.; Kin.; Japan Omine	
954909	Thomas	George	Gnr.	Ch.; Rw. Track; Saigon	
987298	Thompson	Robert L.	L/Bdr.	Ch.; Kin.; T6 (died)	Sai Wan V L4
1105148	Thomson	David	Gnr.	Ch.; Rw. Track; Japan Funa.	
134472	Tinsley	John B.	Lt.	Ch.; Rw. Track	
322642	Tole	Jack	Gnr.	Ch.; Rw. Track; Japan Funa.	
324679	Tominey	James	Gnr.	Changi	
933879	Topping	John F.	Gnr.	Ch.; Kin. (died)	Sai Wan V1 K10

209

ASN	Surname	First Name	Rank	POW Camps	Place of burial/Commemoration
325749	Tough	Robert	L/Bdr.	Ch.; Kin.; T6	
963171	Townley	Walter	Gnr.	Ch.; Kin.; T6	
963492	Toye	Cyril W.D.	Gnr.	Injured, evacuated 15.1.42	
987299	Tuck	Stewart H.	Gnr.	Ch.; Kin.; Sh. (died)	Sai Wan V M6
325758	Tudehope	Walter	Gnr.	Ch.; Rw. F Force; Ch.	
960018	Turner	William J.	Gnr.	Ch.; Rw. Track; Saigon	
934545	Tuthill	George W.	Gnr.	Ch.; Kin.; Kuk.	
936646	Twist	Frederick P.	Sgt.	Ch.; Rw. Track	
322866	Tyrie	Matthew	L/Bdr.	Ch.; Rw. H Force; Ch.	
885144	Vacher	Gordon W.	Gnr.	Ch.; Kin.; T6	
864848	Vacher	Walter M.	L/Bdr.	Ch.; Kin.; Kuk.	
996455	Vanstone	Richard H.	Gnr.	Ch.; Kin.; T6; Sh. (died)	Kranji Mem. Col. 38
326799	Vere	Andrew	Gnr.	Ch.; Kin.; Sh. (died)	Sai Wan V1 H3
963495	Viccars	John V.	L/Bdr.	Ch.; Kin.; Kuk.	
996569	Vickery	Arthur H.S.	Gnr.	Ch.; Rw. Track; Japan Funa.	
953828	Wain	Frederick	Gnr.	Ch.; Borneo Kuch.; Lab. (died)	Kranji Mem. Col. 38
996883	Waldron	Thomas J.	Gnr.	Ch.; Kin.; T6; Japan Hak. 2	
960019	Walker	Arthur (Titch)	Gnr.	Ch.; Kin.; Kuk.	
963174	Walker	J.L.	Gnr.	Ch.; Rw. Track	
322012	Wallace	Joseph	L/Bdr.	Ch.; Kin.; Kuk.	
982215	Walsh	Henry	Gnr.	Ch.; Kin.; T6	
961375	Ward	Ernest L.J.	Gnr.	Ch.; Kin.; T6; Japan Hak. 2	
1105180	Ward	Thomas B.	Gnr.	Ch.; Kin.; Kuk.	
943146	Warner	Joseph	Gnr.	Ch.; Kin.; T6; Sh.	
1105181	Warnock	Hugh	Sgt.	Ch.; Kin. (died)	Sai Wan V1 G12
317978	Warwick	Richard	Sgt.	Ch.; Kin.; Japan Omine	
325747	Warwick	Robert A.	Gnr.	Pudu; Ch.; Rw. F Force; Ch.	
963201	Wass	Leonard	Gnr.	Ch.; Rw. F Force; Ch.	
317989	Watson	James	Sgt.	Ch.; Kin.; Sh.	
318288	Waugh	John D.	Sgt.	Ch.; Kin.; Japan Omine	

ASN	Surname	First Name	Rank	POW Camps	Place of burial/Commemoration
326870	Wearing	George W.	Gnr.	Ch.; Kin.; Kuk.	
4687344	Webster	Edgar	Gnr.	Ch.; Rw. Track; Mergui (died)	Kanburi 6 D74
969560	Weedall	Eric	Gnr.	Ch.; Kin.; T6; Sh.; Japan Fuk. 9	
1105182	White	Blades	Gnr.	Ch.; Rw. Track; Japan Funa.	
950103	White	George	Gnr.	Ch.; Kin.; T6; Japan Hak. 2	
941794	White	John G.	L/Bdr.	Ch.; Kin.; Japan Omine	
998866	White	Robert S.	Gnr.	Ch.; Rw. Track	
951195	Whitehead	John H.	Gnr.	Ch.; Kin.; T6; Japan Hak. 2	
999649	Wileman	Joseph H.	Gnr.	Ch.; Sh.	
7874419	Williams	Ernest	Gnr.	Ch.; Kin.; Japan Omine	
997366	Williams	Frederick S.	Gnr.	Ch.; Rw. Track	
325757	Williams	George H.	Gnr.	Ch.; Kin.; Kuk.	
926871	Williamson	William B.	Gnr.	Ch.; Kin.; Kuk.	
905519	Wilmer	Joseph	Lt.	Pudu; Rw. 14.10.42	
963217	Wilson	Frederick A.	Gnr.	Ch.; Rw. F Force; Ch.	
42299	Wilson	John	Major	Killed in action	Kranji 18 D4
326281	Wilson	Samuel W.	Gnr.	Ch.; Kin.; T6	
960021	Winslow	Walter	L/Bdr.	Killed in action	Kranji Mem. Col. 38
996517	Wintle	William G.	Gnr.	Ch.; Rw. Track; Saigon	
1557949	Wiseman	Jack	Gnr.	Ch.; Kin.; T6; Japan Hak. 2	
963503	Woodcock	Leonard S.H.	Bdr.	Ch.; Rw. Track; Ch.	
961128	Woolley	Frederick C.	Gnr.	Changi	
942992	Wrightson	Alan B.R.	L/Bdr.	Ch.; Rw. Track; Saigon	
317810	Wyllie	John S.	B.Q.M.S.	Ch.; Kin.; T6	
317891	Wyllie	Thomas C.	Bdr.	Ch.; Kin.; Kuk.	
164312	Wynne	Jack G.	2/Lt.	Killed in accident	Kranji 36 G13
1105183	Young	Harry	Gnr.	Ch.; Rw. Track	
325758	Young	William G.	Bdr.	Ch.; Rw. Track	

Order of Battle on Japanese Invasion on 8 December 1941

HQ Malaya Command

Singapore Fortress
1st Malaya Brigade: 2nd Loyal Regiment, 1st and 2nd Malay Regiments
2nd Malaya Brigade: 1st Manchester (Machine Gun Battalion), 2nd Gordon Highlanders, 2/17th Dogras

111 Indian Corps
Corps Troops: 5/14th Punjab, 1st Hyderabad
28th Indian Brigade: 2/1st, 2/2nd and 2/9th Gurkha Rifles

9th Indian Division
Divisional Troops: 5th and 88th Field Regiments
8th Indian Brigade: 2/10th Baluch, 1/13th Frontier Force Rifles, 3/17th Dogras
22nd Indian Brigade: 5/11th Sikhs, 2/12th Frontier Force Regiment, 2/18th Garhwal Rifles

11th Indian Division
Divisional Troops: 3rd Cavalry, 137th and 155th Field Regiments, 80th Anti-Tank Regiment
6th Indian Brigade: 22nd Mountain Regiment, 2nd East Surrey, 1/8th Punjab, 2/16th Punjab
12th Indian Brigade: 2nd Argyll and Sutherland Highlanders, 5/2nd Punjab, 4/19th Hyderabad
15th Indian Brigade: 1st Leicestershire, 2/9th Jat, 1/14th Punjab, 3/1st Punjab

8th Australian Division
Divisional Troops: 2/10th and 2/15th Field Regiments, 2/4th Anti-
Tank Regiment
22nd Australian Brigade: 2/18th, 2/19th and 2/20th Infantry Battalions
27th Australian Brigade: 2/26th, 2/29th and 2/30th Infantry Battalions
Malaya Volunteer Forces, including 1st, 2nd, 3rd, 4th Straits Settlement
Volunteer Force
1st, 2nd, 3rd, 4th Federated Malay Straits Volunteer Force

During January 1942, reinforcements arrived in Singapore. They included
the 44th and 45th Indian Brigades, largely made up of young men who
had not been properly prepared for what they were about to meet. A
British Force, the 18th Division, which had been destined for North
Africa, was disastrously diverted to the Far East and on arrival at
Singapore was immediately thrown into action. The division, made up
of the following units, was initially caught out but once settled, gave a
good account of itself.

18th British Division
Divisional Troops: 118th, 135th and 148th Field Regiments, 125th Anti-
Tank Regiment, 9th Northumberland Fusiliers and 18th Battalion
Reconnaissance Corps
53rd Brigade: 5th and 6th Royal Norfolks, 2nd Cambridgeshire
54th Brigade: 4th Royal Norfolk, 4th and 5th Suffolks
55th Brigade: 5th Bedfordshire and Hertfordshire, 1/5th Sherwood
Foresters, 1st Cambridgeshire

Japanese 25th Army
Imperial Guards Division
3rd, 4th and 5th Guards Regiments

5th Division
9th Brigade: 11th and 41st Regiments
21st Brigade: 21st and 42nd Regiments

18th Division
23rd Brigade: 55th and 56th Regiments
114th Regiment

Short Bibliography

Unpublished sources

Barnes, W., short unpublished memoir, Imperial War Museum.

Bruton, P., *The Matter of a Massacre, Alexandra Hospital, Feb. 1942*, unpublished manuscript.

Cresswell, J., *The Prisoner of War Diary of Sgt Jack Cresswell*, unpublished memoir.

Fasson, Lt. Col. J., papers, privately held.

Gold, Lt. Col. P., *Notes on the history of the 155th (Lanarkshire Yeomanry) Field Regt, RA*, National Archives, Kew.

Gwillim, R., *Every Day a Bonus*, short unpublished memoir, privately held.

Mather, J., unpublished diaries, privately held.

Murdoch, Lt. Col. A., letters, privately held.

Seed, Captain P., MO, 155th Field Regt, private papers, Imperial War Museum, ref 91/35/1.

Sewell, E.R.A., private papers, RA Museum and Library, Woolwich.

Smith, A., *The Knights of Kinkaseki*, unpublished memoir, Imperial War Museum.

Published sources

Alexander, S., *Sweet Kwai Run Softly*, Merriotts Press, Bristol, 2006.

Allbury, A.G., *Bamboo and Bushido*, Robert Hale, London, 1955.

Barks, B., *Yasumi – The Rising Sun has Set*, UPSO Ltd, 2005.

Barwick, I.J., *In the Shadow of Death*, Pen & Sword, Barnsley, 2005.

Benford, E.S., *The Rising Sun on My Back*, Lane Publishers, Stockport, 1997.

Boden, T., *Changi Photographer*, ABC Books, Sydney, 2001.

Braddon, R., *The Naked Island*, Pan Books, London, 1952.

Burton, R., *Railway of Hell*, Pen & Sword, Barnsley, 2010.

Chippington, G., *Singapore: The Inexcusable Betrayal*, Worcester, 1992.

Chye Kooi Loong, *The History of the British Battalion 1941-1942*, privately published, 1984.

Clarke, H.V., *A Life For Every Sleeper*, Allen & Unwin, Australia, 1988.

Coombes, J.H.H., *Banpong Express*, privately published, 1948.

Dunlop, E.E., *The War Diaries of Weary Dunlop*, Penguin Books, Australia, 2009.

Durnford, J., *Branch Line to Burma*, MacDonald & Co., London, 1958.

Edwards, J., *Banzai, You Bastards*, Corporate Communications, Hong Kong, 1991.

Falk, S.L., *Seventy Days to Singapore*, Robert Hale, London, 1975.

Farndale, General Sir M., KCB, *History of the Royal Artillery, Far East Theatre 1941-46*, Brassey's, London, 2002.

Farrell, B.P., *The Defence and Fall of Singapore*, Tempus, Gloucester, 2005.

Godman, A., *The Will to Survive*, Spellmount, Kent, 2002.

Kershaw, G.F., *Tracks of Death*, Book Guild, London, 1992.

Kinvig, C., *River Kwai Railway*, Brassey's UK, 2003.

Lane, A., *Lesser Gods, Greater Devils*, Lane Publishers, Stockport, 1993.

McEwan, J., *Out of the Depths of Hell*, Pen & Sword, Barnsley, 1999.

McGowran, T., *Beyond the Bamboo Curtain*, John Donald Publishers, Edinburgh, 1985.

Mackenzie, C., *Eastern Epic*, Chatto & Windus, London, 1951.

Michno, G.F., *Death on the Hell Ships*, Leo Cooper, 2001.

Modder, R., *The Singapore Chinese Massacre*, Horizon Books, Singapore, 2004.

Pavillard, S.S., *Bamboo Doctor*, Macmillan, London, 1960.

Peacock, B., *Prisoner on the Kwai*, Blackwood & Sons, London, 1966.

Peek, I.D., *One Fourteenth of an Elephant*, Bantam Books, London, 2005.

Percival, A.E., *The War in Malaya*, Eyre and Spottiswoode, London, 1949.

Rhodes, P., *To Japan to Lay a Ghost*, Changi University Press, Singapore, 2008.

Russell-Roberts, D., *Spotlight on Singapore*, Times Press, London, 1965.

Shuttle, J., *Destination Kwai*, Tucann Books, Lincoln, 1994.

Simson, I., *Singapore: Too Little, Too Late*, Leo Cooper, London, 1970.

Smith, D., *And All the Trumpets*, Geoffrey Bles, London, 1954.

Smyth, J., *Percival and the Tragedy of Singapore*, MacDonald & Co., London, 1971.

Summers, J., *The Colonel of Tamarkan*, Simon & Schuster, London, 2005.

Tanaka, Y., *Hidden Horrors*, Westview Press, London, 1996.

Thompson, P., *The Battle for Singapore*, Portrait, London, 2005.

Tsuji, M., *Japan's Greatest Victory, Britain's Worst Defeat*, Gloucester, 2007, first published Singapore, 1960, as *Singapore: The Japanese Version*.

Wall, D., *Kill the Prisoners*, Don Wall Publications, Australia, 1997.

Warren, A., *Britain's Greatest Defeat*, Hambledon & London, London, 2002.

Watson, J.L., *Memoirs*, privately published.

Woodburn Kirby, S., *The War Against Japan, Vol 1*, HMSO, London, 1957.

Woodburn Kirby, S., *Singapore: The Chain of Disaster*, Cassell, London, 1971.

Wood-Higgs, S., *Bamboo and Barbed Wire*, Roman Press, Bournemouth, 1988.

Wyatt, J., & Lowry, C., *No Mercy from the Japanese*, Pen & Sword, Barnsley, 2008.

Other published sources

Handbook on Japanese Military Forces, US War Department (London 1991), first published as War Department Technical Manual TM-E 30-480 in 1944.

How the Jap Army Fights, A Penguin Special, Middlesex.

Tett, D., *A Postal History of the Prisoners of War and Civilian Internees in East Asia During the Second World War, Vol 1, Singapore and Malaya 1942-1945*, BFA Publishing, Herts, 2002.

Index

Adams, Lieutenant Geoffrey, 94–5
Ahmednagar, 11
Alexander, Second Lieutenant Stephen, 80
Alexandra Hospital massacre, 58–9
Allbury, Gunner Arthur, 75
Anderson, Captain Michael, 45, 178
Askew, Lance Bombardier Harold, 155, 179
Aspinall, Private George, 116, 124
Atomic bomb, 185
Australian Army units:
  8th Division, 41, 53
  27th Brigade, 42
Ayer Hitum, 42

Barnes, Gunner William, 25
Barwick, Regimental Nursing Orderly Idris James, 113–14, 117, 123
Batu Pahat, 42, 44–7
Benford, Lance Bombardier Ernest, 104, 106
Bennett, Bombardier George, 23
Beriberi, 65, 115, 122

Billings, Battery Sergeant Major Francis, 35–6
Birdwood Camp, 64
Bockscar (B29 Superfortress bomber), 185
Bombing of POW camps:
  Taiwan POW camp:
    Heito, 168
  Thailand POW camps:
    Non Pladuk, 97
    Tamarkan, 97
Bourke, Father Gerard, 70, 97
Braddon, Gunner Russell, 129, 131
British and Indian army units:
  215th Anti-Tank Battery, 22
  2nd Argyll and Sutherland Highlanders, 33, 51
  2nd Cambridgeshire, 42
  2nd East Surrey, 15, 19, 21, 25
  137th Field Regiment, RA, 26, 33–4
  198th Field Ambulance Company, 47
  2/1st Gurkha, 20–1
  2/2nd Gurkha, 26
  2/9th Gurkha, 34
  4/19th Hyderabad, 33–4
  2/9th Jats, 15, 19, 21, 24
  1st Leicestershire, 15, 19, 21–5

5th and 6th Norfolks, 42–3
1/14th Punjab, 15, 20–1
2/16th Punjab, 21
5/2nd Punjab, 33
5/4th Punjab, 33
5/14th Punjab, 33–4
Brooke-Popham, Air Chief
    Marshal Sir Robert, 15
Brown, Captain Charles Gordon,
    36–8
Brown, Lieutenant Michael, 143,
    157, 159–60, 163
Bruce, Private Arthur, 59
Buchanan, Gunner Roy, 152, 168
Bukit-Pelandock defile, 42
Burton, Captain Reginald, 131

Campbell, Bombardier Patrick,
    19, 31–2, 36, 66, 69, 92, 96,
    108, 189
Canning Camp, 14
Changi, 62, 111, 127–8, 139, 174
Chinese massacre, 61–3
Chippington, Lieutenant George,
    24
Cholera, 93–4, 106, 119–20
Chunglan Bridge, 20
Coogan, Gunner Andy, 146, 156
Cresswell, Sergeant Jack, 154,
    169, 178
Cross, Lieutenant J.T.N., 150
Crossley, Major James F., 143, 152

Death Railway:
  Bridges:
    Hintock, 134–5
    Pack of Cards, 135
    Songkurai, also known as
        The Bridge of Six
        Hundred, 123
    Tamarkan, 79–80, 90
    Three Tier Bridge, 135
  Cuttings:
    Kanyu, 105
    Kinsaiyok, 95
    Tonchan, 81
  Embankments, 79–80, 82, 103,
    136

Denys-Peek, Ian, 105–106
Douglas, Lance Bombardier
    John, 163, 187–8
Douglas-Home, Lieutenant The
    Hon. Edward, 25
Dragonfly, HMS (gunboat) 49
Duckworth, Padre Noel, 46–7
Dunlop, Lieutenant Colonel
    Edward 'Weary', 103
Durnford, Lieutenant John, 72–3,
    76–7, 84, 102, 133, 188, 190
Dysentery, 66, 115, 120–1, 149–50

Edwards, Sergeant Jack, 51, 59,
    61, 63, 145
Ekma, SS (troopship), 13
Empire Pride, SS (troopship), 188
Enola Gay (B29 Superfortress
    bomber), 184
Eustace, Lieutenant (later
    Captain) Maurice, 34, 36, 57

Farmer, Lance Sergeant John,
    154, 167
Fasson, Lieutenant Colonel
    James, 138, 142, 148, 155
Fergusson, Bombardier James,
    39, 177
Ffolkes, Lieutenant David, 72, 181
Final Disposition, 162, 167, 173,
    178, 184–5
Findlater, Lance Sergeant Robert,
    89–90, 94, 189
Forster, Captain Alfred, 23
Frew, Gunner Samuel, 7, 69

Gemas, 42
Great World POW camp, 69
Gold, Major (later Lieutenant
    Colonel) Philip, 39, 54, 59
Gough, Bombardier Benjamin,
    65, 142, 160
Gurun, 27–9
Gwillim, Gunner Richard, 3, 5–7,
    47, 58–9, 189

Haigh, Padre John Foster, 114
Hannah, Gunner Thomas, 4, 10,
    12, 22, 67–8, 79, 83, 117, 187–8
Harris, Lieutenant Colonel
    Stanley W., 128, 136–7
Hellfire Pass, 107
Hellships:
    De Klerk, 171
    England Maru, 138–40
    Haruyasa Maru, 179–80
    Kachidoki Maru, 175–6
    Melbourne Maru, 177
    Taiko Maru, 177
    Wales Maru, 173
Hirohito, Emperor, 186
Humphries, Lieutenant Colonel
    H.R., 128, 136–7

Indian National Army, 64
Indomitable, HMS (aircraft carrier),
    16
Intelligence Report: Formosa
    Camps, 147–8, 156

Japanese Army units:
    25th Army, 16–7
    9th Division, 42, 53
    18th Division, 53
    9th Infantry Brigade, 27
    Imperial Guards, 42, 55
Johnston, Gunner James W., 11,
    14

Kane, Gunner John 'Dempsey',
    92, 146
Keen, Sergeant Oliver, 35–8
Kelly, Lance Bombardier John
    McKay, 56, 127, 189
Kepple, Lieutenant Martin, 35, 59
Kota Bharu, 17

Lockhead, Lance Sergeant
    Samuel, 55
Lowther, Sergeant (later Battery
    Sergeant Major) Charles
    'Chuk', 9

Macdonald, Major Ian, 93, 96
Mackenzie, Captain James, 24,
    30–1, 35–6, 40
McCready, Gunner Patrick, 67,
    72, 83
McEwan, Gunner John, 1, 38, 63,
    144, 165, 186, 189
McKie, Gunner Thomas, 3, 5–7,
    40, 48–9, 63, 70, 94–5, 181–2,
    188–90
Mair, Lance Bombardier George,
    36–7, 174
'Malayan Dunkirk', 49
Marmite, 65
Matador, Operation, 15
Mather, Bombardier John, 139,
    157, 161
Monsoon, 91, 103–104, 115, 124,
    135
Murdoch, Lieutenant Colonel
    Alan, 3, 29, 35, 39
Murray-Lyon, Major General
    D.M., 20

Newey, Lieutenant Colonel
    Thomas H., 131

Ogden, Gunner John, 37

219

Pampanito, US (submarine), 176
Parit-Sulong massacre, 47
Patani, 17
Pavillard, Doctor Stanley, 74, 93
Peacock, Major Basil, 129
Percival, Lieutenant General
    Arthur, 15, 29, 33, 53
Pett, Gunner Ken, 158, 162, 165–6
POW camps:
  Borneo POW camps:
    Kuching (Batu Lintang),
        171–3
    Labuan, 172–3, 184
  Borneo POW camp guards:
    Sugino, Sergeant Major, 173
  Japan POW camps:
    Bunka, 174
    Fukuoka 5B (Omine), 177–8
    Fukuoka 9 & 12 (Miyata),
        178
    Fukuoka 24B (Senryu), 178
    Funatsu Nagoya, 174–5
    Hakodate, 174, 177
    Omori, 174
    Shinkai, 176
  Manchuria POW camp:
    Hotten, Mukden, 178
  Taiwan POW camps:
    Heito, 167–8
    Inrin, 169
    Kinkaseki, 140–64
    Kukutsu, 164, 185–6
    Oka, 167, 185
    Shirakawa, 169
    Taichu, 168
    Taihoku 6, 156, 166
    Toroku, 169
  Taiwan POW camp guards:
    Cho Kon Toku (Frying Pan),
        159
    Immamura, Captain
        Yaychachi, 158

  Kakegoro Nagi (The Ghost),
      150
  Korai Fuku (The Nasty
      Carpenter), 214
  Kurabayashi, Corporal
      Shigeru (So-So), 142
  Mishima, Gunso, 160
  Moruyama, Gunso, 160
  Suzuki Lieutenant Nobuo
      (The Count), 160, 186
  Tamakai, Lieutenant (The
      Mad Man), 165
  Tashiro, Sergeant (Sanitary
      Sid), 142, 149, 159
  Ueno, Corporal Mitsuo
      (Lancho), 142, 159
  Wakiyama Yoshio, 140, 158
Thailand POW camps:
  Ban Pong, 74–5, 77, 88, 114
  Chungkai, 84, 108
  Hintock, 104, 131
  Kanchanaburi, 90, 116, 126–7
  Kanyu, 83, 104–105
  Kinsaiyok, 94
  Konkuita, 97, 135
  Nakon Pathon, 97
  Non Pladuk, 89, 97
  Tamarkan, 78, 85, 97
  Tarsau, 76, 102
  Tonchan, 76–7, 80–1, 92, 131
  Wampo, 91
Thailand 'F' Force camps:
  Changaraya, 118–20, 124
  Kami Songkurai, 118, 124,
      125
  Nikki, 118
  Shimo Songkurai, 118
  Songkurai, 118–20, 124
  Thanbaya, 122, 124, 126
Thailand POW camp guards:
  Aitaru Hiramatsu, Sergeant
      Major (The Tiger), 133

220

Banno, Colonel, 114
Kosakata, Lieutenant, 79
Kuwabara, Captain, 131
Saito, Sergeant Major, 79
Ukemi, Gunso, 91
Prince of Wales, HMS (battleship),
    16, 20

Queen Mary, SS (troopship), 188

Raids Behind Japanese Lines,
    British Army information
    document, 101
Repulse, HMS (battlecruiser), 16,
    20
Rhodes, Gunner Peter, 8, 10, 30,
    52, 60, 63, 173, 186
Road-night, Battery Sergeant
    Major Charles, 38, 43, 60
Ronaldson, Lieutenant Patrick,
    35–7, 139, 148
Russell, Sergeant Roy, 10, 189

Scorpion, HMS (gunboat), 49
Scullion, Regimental Sergeant
    Major Peter, 54, 60–1, 145
Seed, Captain Peter, 139, 141,
    154–5, 161, 163
Selerang Incident, 71
Serendah, 40–1
Sewell, Lieutenant (later Captain)
    Andrew, 28, 42–4, 151
Shannon, Gunner George, 67, 72
Shone, Bombardier Joseph, 43–4

Singora, 17
Smith, Gunner Arthur, 139, 147,
    166, 177
Smith, Lance Corporal William,
    112, 114, 126
Stewart, Captain Fraser, 26, 161,
    163, 170
Strathmore, SS (troopship)

Telaga Jetty, 42
Toosey, Lieutenant Colonel
    Philip, 75, 77–8, 85
Tropical ulcers, 96, 106, 108, 122,
    126

Walker, Gunner Arthur 'Titch',
    19, 31–2, 36
War Crimes Trials, 159, 175, 184
Warwick, Gunner Robert, 35, 89
Watson, Sergeant Jim, 18, 22,
    45–7, 57, 149–50
Wavell, General Sir Archibald,
    41, 54
Wheeler, Major Ben, 156–7, 162
Wild, Major Cyril, 115, 124
Williamson, Gunner William,
    150, 186
Wilson, Major John 'Jock', 5, 41,
    45–6
Wood-Higgs, Nursing Orderly
    Stanley, 117, 121–2

Yamashita, General Tomoyuki,
    42